C. S. Lewis

C. S. Lewis

A Life

MICHAEL WHITE

CARROLL & GRAF PUBLISHERS
NEW YORK

C. S. LEWIS
A Life

Carroll & Graf Publishers
An Imprint of Avalon Publishing Group Inc.
245 West 17th Street, 11th Floor
New York, NY 10011

AVALON
publishing group incorporated

First Carroll & Graf edition 2004

Simultaneously published in Great Britain by Abacus, an imprint of
Time Warner Book Group UK

Library of Congress Cataloging-in-Publication Data is available.

ISBN: 0-7867-1376-3

Printed in the United States of America
Distributed by Publishers Group West

For Australia

Contents

Introduction

An abiding interest in C. S. Lewis came to me young and from several directions. When I was seven or eight years old I saw *The Lion, the Witch and the Wardrobe* read on a wonderful BBC children's television programme called *Jackanory*. I was immediately captivated by C. S. Lewis's fantasy world and read all the Narnia books, one straight after the other. Not so long after this I began to acquire a taste for science fiction and a school friend recommended that I try Lewis's space series – *Out of the Silent Planet*, *Perelandra* and *That Hideous Strength*. I loved them instantly and, just as with the Narnia tales, as soon as I put the first one down I began the second and then the third. I found they got better as they went on and I was left despondent when the trilogy had come to an end. It felt as though I had been cut off from a universe that, for a short while, had been more genuine and more welcoming than the real world of homework, exams and school bullies.

The third direction from which Lewis's ideas and writings came to me was through my elder sister, who had become a huge fan of the man and pressed into my adolescent palm a copy of *The Screwtape Letters*, urging me to read it.

I have remained grateful ever since because in some ways I found *The Screwtape Letters* the most satisfying of all Lewis's books. Maybe it was because I was slightly older when I read it, or perhaps the humour of the story captured me. But the fact that I had never seen

ascerbic tongue

anything like it before (nor have I since, come to that) ensured that I was gripped for the single evening it took to complete this great story. And, although I consumed the book quickly and with almost as much appetite as Screwtape expressed for his wayward nephew, Wormwood, it stuck with me long after I had put it down, so that I could clearly recall whole chunks of the story decades later when I came back to it as part of the research for this biography.

So, what drove me to write a life of C. S. Lewis? I think my reasons have been different to those that inspired his earlier biographers. Most of those who have written about Lewis have been deeply religious people or academics, so they have concentrated on these aspects of his life. For a large part of his life Lewis was a devout Christian and a significant aspect of his fame came from his books of religious apologetics. Until he found literary success he earned his living as an academic and he remained one almost until the day he died. But there was, I believe, much more to the man, however important these elements were in shaping him.

I wanted to consider C. S. Lewis from the position of a fan, certainly, but I did not want to dwell too much on his religious devotions or his academic accomplishments. In many ways I am the polar opposite of my subject. I am an atheist and I very much enjoy the twenty-first century, whereas Lewis had little time for the era in which he lived. Throughout his life he was intimately attached to his own childhood, whereas I have little conscious empathy with my own and my inclination is to focus on the present and the future, something Lewis seemed to do only rarely.

The things that drew me to Lewis were his fiction, his creativity and his ability to express himself in such diverse ways. Lewis lived to write and he had an interest in all sorts of writing – he had published dozens of non-fiction books as well as collections of poetry, academic treatises, histories, autobiography, science fiction, children's fantasy and religious satire. He was an extremely amusing man with a sharp wit and an often acerbic tongue, he was jolly company (despite his chauvinism – a trait that was far from abnormal in the age and society in which he matured). Most of all he had

Pigeonholed —
Typecast —

a tremendous gift for conveying complex ideas in a brilliantly clear fashion; he could write as he spoke, with a wonderfully warm, welcoming, encouraging voice.

In a sense Clive Staples Lewis is someone whose literary gifts I aspire to: I can identify with his interest in a range of expression and his resistance to being pigeonholed or typecast. There is nothing at all wrong with earlier biographies of the creator of Narnia, but hopefully the fact that I am coming to Lewis from a different direction to my eminent predecessors has allowed me to offer a fresh perspective on his life. I write as a devotee certainly, but as someone less absorbed by my subject's religious or even his academic world. I hope this has led me to offer up a revealing yet balanced portrayal of one of the twentieth century's more endearing and enduring weavers of fantasy. For his skill as a storyteller was, I am sure, the very essence of the man.

Michael White
Perth, Australia
June 2004

I

'Call Me Jack'

Evening in Oxford, a few days before Christmas 1940. A bracing wind sweeps along St Giles and it is threatening to snow. Ensconced in their favourite pub, the Eagle and Child, a group of men sit around a plain wooden table each nursing a pint of beer while a few cup their pipes or draw on cigarettes. The room is filled with smoke and talk. Then one of the men, portly, balding and ruddy-faced, stands up and the others stop talking. Into the quiet fall the sounds from the pub: the hubbub of men making merry at the bar, the clink of glasses, laughter and raised voices.

The man clears his throat and tells the gathering that he has something a little different for them and that he hopes they'll like it. It's a piece of comic drama, he says, written in the form of letters from a senior devil to his nephew, an apprentice demon, in which he offers advice concerning the best way to capture the soul of a human. A couple of the party laugh briefly and there are smiles all round as the reading begins.

The reader is Clive Staples Lewis, always known to his friends and family as Jack. We are eavesdropping on a meeting of the Inklings, an informal literary group who, for more than twenty years between the early 1930s and the 1950s, gathered at least twice a week in pubs and college rooms in Oxford. At these meetings the members, most of them university dons and writers, read to the others their latest efforts and appraised each other's work as the beer flowed.

Lewis speaks eloquently, telling his story in a deep, resonant tone, his rounded, precise English tinged with a faint Irish accent. Adopting voices and pulling faces, he enthrals his listeners, recounting his tale for fifteen minutes before returning to his chair to hand the floor to the next reader. A few moments later a chair shuffles across the wooden floorboards and Professor Tolkien stands up, pipe in hand. He takes a sip of beer, arranges his papers as the others look on and then begins to read.

This is a time when the Inklings were at their height and on such an evening perhaps seven or eight of the club members would be seated around the table. The group's founders, C. S. Lewis and J.R.R. Tolkien, would usually be joined by Lewis's elder brother, Major Warren ('Warnie') Lewis, recently returned from the beaches of Dunkirk. If the trains were running properly Hugo Dyson would have travelled up from Reading University, some twenty-five miles away. A relatively new member in 1940 was a particular favourite of Lewis's, the writer and editor Charles Williams, and from their colleges in Oxford came dons, Nevill Coghill and Lord David Cecil. They usually met twice weekly. The gatherings at the Eagle and Child most often took place on a Tuesday morning, but occasionally of an evening, and on Thursdays around 8 p.m. the group would meet in Lewis's rooms in Magdalen College or rather less frequently in Tolkien's in Merton.

By 1940 both Lewis and Tolkien were published authors. Tolkien's children's story *The Hobbit* had been well received after its publication in 1937 and Lewis was already an accomplished author with seven books to his name. On a night such as the one described, during the early years of the Second World War, Tolkien would have read a passage from his new work-in-progress, which he called 'the New Hobbit', later entitled *The Lord of the Rings*. Lewis meanwhile read the latest instalments of his new project, a story that would become one of his most famous, the tale of devilry and seduction published in 1942 as *The Screwtape Letters*.

The Inklings were only a loose grouping of literary figures with no manifesto or shared aims, but at their core they were a close-knit group, and although some associations within the company were closer than others, they were all Jack Lewis's friends. More often than not, it was he who introduced new members to the group and he remained the driving force behind this affiliation of like-minded men.

As the evening draws to a close, the readings done and the critical appraisals made, discussion turns to news of the war and then to lighter fare – favourite anecdotes and university intrigues – until the landlord manages to coax them to the door of the pub and bids them all a friendly goodnight.

Outside, snow has fallen and the pavement is wet. In the icy wind further talk is kept to a minimum and the men stamp their feet and rub their hands together. Tolkien pulls on his gloves and clambers on to his bicycle. With a wave he heads off into the cold darkness of the blackout, returning to his family home some half a mile away in north Oxford. Coghill, Williams and the others, with scarves around their ears and hats pulled down tight, stride off, struggling against the wind to reach their university rooms or their private digs.

After making their farewells, the Lewis brothers begin the ten-minute walk back to Magdalen College, towards the other end of The High. Jack sleeps in his rooms during the week and spends each weekend at The Kilns, his house on the outskirts of Oxford.

Jack and Warnie have little concern for the cold – they are big men and wrapped up warm – and they let the topics of the evening run on into their conversation as they walk. Above them the stars are especially bright. Thanks to the blackout, street lights have been turned off and all the college buildings along The High and the shops and public buildings in the city centre stand in complete darkness.

Reaching his rooms, Jack makes a beeline for the kettle and he and Warnie settle into one of the scruffy sofas that dominate the middle of the sitting-room. The brothers talk for perhaps another hour over several more cups of tea and then they set up a camper bed for Warnie before Jack heads off to his bed in the adjoining room.

After saying his prayers he sits up in bed to gaze out of his window looking out on to the icy fields of Magdalen deer park. Beyond the glass and overhead the speckled splendour of the Milky Way dominates the chill night sky. What, we may wonder, would have been his thoughts on a night such as this? As the alcohol coursed still through his veins and the conversation of his intellectual friends ran through his mind, did he sit and ponder the heavens above and begin to dream perhaps of imagined worlds, settings for the Ransom trilogy, his science-fiction epic, the first volume of which had already been published? Or did his thoughts turn to God? For, by this time Lewis was a devout Christian and becoming famous as a Christian apologist.

Perhaps instead he considered more prosaic matters; the woman he lived with at The Kilns, Janie Moore (whom he habitually referred to as 'Mother'); his past growing up in Belfast, the death of his real mother when he was only nine. Maybe, as he cleared his mind and tried to rest, his concerns became those of most ordinary men, concerns that lay far from the lofty discussions and debates that occupied most of his waking life. Perhaps as sleep approached, he felt the same fears for the future as his fellow countrymen, for the war was going badly. Maybe he began to scrutinise his career, his prospects, his hopes. But then again, as he slid into sleep, maybe visions took shape in his mind, images of something less prosaic, something altogether otherworldly: a wardrobe door opening, a faun, a snow-laden landscape and, on the tip of his tongue, the taste of Turkish Delight.

When, in middle age, Warren Lewis began a family archive (today kept in Wheaton College in Illinois, USA, and known as the Wade

Collection), he was able to trace his and Jack's ancestors back to the sixteenth century. Yet, although the Lewis brothers always considered themselves Irish, and in particular, Ulstermen, only the maternal line could claim Irish roots dating back more than two generations.

Jack's paternal grandfather, Richard Lewis, the son of a Welsh farmer, was an émigré who worked his way up the ladder to become a partner in an engineering and shipbuilding business in Belfast. Completely self-made, he was responsible for elevating the Lewises from the lower middle class to the genuine bourgeoisie, and in the process he succeeded in giving his children the opportunity of a proper education.

Richard Lewis and his wife, Martha, met in Belfast and for ten years they led a peripatetic existence moulded by career moves that took them around Ireland while their six children came into the world. Their youngest child, Jack's father, Albert, was born in 1863, by which time the family was living in Cork, where Richard worked for a growing engineering company. But, before Albert's first birthday, they had made another move, this time to Dublin, after Richard was headhunted as manager of the shipbuilding firm of Walpole, Webb and Bewly. Then, four years later, in 1868, they were all back in Belfast again and Richard embarked on the greatest gamble of his life when he went into business with a friend named John MacIlwaine to create 'MacIlwaine and Lewis: Boiler Makers, Engineers, and Iron Ship Builders'.

The gamble paid off. By 1870, during the halcyon days of the British Empire and with the demand for ships designed and built in Britain at its very peak, MacIlwaine and Lewis had started to turn a handsome profit. Richard could end his days of wandering and climbing the employment ladder and was able to settle his family into a comfortable home in the desirable Belfast suburb of Lower Sydenham, where they remained until some years after all the children were married.

With this move the Lewises began to mix in more elevated circles. Many of their neighbours were doctors, lawyers, professors and successful business families similar to themselves. But the most significant new acquaintances arrived a few years after the move, when Thomas Hamilton was appointed as the new rector of the parish of St Mark, Dundela, into which Lower Sydenham fell. The Hamiltons and the Lewises struck up a friendship immediately. They soon began to share a close-knit social circle and their children frequently played together.

On the surface at least, the two families were quite different. Thomas Hamilton was a highly educated man who had taken a First in Theology at Trinity College, Dublin. His grandfather had been a Fellow of Trinity and had gone on to become Bishop of Ossory, the oldest bishopric in Ireland. Thomas's wife, Mary, was the daughter of Sir John Borlase Warren. She was a very intelligent and eloquent aristocratic woman, who, but for her sex, may well have become far more accomplished than her husband.

Thomas Hamilton was no ordinary preacher; he was a religious zealot who delivered fire-and-brimstone sermons. Although many people felt overpowered by his extreme religious views, he remained a popular and well-liked figure because he was a great conversationalist. He loved to entertain and was said to be an excellent companion on the long country walks he so favoured. However, unknown to almost everyone outside his immediate family, Thomas was also a prolific writer. As a naval chaplain during the Crimean War, some twenty years before settling into the rectorship of St Mark, he had kept a detailed travel journal recounting his adventures and for the rest of his life he continued to put his thoughts down on paper. Although Jack and Warnie were never shy to admit a certain admiration for their maternal grandfather, when Warnie discovered his ancestor's writings he was immediately repelled by Thomas Hamilton's surprising lack of literary skill, but even more by his racism and almost total intolerance of other religions and cultures.

Richard Lewis was a very different social animal. Future generations would have called his type *nouveau riche* and on this side of the family there was no trace of any academic heritage. As well as being self-made, he was self-educated, a man who read widely and was also a keen amateur writer. In his autobiography, *Surprised by Joy*, Jack Lewis tells us how, during the time his grandfather worked as a manager in Cork, he wrote a series of intense and carefully worded theological papers which he delivered during evening reading sessions attended by the workmen he managed at the engineering plant. More surprisingly perhaps, Richard Lewis also wrote proto-science fiction which he read to his children. Many of these stories were set on the moon, and as one would expect from the mind of a self-educated engineer, his characters invariably became involved in building elaborate machines and strange, complicated devices with which they could extricate themselves from the tight corners into which the plot had taken them.

It is easy to see how a grandson of Thomas Hamilton and Richard Lewis found it natural not only to write in a variety of forms and across so many different genre, but to be happy to read his work in development to his friends and associates, for it was almost a family tradition. One might ponder what both grandfather Lewis and grandfather Hamilton might have thought of a C. S. Lewis performance at a gathering of the Inklings.

Albert Lewis was seven when the family settled in Lower Sydenham and he and his five siblings, each according to their age, interacted with the Hamiltons' four children, Lilian, Florence, Hugh and Augustus. Florence (or Flora) was a year older than Albert and the two of them formed an especially strong bond.

From an early age Albert was a lively, playful character, fond of making up tall tales and telling jokes. He was also very bright and was considered a star pupil at Lurgan College in County Armagh. The headmaster there, a logician named William Kirkpatrick, took a particular shine to the boy and suggested to Richard Lewis that he encourage his son to study law. So, after finishing school, Albert took the road south to Dublin, where he studied with the firm of Maclean, Boyle & Maclean before returning to Belfast six years later to start up his own law practice.

Reading Jack Lewis's autobiographical writings and his father's own journals, it is impossible to ignore the sense that Albert Lewis was a man who never truly came close to fulfilling his potential. He wanted to read for the Bar, but, lacking the necessary financial support, he was obliged to give up this idea and start making a living as a solicitor as soon as he qualified. He also appears to have had serious political ambitions and had, from the start, viewed the study of law as a means to an end, a route into politics. He was a very good speaker, self-confident and strongly opinionated. Vehemently opposed to Home Rule for Ireland (effectively the creation of a state independent of the rest of the United Kingdom), he argued publicly against the most famous politician of the day and the great advocate of British withdrawal from Irish politics, William Gladstone.

For a few years during his twenties Albert was ambitious and determined enough to push himself forward as a political advocate and he delivered public speeches in Dublin and Ulster arguing strongly against Home Rule. But success as a politician was to elude him. Instead he spent his entire career as a rather ordinary solicitor working as a police prosecutor in the local courts. Along this path lay precious little glamour, but it was a secure career and promised a prosperous, comfortable, if rather mundane existence for him and his future wife. If nothing else, this made him something of a good catch. Albert was not a terribly handsome man but he had an active imagination and a cosy wit. He had a lot to offer and was therefore more than a little surprised when, after turning his attention towards his childhood friend Florence Hamilton and eventually proposing to her, she turned him down flat.

Florence appears to have felt nothing more than a warm friendship for her young suitor. She was an exceptionally intelligent woman, certainly Albert's intellectual superior, but she was also a little cold when it came to romance. While Albert had been busy qualifying as a lawyer in Dublin, Florence had, most unusually for the time, spent five years studying mathematics at Queen's College, Belfast. In 1885, just as Albert travelled back up from Dublin and laid plans to establish his own law firm, Florence had obtained First Class Honours in Logic and a Second in Mathematics.

To make things more difficult for Albert, there was also a social hurdle he was obliged to overcome. The Hamiltons considered the Lewis family to be friends, but Albert Lewis was not quite what they had hoped for in a prospective son-in-law. Mary Hamilton was particularly fond of Albert and enjoyed lengthy political discussions with him. He was a respectable young man who could clearly offer much, but when it came to considerations of marriage, rather traditional Victorian families such as the Hamiltons often had old-fashioned and frankly unrealistic expectations.

But Albert was nothing if not determined. He was not put off by Florence's rejection, and if anything, the friendship between the pair grew stronger after she rejected his offer of marriage. Although they lived less than a mile apart they wrote to each other almost daily and when Florence became a freelance magazine journalist, Albert, who had a superior knowledge of English literature, was always there to help her with her grammar. At the same time Albert must have been quite conscious of the delicate social manoeuvring involved in winning the approval of the Hamiltons and he worked hard to build his friendship with them and to impress them with his own successful career.

So, after Albert had persisted for almost eight years, finally, in 1893 (by which time both he and Florence had entered their thirties), Florence agreed to accept his latest marriage proposal. But even then the relationship seems to have been rather one-sided. While Albert appears to have remained besotted with his fiancée, Florence displayed an unusual detachment. In a letter written to Albert shortly before their wedding day she asked: 'I wonder, do I love you?' She knew she was very fond of him and would never love anyone else, but even so, did she really love *him*?

While many men would have found such remarks difficult to accept, Albert took them all in his stride and simply accepted such doubts and personal independence as part and parcel of the woman he knew he loved. For her part, Florence appears to have simply told herself that she would try to find love for Albert and that he was the best she could hope for. And so the wedding went ahead on

24 August 1894 at St Mark's Church, Dundela, and the couple honeymooned in North Wales before returning to Belfast and a semi-detached house at Dundela Villas, about a mile from Albert's family home.

With such a drawn-out courtship behind them, the couple wasted no time in starting a family, and by Christmas 1894 the Hamiltons and the Lewises were celebrating the news that Florence was pregnant. Six months later, in June 1895, a boy they named Warren was born. It is possible they had planned to stop after one child because another three and a half years were to pass before Clive Staples was born on 29 November 1898.

As the family grew, Albert's law firm prospered and became one of the most in-demand legal practices working with the Belfast police. For the Lewis boys this provided a stable and comfortable environment in which to grow up, a cocoon that would greatly influence their personal development.

Many of Jack's earliest memories came from books and stories rather than any real-life experiences. He became terrified of insects thanks to a pop-up book that his elder brother taunted him with and this phobia remained with him his entire life – years later he could vividly remember tales of goblins and ogres read to him in the nursery. It was in the rather overcrowded Dundela Villas that he and Warnie first formed the special bond that would last their entire lives and here that the four-year-old Clive Staples announced one day that he wished to be known as 'Jack' or 'Jacksie'. The name stuck.

But, aside from these associations, few recollections of this first family home stuck in Jack Lewis's mind. In 1905 the Lewises moved to Little Lea, a large house built to Albert's design in a more salubrious neighbourhood just outside Belfast. It was this house that provided the backdrop for Jack's childhood and the setting for all his family memories.

Today Little Lea stands amid other rambling homes in the heart of the leafy, middle-class Belfast suburb of Strandtown. But at the start of the twentieth century it was surrounded by fields. To the north there were almost uninterrupted views of the city and to the south lay great swathes of County Down countryside. By 1905 Belfast was one of the most important shipbuilding cities of the British Empire, powering the Royal Navy and the merchant fleet. From the upper windows of Little Lea, Lewis could just about see the shipyards, the great cranes towering over the carcasses of half-built freight carriers, and around the yards the endless streets of packed, grimy terraces and blackened brick chimneys spewing out thick smoke.

Little Lea was actually a rather ugly house, and as adults both Lewis brothers concluded that their father had been resoundingly conned by its builders. Jack once claimed that Albert had 'more capacity for being cheated than any man I have ever known',[1] and they referred to the place as being one of the worst-designed houses they had ever seen. It was draughty, badly lit and, according to Warren's memory at least, contained long corridors with cupboard-sized doors that led to empty voids and roof spaces. Yet, in spite of all its faults, Jack would later claim that Little Lea was an integral part of his life story, a place that provided the inspiration for many of the old houses described in his works of fiction.

Little Lea was filled with books and too much bulky furniture. In the winter it was chilly, as the wind blew through the rafters, but in the summer the Lewises enjoyed the large garden, where the adults took tea on the back lawn while the children played. The house was big enough for Warnie and Jack to get lost in, and by the time Jack was about four and Warnie seven an attic room at the end of a long corridor they called the 'Little End Room' had become the focal point for the boys, a place they could turn into a hideaway, a private den where they could do pretty much what they wanted.

By the time the family moved to Little Lea, both Jack and Warnie were avid readers. As small boys their nanny, a young woman named Lizzie Endicott, had recounted frightening tales of their native Ireland, legends about leprechauns, ogres and giants, and this had sparked their imaginations. The first books Jack tried to read were *The Tale of Squirrel Nutkin* and other Beatrix Potter stories. He was particularly taken with the illustrations, and according to his own recollections of childhood, this fuelled a fascination with the idea of animals dressed as humans. A few years later and several steps up the literary ladder, he was digesting more adventurous fodder such as Mark Twain's *A Connecticut Yankee in King Arthur's Court*; E. Nesbit's *Five Children and It*, *The Phoenix and the Carpet* and *The Story of the Amulet*; and, most importantly, the adventure stories of Sir Arthur Conan Doyle that appeared in the short-lived monthly publication the *Strand Magazine*.

In his autobiography Lewis tells us that his parents were very different types. His mother he described as calm, cheerful and tranquil, her family 'cool' and 'ironic', whereas he defined Albert as overly emotional, a lover of oratory and something of a showman. Both were 'sentimental', 'passionate' and brought easily to anger and laughter.

Florence appears to have been the more introverted and insular of the two and Lewis understandably deified her in his autobiography, written some half a century after her premature death. As we shall see, the relationship between the adult Jack Lewis and his father was often turbulent, and much about the Albert Lewis described in *Surprised by Joy* is tainted by prejudiced memory and lack of objectivity, making it difficult to glean from the book his real personality.

While Florence exuded a sense of inner calm, Albert was fretful and overbrimming with energy. He was certainly thwarted and frustrated and this showed itself in his love of political argument. A dinner party or a summer luncheon with friends on the lawn at Little Lea was incomplete without an intense political debate, usually revolving around the 'Irish Question': the matter of Home Rule and the growing antagonism between Dublin and London.

From an early age Jack and Warnie were there to hear the arguments and the rhetoric, and rather than being inspired by such discussions, each acquired from them a lifelong distaste for any form of politics. Although in middle age Jack became something of a crusty conservative with a small 'c' and bemoaned the post-war successes of the Labour Party, he was never the slightest bit interested in talking politics with his friends. Indeed, such was his dislike of political debate that he would make a point of changing the subject whenever a conversation threatened to move into that area.

The upside of Albert Lewis's fascination with political debate and his thwarted career on the soapbox was that he developed a love for public speaking and was, according to all who knew him, a marvellous story-teller. Jack was fond of this aspect of his father's character and went as far as to describe him as 'the best raconteur he had ever heard'.[2] Nothing pleased Albert more than to spend an afternoon at home with a good port and two or three of his close relatives or lawyer friends sharing amusing anecdotes, or what they called 'wheezes'. And if Lewis's autobiography is shot through with poorly disguised bitterness towards the man, it is also clear that it was the raconteur and the confident, outspoken debater in him that he loved most and remembered best.

The pleasure Lewis senior found in the art of debate clearly rubbed off on his younger son. So too did the family obsession with books. Lewis recalled how Little Lea was crammed to the draughty rafters with them. His father could never throw away a book and so volumes would spill out of every cupboard and they stood two-deep in the bookcases that lined the corridors of the house. Both Florence and Albert had eclectic tastes, but neither was at all interested in the romantic literature that was to so captivate their son in later years. As well as this gap in their reading, according to Lewis, his mother had absolutely no interest in any sort of poetry, and the family favourites were Dickens and the political novels of Anthony Trollope, which Jack believed offered his father a chance to quell his frustrations by living out a political career vicariously.

Like all children, Jack and Warnie needed their own private universe and they delved deep into worlds drawn from their overactive imaginations. At first they took to drawing fantasy realms and they covered the walls of the Little End Room with their efforts. Warnie was very much taken with machines, gadgets and mechanical devices, spending hours drawing ships and guns and battle scenes in the

most intricate detail. Then, from the age of six or seven, he became
enamoured with India and fantasised about the Raj. Jack was not so
keen on such things and instead drew, and later wrote about, his
twin obsessions of the time, knights in armour and (thanks to
Beatrix Potter) 'dressed animals'. Originally at Dundela Villas, but
later in the Little End Room, Jack began to combine these two
interests. The result was what he called 'Animal Land', a fantasy
realm inhabited by animals with human characteristics.

Some of the tales set in Animal Land and written by Jack when
he was eleven or twelve years old have survived. They may be found
in the Wade Collection. Reading them now it is difficult to see even
the first glimmer of the future creativity that would make Lewis
famous and his writing loved by millions of readers. The tales of
Animal Land, or Boxen as the setting became known, are extremely
dull.[3]

Instead of writing about the characters living there, Jack had
become obsessed with the geography, languages, culture and history
of this realm. There is no sense of drama or plot in the stories and
the characters are one-dimensional; it is all analysis and background.
As an adult, Lewis himself had to admit that there had been no element of romance or poetry in his Boxen stories, and because of this
Boxen bears no comparison with Narnia. Lewis's adult fantasy writing pivots on what is glaringly missing from the Boxen narratives –
romance and poetry. It is as though the young Lewis, lost in his fantasy world, snug in his comfortable home environment, was
interested only in the nuts and bolts of creation. There is no
humanity, no reversals of fortune, no pain in Boxen. But up to the
age of ten, by which time most of the history and geography of this
imaginary land had been chronicled, Lewis had experienced very
little beyond the rather humdrum life he led in his parents' house.
As a middle-aged man who had known war, grief, love and toil, he
could express himself in an altogether different way.

Although the creation of Animal Land was almost entirely an
intellectual exercise, it was also an escape route into an inner world,
the place where Jack could find solace when his brother went off to

boarding school. It was a private thing, something only they shared and it excluded the grown-ups. As dull as these early efforts may have been, they were, as Lewis later realised, the perfect training for a literary career.

From the time Warnie left for school in England in March 1905, Jack led a rather solitary existence. He was taught at home by a governess named Annie Harper of whom he appears to have been quite fond, once commenting that, for a governess, she was fairly nice. He had pets, a dog named Tim, Tommy the mouse and Peter the canary, and he was friendly with the servants, Martha the cook and Maude the maid. His mother he described as being, like most ladies of her age, spectacled, stout and keen on knitting, while his father was generally grumpy and at home dressed in a scruffy jumper. Jack also got on well with his grandfather, Richard Lewis, who had lived with his son's family since 1903, when his wife Martha died. Jack remembered him as a fine old gentleman with a raw sense of humour, but he had aged prematurely so that by his early sixties he was deaf and housebound. Jack spent many hours in the old man's room looking through ancient books and photo albums and hearing his tall tales.

Jack was lonely, yet he grew to love the freedom and independence this lifestyle brought him. And, of course, he had the time to devour any book he wished from the huge choice in the house. Even so, as school holidays approached, he longed for his brother's return. He would confide to his diary that he had been thinking of him and missing him desperately. In his mind, on the days Warnie was due home he fancied he could hear him stomping up the stairs and rushing along the corridor to the Little End Room. He imagined to himself how his brother would come into the room and they would shake hands and begin talking right away as though he had only gone away earlier that day.

Lewis described his childhood as 'humdrum', a prosaic happiness, that, he claimed, made it difficult for him to remember at all; and it reveals much that he began his autobiography with a quote from Milton: 'Happy, but for so happy ill secured.' This is both accurate and apt. Until the dreadful year of 1908 Jack was a closeted child, overprotected and almost entirely isolated from the real world. Perhaps because of this, when his previously secure family life began to disintegrate with horrible speed, it was to scar him for the rest of his life and influence the development of his character more than anything else he ever experienced.

Jack's troubles began in the early spring, when Florence Lewis became seriously ill. The doctors could not reach a diagnosis for some time, and simply advised bed rest. This meant that grandfather Lewis was obliged to move out. Tragically, within two weeks, he had died from a stroke.

Feeling overwhelmed with guilt and anxiety for Florence, Albert Lewis became depressed and inward-looking. His mental state grew far worse when the doctors attending his wife concluded that she was suffering from cancer and could not be expected to live long. Florence underwent an operation conducted by a surgeon who visited the house, and for a short time this seemed to halt the progress of the disease. Jack visited his mother and stayed in her room for part of each day throughout that summer, and for a while Albert, the doctors and the family visitors may have cherished a distant hope that Florence would pull through. But there was little room for genuine optimism.

At first Jack and Warnie had hardly any idea of what was happening, but when in mid-summer Florence's symptoms returned and grew rapidly worse, it became obvious to the boys that their mother was now gravely ill. Warnie, who turned thirteen in June, was terrified she would die while he was away at school. During the final term of the school year Albert wrote to warn him that the worst may happen very shortly, and Warnie could do nothing but write back asking simply to be kept informed of everything.

Throughout this time Jack was even more lonely than usual. Depressed and detached, his father could offer little comfort, his grandfather was dead, and each day it became clearer to the nine-year-old that his beloved mother might never recover, that she might never again play with him on the lawn or take him into town for a tram ride or go on long walks in the nearby countryside.

The summer holidays brought Warnie home, but at the same time Florence grew dramatically worse. Now the boys could spend only short spells with her and each day they saw her face become more gaunt and the light slowly fade from her eyes. A few days before Warnie was due to board ship for the new school term in England, Florence Lewis slipped into a coma from which she never regained consciousness. She died early on the morning of 23 August 1908, aged forty-six.

2

The Call of Learning

According to Lewis's own account of the period, the weeks leading up to the moment his mother died were in many ways worse than her death itself. In late middle age he would painfully recall how months before her passing the house had become something of an alien place. He remembered the smell of morphia, the silent, ashen-faced strangers passing in and out of his mother's room. Fifty years after these events he could conjure up the sounds of his mother's suffering and the palpable dread that pervaded Little Lea.

Soon after his mother died, Jack was taken to see her body. She lay under the neatly arranged bedcovers, her face rouged. To the boy, these things were jarringly ephemeral. Overriding all details, mocking the euphemisms was what he described as 'the total disfigurement of death itself'.[1] The funeral was almost too much to bear and he loathed the ritual, which, even as a child, he considered ridiculous flummery. It left him with a loathing for everything associated with public formality, a distrust of the slavish way most people followed convention.

Albert had suffered a terrible year. During the course of one season he had lost both his father and his wife, and only two weeks after Florence's death his brother Joe also died unexpectedly. Jack later reported that he knew his father had never been a man possessed of steady nerves, but, hit by this succession of calamities, Albert was simply overwhelmed. He turned inwards, unable to spare any thought for his sons; and, to make things worse, he began to drink heavily.

According to Lewis, during this period his father seemed quite incapable of controlling his emotions. He would fly into a rage over some small matter and scream at Jack for the most trivial reasons. Under the influence of alcohol, he would collapse in tears one moment and shout and rant the next. Warren stayed home for a short while after the funeral, and during this time, with no one else to turn to for emotional support, the brothers drew closer together. At the same time, emotionally traumatised and unable to relate to his sons, Albert, in his grief, was causing irreparable damage to the solid relationship he had until then enjoyed with them, and this caused a deep wound that was never really healed. 'Thus by a peculiar cruelty of fate . . . ,' Lewis wrote, 'during those months, the unfortunate man, had he but known it, was really losing his sons as well as his wife.'[2]

Although it is perhaps spurious to compare too closely the way lives of creative people have been shaped in part by childhood trauma, some small insights may be gained from considering the remarkable similarities between the tragedy that befell C. S. Lewis at the age of nine and a comparable calamity in the childhood of his close friend and fellow author J.R.R. Tolkien.

After being widowed at a young age, Tolkien's mother Mabel became a devout Catholic. This was a brave decision as all her family were Protestants, and she was ostracised because of it. The immense stress this caused Mabel was, Tolkien always believed, a major factor in precipitating her premature death (aged just thirty-four). Tolkien's mother remained at the heart of her son's emotional being his entire life and her memory acted as both guide and muse for his creative self. More specifically, Tolkien's literary output was enormously influenced by his powerful need to somehow reclaim his lost childhood. In his own mind he associated the fantasy realms he created with a time before his mother's death. This was more than simply a form of subconscious escapism. By constructing his incredibly complex imaginary world of Middle-earth, Tolkien succeeded in losing himself in memory and nostalgia.[3]

In an almost identical fashion, a few years after the death of his mother Jack discovered the pull of fantasy fiction and was drawn towards vivid recollections of the 'atmosphere' of his childhood, the innocent, happy, secure time before death stalked Little Lea and cast a dark shadow over the Little End Room. The death of his mother snapped a cord and exposed him to the real world. It ended for ever those blissful nursery days, days that had in fact already been allowed to run on too long. As an adult, more than four decades after his mother's death Lewis created his own Middle-earth, the land of Narnia, and the stories he set there came from the child he held in aspic somewhere deep in his own mind.

After the initial chaos, decisions about the future of the Lewis boys had to be made. If not exactly happy, Warren was, it seems, at least settled at Wynyard House, near Watford, Hertfordshire, where he had been sent three years earlier in 1905. But what to do with Jack?

Immediately after Florence's death, Albert and his younger son could barely communicate and Jack was feeling extremely uncomfortable at home. The only person he could talk to was Warnie, and so it seemed obvious that he too should be enrolled at Wynyard House, where he would at least have his brother's company. Warren could show him the ropes, and the company of boys of his own age would offer him a healthier environment in which to recover from the family's tragedy.

At least this was the considered view of Albert and of Jack's surviving grandparents. In reality it merely sidestepped the emotional issues facing the Lewises. What Jack really needed was some support from the adults around him. Being bundled off, so soon after losing his mother, to a foreign country and a new school full of boys he had never met before, with only his elder brother for company, only deepened Jack's misery. It was a decision that caused further damage to his relationship with his father, and he never forgot it.

Albert Lewis made many mistakes, but there is no denying that his son was unduly harsh in his recollections of him. At one point in *Surprised by Joy* Lewis refers to his father as 'a man not easily informed' and elsewhere he describes him as 'a simple man who thinks he is a subtle one'. Such comments were unfair, but they stemmed from genuine pain and his father's mishandling of the melodrama into which their lives had descended. If, instead of collapsing under the emotional burden of bereavement, Albert had somehow managed to find fortitude, some inner strength; if he had been able to demonstrate this to his sons, or even turned it into a performance much like the speeches for which he was famed, he may have enjoyed a far better future with them. He may also have been painted in a far better light for posterity. 'They say that shared sorrow draws people closer together,' Lewis wrote. 'I can hardly believe that it often has that effect when those who share it are of widely different ages. If I may trust my own experience, the sight of adult misery and adult terror has an effect on children which is merely paralysing and alienating.'[4]

For Jack, who turned ten just before enrolling at Wynyard House, embarrassment and shame over his father reached a peak as he and Warren boarded the ship bound for Liverpool. On the quayside, Albert wept uncontrollably, but he could not bring himself to share his emotions with his sons, who simply stood in silence concealing their own anguish.

Much that went into shaping the adult C. S. Lewis derived from the events of 1908. His character was moulded by the pain of loss, followed by the agony of isolation, the suppression of emotion, the claustrophobia of life at Little Lea and then the wrench away from all that was familiar. As well as playing a role in framing his direction as a writer, this childhood trauma endowed him with a certain theatricality, a device that also served to protect him. It led him to become extrovert and confident in demonstrating his intellect. But, when it came to expressing emotion to anyone other than intimates, he was closed off, dysfunctional. Lewis was a great self-publicist, a man totally at ease before a microphone or addressing a gathering of scholars, but not even his closest friends could recall any occasion when he talked freely about his own life, his feelings, his dreams, his hopes. And even this character trait played a role in Lewis's creative life. Famed as a religious commentator, a proselytiser of Christianity and author of what might be called 'moralistic fiction', such as *The Screwtape Letters*, he succeeded in pouring his heart on to the page. Here he could comfortably expose every fibre of his inner self, because in this way he could intellectualise his emotions to the point where they were almost no longer emotions at all.

Lewis's initial impressions of England were bad. He found everything unsettling. The first thing he saw when the ship entered Liverpool were the huge dockyards, beyond which lay the flat, featureless landscape of Lancashire. And then there was the train journey from Fleetwood to Euston in London, through what he considered the 'dullest and unfriendliest' strip of land in England. But if the landscape was not much to his liking, it was as nothing compared with the horrors of his new school, a place he later habitually referred to as 'Belsen'.

At one time Wynyard House had been a modestly successful little private school and had even managed to secure a scholarship for one or two of its more promising pupils. However, in 1901, seven years before Lewis junior arrived there, an aggrieved parent had brought a brutality case against the headmaster, Reverend Robert Capron. This was eventually settled out of court, but it had the effect of tarnishing the reputation of the school. By the time Lewis joined his brother there were fewer than twenty pupils (only a dozen of whom were boarders) and Capron was still running the place with his customary brutal methods.

Wynyard House no longer exists and we only have Lewis's personal account of the place to go by, but there is no reason why we should not believe his descriptions, even if his recollections are stamped with an undying hatred for everything to do with the school. As a place of learning it was woefully inadequate. The staff, consisting of 'Oldie' Capron, his son, nicknamed 'Wee-wee' by the boys, and one of Capron's daughters, were joined by a succession of 'ushers' or assistants, some of whom lasted in their position for less than a week. There were no sports, no library and just a single shared bathroom where, once a week, the boys bathed in ice-cold water.

The curriculum was ludicrously narrow and consisted of little more than mathematics, the only subject Capron was interested in. The boys spent every morning going through endless calculations written out on their slates. After the sums were corrected by Capron and he had handed out beatings even for minor errors, one of the boys would be called on to 'say a lesson', which involved reading a passage from the Bible or something prepared by Capron.

Lewis claimed he learned almost nothing during his entire time at the school. When he arrived there he knew a little Latin grammar and just before he left eighteen months later he was still covering the same material. He gained nothing from the endless algebra and geometry lessons. Geography, history, literature and science were never even mentioned. All of this could easily have destroyed any chance he may have had of ever becoming an academic.

Yet the quality of schooling at Wynyard House was not Jack's main concern; he was far more disturbed by the living conditions there and the mentality of the headmaster. The school was filthy, unsanitary, freezing cold in winter and stiflingly hot in summer. The buildings were dilapidated and the furnishings utilitarian in the extreme. But, most importantly, Capron was a master of cruelty.

A big, hairy man with a massive bearded face, Reverend Capron was physically strong, exuded appalling body odour and took sadistic pleasure in torturing many of the boys in his care. He had a particular loathing for the sons of those he considered his social inferiors and duly tormented them with relish.

Lewis recalled vividly how some of his school friends suffered terrible abuse at Capron's hands. On one particular occasion 'Oldie' thrashed the son of a dentist after the boy had committed some trivial offence. To deliver his strokes he ran the length of the room before striking the cane viciously hard across the boy's backside. The poor child had apparently become so used to being flogged by the headmaster that he made almost no sound at each fall of the cane. He merely emitted a barely audible grunt of resignation and relief as the thrashing finally came to an end.

Jack wrote long letters home describing the torment of each day at Wynyard House. He wrote of the complete ineptitude of the staff, the horrendous living conditions and the physical and mental abuse he and the other boys suffered; but his complaints were ignored. During holidays the subject of school was never discussed at home because Albert simply could not stomach such conversation. For his part, Jack could not, as he saw it, demean himself by confessing his misery.

But things grew far worse soon after the start of his second year at the school. During the summer holiday of 1909 Capron's wife died. Rather than taming the sadism of the man, his grief merely served to exaggerate it. The beatings he doled out grew more savage and they were administered more frequently. For Jack, all of this represented a disturbing repetition of history. Capron, it seemed, was another adult who fell apart at the loss of his wife and this collapse worsened an already bad environment. Jack reacted in the same way as he had at home: he turned even further into himself and found some solace in fantasy and inner wanderings.

About this time he began to write more Boxen stories and he started what he later described as a 'novel', a piece of historical fiction he called 'The Ajimywanian War'. He managed to keep it up for a few dozen pages, but only a fragment has survived. As with his earlier stories, reading this one reveals almost nothing of the later Lewis, and even he considered it to be as dry as dust. Having made little headway with this novel, he next turned his mind to an auto-biographical piece which told of life at a decrepit English private school where the teachers were called 'Oldie' and 'Wyn'. But this too fizzled out after only a few chapters.

Fortunately, Jack's time in this purgatory was relatively short.

Late in 1909 the parents of a pupil at the school learned that their son was suffering repeated and unwarranted beatings from Capron and took out a High Court action against him. This time it led to a trial, and although the case was dropped, the bad publicity it generated ripped away any credibility Capron had and Wynyard House was forced to close. By the end of the year Warren had left for Malvern College and Jack, who then had to suffer six months without his brother, was finally shipped back to Ireland in the summer of 1910 with no clear idea of where he would be educated next.

As for Capron, although the trial ruined him, he succeeded in wheedling his way back into a less-than-choosy Church and secured for himself a rectorship at the village of Radstock, a few miles from the school. There he slid into severe mental illness, was certified as insane a few weeks after taking up his appointment and died in an asylum in 1911 aged sixty.

In view of the astonishing degeneracy of Capron's establishment, which, even by the standards of the time, was an illegal mockery of a school, it is rather surprising that Albert Lewis not only sent his son there in the first place but kept him there in spite of the constant stream of letters from the boy begging to be allowed to come home. Even more striking is the fact that Warren didn't warn his father off the idea of enrolling Jack at Wynyard House. We can only assume he was so keen to have his brother's company that he didn't care how bad the place would be for him.

In spite of all the great negatives associated with Wynyard House, even Lewis could not deny that he did get something out of his time there. He suffered more than he gained, but there were some positive aspects to the entire experience. He learned the value of camaraderie. All the boys at the school were in the same vile predicament, and because it was on its last legs there were no new boys, which made it a close-knit community.

When not in class the boys were pretty much left to their own devices and so Lewis was able to read anything he liked. He formed a club with some of the other boys and acquired copies of all the latest boys' magazines, including the *Strand* with its stories by acclaimed authors such as Conan Doyle, H.G. Wells and Ryder Haggard. In these stories Lewis discovered the seed of imaginative fiction that was to influence his own writing enormously, and it awoke in him a sense of wonder, the realisation of a place far from the prosaic, everyday world.

At Wynyard House Lewis also had his first taste of religion. In *Surprised by Joy* he described how, when he discovered his mother was dying, he went through what he later viewed as a 'phoney' religious phase. At the beginning of this he had called on his personal vision of God to intercede in the tragedy facing the Lewis family and to heal his mother of cancer. When, in spite of his prayers, she died, Jack convinced himself that this was not the end, that he would witness a miracle. His mother, he believed, would rise, Lazarus-like, from her deathbed. When this did not happen either, he merely accepted it as a failure like any other, realising there was really no alternative.

It is perhaps surprising that this experience did nothing to damage his subsequent awakening to a genuine religious sense. But Lewis later concluded that this had not in fact been an authentic religious experience at all, merely a childhood fantasy. He had perceived God to be some sort of magician who he hoped would perform miracles, a conjurer who could wave a wand and make everything instantly better.

At Wynyard House Lewis was introduced to the Anglo-Catholicism that had dominated Capron's own distorted psyche. The headmaster took the boys to the local church twice each Sunday, and there Lewis, the product of a family of Irish Protestants who had rarely stepped into a church, first encountered High Church traditions. This was his first experience of hymns sung kneeling and hour-long, largely meaningless sermons delivered by the local rector. And they succeeded in their purpose, terrifying the boy into acquiescence. All of this was far removed from the vision of God he had found through his own mental voyages at Little Lea. After this initiation, and thanks to the power of ritual and fear, he began to read the Bible and to engage in earnest religious conversation with some of the other boys who had also been swept up in the heady atmosphere of suffering and salvation.

But even this did not last long. With the school closed down suddenly, Lewis was soon saying his farewells to his comrades in misfortune and before long found himself at Liverpool docks to take the ship across the Irish Sea and home. Back in the familiar surroundings of Belfast, he started at a new school called Campbell College, close to his father's house.

However, he was not there for long. Jack had been a rather sickly child, and since the age of three he had gone through a long succession of throat infections, stomach upsets, bouts of flu and colds. For the most part he had thoroughly enjoyed his childhood illnesses, for at these times he was pampered and nursed. He had been allowed to spend all his time reading what he wanted, and was completely relieved from any schoolwork. But the conditions at Wynyard House, the uncomfortable 'dorm' and the general squalor of the place had aggravated his delicate constitution. He had undergone an operation on his adenoids towards the end of his time at the school, and when, after only a few weeks at Campbell College, he fell ill again, Albert decided he should come home.

Nevertheless, this decision presented Albert with quite a problem, as he could not face having Jack at home all the time. In search of a solution, he turned to a tutorial college and educational consultancy in London named Gabbitas & Thring, which specialised in placing boys in appropriate private schools around the country. After some deliberation Albert settled on Cherbourg House, a small prep school in Malvern, Worcestershire, very close to where Warnie was by now in his second year at Malvern College.

For Jack, the Christmas of 1910 was a surprisingly happy time. He had recovered from his latest illness, Warnie was home and Wynyard House was nothing but a sour memory. He was also excited by the prospect of a new, and by all accounts, infinitely better school than either Wynyard House or Campbell College. With the holidays over, early in the new year the brothers set off through driving snow and sub-zero temperatures for another journey by sea to England, and for Jack, his third school in two years.

The town of Malvern was far more prepossessing than the environs of Wynyard House, and Warnie had almost certainly told his brother all about the place in advance. By 1911 it was already a good-sized town that had grown threefold since the middle of the previous century, when it had sprung up around a fashionable spa. The fashionable but entirely bogus remedial treatments offered in Malvern had made several unscrupulous businessmen small fortunes, and they had gone on to build fine homes and sponsored local amenities.

Happily for Jack, the move to Cherbourg House was to mark the real beginning of his education. Academically strong, with a staff of reasonably competent teachers, it soon remedied the educational failings of Wynyard House. It was a time during which Jack matured enormously, and for much of this we can thank Warnie, who was now in his mid-teens and something of a 'boy's boy'. He had been at Malvern for almost a year and a half, and in that time he had acquired some habits that were to impress and influence Jack.

Warnie knew the shops that sold cigarettes to schoolboys, the best places to buy comics and cheap novels and where the underaged could drink, and soon after Jack's arrival in Malvern, Warnie introduced him to the pleasures of tobacco and gambling, although neither brother appears to have shown much interest in the local girls. Jack and Warnie could meet up only occasionally and it was risky to take too many liberties in such a small community, but they made the most of it. Jack's fondest memories of the time were of the journeys to and from school at the beginning and end of each term. On their way from Belfast the brothers would take an early train from Liverpool to London and then leave London at the last possible moment, boarding the late train they knew would get them to Malvern just in time for registration. During these few snatched hours beyond the reach of parent or school they would dine at a cheap hotel, go to a music hall and smoke a seemingly endless stream of cigarettes. This pattern of a brief jaunt to London was then joyously repeated on the homeward leg at the start of the school holidays.

Jack had always been 'the clever one', and he was also strong-willed. If anything, he dominated his brother, even though he was over three years younger. Yet Warren was more worldly and he influenced his brother to adopt what they both considered 'grown-up habits'. Even so, Jack was always the more measured and self-possessed of the two. By their early twenties both men had become heavy drinkers, but it was Warren who, in middle age, became an alcoholic who needed to be hospitalised repeatedly and never succeeded in beating his addiction. Each of them treated drink differently. Jack drank socially, as part of the ritual of his life. Warren liked to socialise, but he drifted through life rudderless and never possessed his brother's intellectual prowess, so he relied on alcohol to fill a void. This difference first made itself apparent when they were teenagers and it became more and more significant as they grew older.

Jack enjoyed Cherbourg more than any other school he attended. He was soon singled out as a very strong student with the potential to achieve the highest academic honours. But perhaps the greatest attraction for the place, in his eyes at least, was the young matron, Miss Cowie. Lewis later described her as the best school matron anyone could have had and he grew particularly close to her very quickly.

Miss Cowie was extremely affectionate and attentive, but, most importantly, she appeared in Jack's life at a crucial stage of his intellectual development and his sexual awakening. In letters to Warnie, and later to his lifelong friend Arthur Greeves, Jack made cryptic references to Miss Cowie, for whom he felt an instant overpowering lust. But the matron was more than a mere sexual figure. She was, as Lewis later expressed it, 'floundering in the mazes of Theosophy, Rosicrucianism, Spiritualism, the whole Anglo-American Occultist tradition'.[5] For a boy whose religious faith had been built on shaky foundations and then modified by the half-crazed Christianity of Capron, an attraction to the sort of exotica Miss Cowie favoured must have been quite irresistible.

Lewis claimed that she was primarily responsible for leading him to reject the Christianity he had so recently found. But it is probably more accurate to say that she merely confused him over matters of religious ideology. The fire and brimstone of Capron, Albert's luke-warm Protestantism and the alternative philosophies of the matron all went into the melting pot. Like many young people, Lewis searched within, and his introspection took him through many stages of thought about religion. Miss Cowie was to push him on to another level of thinking, to make him consider unorthodox religious and spiritual ideas.

Sadly for Jack, the matron was not so popular with the head-master and the teachers as she was with the boys and she was dismissed only a few months after his arrival. He never discovered the precise reason she was sacked, but according to his later recol-lection of events, the headmaster had apparently found the matron one day cuddling one of the boys in a fashion he did not much care for. There had also been an earlier incident in which, in front of the boys, Miss Cowie defied one of the senior teachers.

Lewis took a long time to get over her dismissal and in his auto-biography he remembered her with an affection he rarely bestowed on memories of his own relatives. The world Miss Cowie had begun to illuminate for him had inspired him, and her sudden departure left a void. But, late in 1911, perhaps just a few weeks after her dis-missal, he stumbled on a substitute, which he later referred to as his fascination with 'Northernness'.

The meaning of this for Lewis was an embracing of an imagined world, a place peopled by ancients, a vision of a place and a time that had never actually existed, a realm of legend. Such a tapestry was woven in music by Wagner, embroidered in Lewis's mind by the drawings of the artist Arthur Rackham and linked by scraps of sur-viving genuine folklore and fragments of English mythology.

Although Lewis was completely swept up by this new enthusiasm and it became a fascination that remained with him throughout his life, such interests were in fact rather voguish in 1911. Wagner's *Ring Cycle* of operas had been completed in 1874 and by the time the thirteen-year-old Lewis discovered an advertisement in a literary journal for a book illustrated by Rackham entitled *Siegfried and the Twilight of the Gods*, a cult had already coalesced around the annual Bayreuth Festival of Wagner's music, which was by then in its thirty-sixth year.

Yet, fashionable as such creations were, their importance for the young Lewis cannot be overstated. Wagner and Rackham became linchpins for a rapid intellectual development that now took over his life. He had always been considered intelligent and had attended to his school work with assiduity, but now he began to literally crave knowledge. It was almost as though a floodgate had opened in his mind. He had discovered a deep yearning for a veiled, imaginary world and this had brought with it a realisation that all knowledge was important and that with discovery came more delicious mystery; answers offered more questions and these could lead you on and on.

Lewis had no conscious realisation that the road into a world governed by books and organised by lines of writing on a page was a path that led away from what most would call 'reality'. He never stopped to ponder the fact that he had embarked on a journey to a place where he would be untouched by the pain of memory. Here the dark, unpalatable tastes of the real world could not reach him. The world of books and music was not the world in which his mother was as dead as a stone; it was a land he could call his own, beyond interference. It would serve him well, but more important still was the fact that one day he could step even further from the nuts and bolts of the here and now to shape fantasy worlds of his own.

Why should he have been aware of any of this at the time? Few intellectuals realise why they follow such a path. Furthermore, for Lewis, his discovery of 'Northernness' in 1911 was but his first career move, the first rung on the ladder that would lead him to become C. S. Lewis, creator of Narnia.

By 1914, aged sixteen, Jack had served his time at Cherbourg House, a school he had liked, and he was sent to Warren's stamping ground, Malvern College. Cherbourg was a small, cosy prep school, where he had made friends easily and felt motivated. The headmaster had considered him to be something of a child prodigy and he had been on good terms with the teachers. In contrast, Malvern made him feel uncomfortable and for the entire year he spent at the school he remained something of an outsider.

This was not helped by the fact that as Jack had entered 'the Coll', his brother was leaving. At the end of the previous school year, in the summer of 1913, Warren had been caught smoking and was about to be expelled when his father successfully persuaded the Principal to allow him to leave voluntarily so that his career plan (Sandhurst and the Army) might not be ruined.

By now Jack had become intellectually independent. He was reading widely and voraciously. He did what was expected of him at Malvern with little sense of inspiration or excitement, but at the same time he was following an autodidactic path that was taking him way beyond Wagner. He had found an important text, *Myths and Legends of the Teutonic Race* by Donald A. Mackenzie, and had also been enthralled by Paul Henri Mallet's *Northern Antiquities*. From these he moved on to the centuries-old *Poetic Edda* (or 'Elder' *Edda*) and *Prose Edda* (or 'Younger' *Edda*), works of Scandinavian mythology written in Old Icelandic.

Jack had also continued with his own writing. Late in 1911 he had composed an essay entitled 'The Great Master of Bayreuth', a finely crafted critical appraisal of his favourite composer. Then, in 1913, he returned to fiction and wrote a short play he described as a 'Norse tragedy', *Loki Bound*. In this he cast as drone-like followers of Thor those he called the 'bloods' of Malvern (the successful pupils, the prefects and those boys most admired by the teachers). At the same time he portrayed himself as an omnipotent voice of pure reason who, through intellectual rigour, takes on and conquers the ultra-conservative followers of the Norse gods.

Loki Bound was pure wishful thinking, of course, and a clear sign that Lewis did not feel at home at 'the Coll'. Fortunately for him, though, his days there were to be cut short. Whether he realised Jack was unhappy at Malvern, or simply because of financial imperatives,

Albert decided that the summer term of 1914 was to be Jack's last at the school.

After leaving Malvern under a cloud, Warnie had been sent to a private tutor in Surrey in order to cram for Sandhurst, and when the boy had surprised everyone by sailing through the entrance exam, Albert quickly concluded that his younger son might also benefit from such individual attention. By this time Jack had decided he wanted to try for Oxford University and it was agreed that a private tutor would offer him a better chance of passing a scholarship examination.

The tutor who had transformed Warnie's academic chances was none other than William Kirkpatrick, Albert Lewis's former head-master at Lurgan College. Now retired, Kirkpatrick, known by the Lewises as 'Kirk' or 'the Great Knock', taught two or three boys at a time in his rambling old house, Gastons, in the village of Great Bookham, some thirty miles south of London. Here his charges were given close individual tuition designed specifically to gain them scholarships and success in entrance examinations.

Jack sailed to England alone, and this time he was travelling through waters watched over by Royal Navy ships on the hunt for German intruders. War had been declared against Germany during the summer holidays, the first spent without Warnie, who was then undergoing intensive officer training. On 19 September, when Jack was heading by train from Liverpool to London, the carriages were filled with soldiers on their way to Southampton and Portsmouth en route to France, and for many of them the journey would end with premature and violent death.

In just six weeks the Great War had escalated from a regional conflict to engulf the world's most powerful nations. But for Jack the only way in which the war had so far entered his consciousness was the fact that his brother was about to leave for France. Disembarking at a tiny railway station where flower boxes in their last bloom lined window sills and the platform was swept clean by an elderly porter, he was about to enter a very different place, a book-lined world of calm and peace.

Kirkpatrick was a tall, lean man who, at sixty-six when Lewis came under his tutelage, was still muscular and fit. He had a deep, booming voice and a heavily whiskered face, and habitually wore such shabby clothes that his new pupil at first mistook him for the gardener. Kirkpatrick was a highly educated man with very strong opinions, and, through the power of his intellect and his exceptional talents as an educator, he was to become one of the most influential people in Lewis's early life.

At Great Bookham Lewis followed a well-organised curriculum centred on Latin and Greek which took him deep into the roots and origins of literature. At the same time he learned from his new guide how to learn. Kirkpatrick was principally a logician, who, given the right student, could work a refined methodology into the learning process to produce very impressive results. He liked both the Lewis boys and had enjoyed having Warnie in his house, but on an intellectual level Jack was an entirely different proposition. Like Warren, Jack was charming, respectful and polite, but he also possessed a versatile and powerful intellect. The Great Knock realised very quickly that the boy's full potential had never been tapped, and that the teaching he had received at a succession of mediocre schools and his dislike of public schools had held him back. He offered Lewis the essential ingredients missing from his education up to that time – discipline and methodology.

A complex man, Kirkpatrick was friendly and often gentle, but, in his utter devotion to logic and intellectual rigour, he hated flabby thinking and had cultivated the outward persona of a man of pure intellect. He had developed the habit of questioning everything and argued over each point of meaning in a sentence, every move or action of an individual. At first Lewis was confused, for he had never met anyone who thought in the way his tutor did, but he was also immediately fascinated by it. Before long he had begun to assimilate Kirkpatrick's approach and this new mannerism stayed with him for the rest of his life. In recalling how Lewis approached conversation, many of his friends and colleagues later described the man's probing manner, his insistence on clarity and refined thinking,

even in the simplest things. For some, this was an intensely annoy-
ing trait, but by the time Lewis had reached adulthood it had
become ingrained into his personality.

As much as Lewis came to admire and like Kirkpatrick, he had
very little time for his wife, Louise. He considered her vulgar and
simple and in his written descriptions he painted her as being interested only in tea parties and sewing. In fact Mrs Kirkpatrick was far
from simple and she tried hard to become friends with her husband's latest charge, accompanying him to the theatre and reading to
him in the evenings. She took him to London to see the Ballets
Russes and even attempted to introduce him to 'modern' authors
such as Virginia Woolf.

Later Lewis wrote in his autobiography that the happiest times at
Great Bookham were when Mrs Kirkpatrick was out of the house,
and almost every reference to the woman is barbed. Such an attitude
towards a soft target like Louise Kirkpatrick is revealing in its unfair-
ness and shows how Lewis had long idealised the memory of his
mother to such an extent that no other older woman could pass
muster. He was also still smarting from the lost affection he had
offered Miss Cowie, and it is striking that, although Mrs
Kirkpatrick tried to introduce Lewis to young women she knew, he
showed them no real interest. After one lame attempt to get to
know a Belgian girl who had been evacuated to the village at the start
of the war, Jack appears to have quickly lost interest and returned to
Dante, Homer and his other favourites.

In all other ways Jack took immediately to life at Gastons. He
was often bored and he missed his brother, but it was an idyllic environment for him. He loved the countryside and had inherited a
liking for long jaunts from his mother's father, Thomas Hamilton,
who would often trek for twenty miles in the rain and claim he
enjoyed it. Jack was surrounded by books, and not only the sort he
had read at home or those he had been force-fed at school. At the
Great Knock's house he began to fully appreciate the vast canon of
Greek literature and history, and he also grew to love Dante, Milton
and Spenser. At the same time he discovered the work of the fantasy

writer George MacDonald and developed a special love for his most famous book, *Phantastes.*

Such discoveries were an important influence on the development of Lewis's imagination and intellect. They were every bit as significant as the material on the curriculum at Gastons. Furthermore, just as Kirkpatrick was transforming Lewis's academic life, he also influenced the young man's thinking in other ways. Brought up as a Presbyterian, the Great Knock had long since relegated all religion to the waste bin of logical absurdity and so, probably for the first time in his life, Lewis was daily in the presence of a dedicated atheist.

He was fascinated with this experience and by the end of the year he was writing to Warnie describing the 'Gastons heresies', with which his elder brother was, of course, already familiar. Warnie, who had embraced Christianity at school, had remained quite unaffected by Kirkpatrick's leanings. Jack, though, was clearly taken with his mentor's stance.

Ironically, just at this time Albert decided that Jack should be confirmed into the Church (even though he was not a religious man himself). However, Jack had reached an intellectual position on religion that he would maintain for another fifteen years. He considered all religions to be mythologies, stories created by simple, primitive people to explain the complexities and terrors of the world, and to him in 1914 Christianity was no different from sun worship or the pagan religions associated with the gods of Olympus. Nevertheless, as a virtual atheist he underwent confirmation for his father's benefit just before Christmas 1914, a process he considered a silly performance in which he was nothing but an actor.

In his autobiography Lewis makes no reference to resenting this ritual but claims that at the time, even if he had wanted to sit down with Albert to discuss such things, he could never have made his father understand his religious feelings. Jack had not been close to his father since Florence Lewis's death some six years earlier, and as he began to develop his own distinct and highly evolved vision of life he found he could barely communicate with his father at all. As far as Jack was concerned, absence did not make the heart grow fonder; for him holidays at home (which from 1914 were spent without Warnie, who had been sent to the Western Front soon after war was declared) became increasingly fraught.

An indication of how much resentment Jack felt towards his father is the fact that some twenty-five years after Albert's death his son could still find few fond words for him and the paternal home. Referring to Little Lea, Lewis wrote of 'home and the way we hated it and the way we enjoyed hating it'.[6] Elsewhere he wrote: 'I thought Monday morning, when he [Albert] went back to his work, the brightest jewel in the week.'[7]

The second statement is strongly reminiscent of what Jack thought of Mrs Kirkpatrick, and in some ways he saw his father and the wife of his tutor in a similar light. In his mind, both of them favoured what he considered 'low-brow' culture. Each was caught up with the minutiae of everyday life to the exclusion of more lofty wanderings.

Behind their father's back, Jack and Warnie referred to him as 'P'daytabird', a name derived from the way Albert pronounced 'potato'. And as Jack's education broadened and he surpassed his father's limited knowledge of art, history and literature, in letters and in private chats with his brother he began to mock their father's 'vulgar' tastes.

For many years Albert remained quite oblivious to Jack's growing contempt. When the boys were home from school, he often took them to popular operas, such as *Carmen*, or to the theatre to see a contemporary musical. Warnie loved such things, but Jack was always a reluctant member of the party and could rarely refrain from comparing them unfavourably (and unfairly) with his beloved Wagner.

It is difficult to know precisely why Lewis was so repelled by his father. The most likely reason is that in some way he blamed him for the premature death of his mother. Of course, there was no logic to this, and if it is the reason, then it came from a subconscious prejudice, an irrational sentiment often felt by the bereaved, a feeling in Jack's case of 'Why did it have to be her and not him?' As a boy he had made a complete emotional commitment to his mother and then she had been cruelly snatched from him. He had had his fingers burned and so at the time he 'felt' (rather than believed) that he could never commit to love again.

Indeed, while he was living with the Kirkpatricks Jack felt almost totally alone in the world. Warnie was far away and leading a quite alien existence. They wrote to each other almost every day and Jack learned of Army life, which his brother enjoyed immensely. In return, Jack reminded him of the characters at Gastons and the daily events in the village. But they were far apart and travelling roads that would not cross again for many long years.

Fortunately for Jack, late in 1914 this vacuum in his life was filled by a new friend who would remain close to him for his entire life. Arthur Greeves, an exact contemporary of Warnie, was a close neighbour in Belfast and had lived with his family almost directly across the street from Little Lea for several years. Arthur and Jack were acquainted but only became close after Jack left for Gastons and Warnie began his military training. Soon Arthur had become Jack's only intimate contact with home, and the two young men wrote very long, deeply personal letters to each other in which they exposed their innermost thoughts, beliefs, hopes and dreams.

The two of them were, in many important ways, very different. Arthur was homosexual and had been aware of his sexual inclinations from his early teenage years. Jack knew he was heterosexual even though he had had no direct experience of sex. From confessions to Arthur, we learn that Jack had started masturbating at Cherbourg, and had been racked with guilt and then thrown into depression because he could not stop himself in spite of the irrational but intense shame he felt. All of this he could share with no one but his friend in Belfast.

Arthur was deeply religious, and Jack, because he had lost his own embryonic faith around the age of fourteen, was keen to argue out the matter with his new soulmate. Arthur was happy to oblige, and so they exchanged long, carefully composed screeds until a particular line of thought had been exhausted. Arthur was an artist and later studied at the Slade in London, but he was also interested in many of the same things as Jack. Arthur had discovered 'Northernness' about the same time as Lewis and he too loved Wagner. What began as a relationship to replace the absent Warnie, and a need to find someone to relate to intellectually, grew quickly to become as important to Jack as any long-standing fraternal feelings. Indeed, as Jack prepared at Great Bookham for the Oxford entrance examination, his friendship with Arthur had become just about the most important thing in his life. In him he had found a friend with whom he could not only share his intellectual discoveries but also compare notes on his deepest drives and the things that influenced him most profoundly.

It was Arthur who first prompted Jack to write about 'Joy'. For Lewis, 'Joy' was a sense, a feeling, a quality difficult to define but which he was sure lay at the heart of all great art. He had first sensed this as a small child looking out at the Castlereagh Hills of Belfast. In those days this response had been a thing without name, simply an emotional reaction. But later, as he found words to define feelings, he gave it the name 'Joy'. For Lewis, 'Joy' was always to be found at the centre of all the things he cherished. It was the sense of wonder that supported the fantasy literature he loved, the music he adored and the beauty he could see in many simple, everyday things. Most crucially, it was 'Joy' that provided the foundation for his own creations. 'Joy' was the cornerstone of Narnia, it imbued the forces of good in his novel *That Hideous Strength* and it is the quality he later believed to be represented by Christian belief. For Lewis, it was the God in all things.

'Joy' was something Arthur understood but a concept Warnie struggled with. It was something which, in Jack's biased opinion, his father Albert could never have comprehended. An appreciation of 'Joy' was something that drew Lewis to those he befriended as an adult, and it was the thing positioned at the epicentre of all learning and the books that so absorbed him for the whole of his life. In 1916, as he sat his Oxford scholarship exam, the search for 'Joy' was the very essence of the reason he was there. He knew even then that within the world of scholarship and academia he could spend his entire life pursuing 'Joy', and, armed with this surety, he gladly allowed himself to be subsumed into the universe it illuminated.

3

Scholarship and War

By the end of 1916 Jack Lewis had been Kirkpatrick's pupil for almost two and a half years and he was now ready to sit the scholarship examination in Oxford. If he could pass this, he would be accepted into a college within the university, given a scholarship worth a little over £100 per year and he would take a huge step towards life as an academic.

Lewis had by now reached the conclusion that he wanted to be a writer. But already he knew this was an extremely difficult profession in which to make a living. Instead he would, he knew, settle, at least temporarily, for the academic life. The Great Knock knew and understood what Jack wanted and had written a letter to Albert Lewis (which Jack only saw many years later) in which he made it clear the boy would be quite useless in any career except that of a scholar or writer and advised Albert to simply accept this as fact.

Lewis's first view of Oxford was both comic and elevating. The day before the first scholarship paper, he travelled by train from Great Bookham, emerged from the wrong side of the railway station and headed off on foot into the rather grim and grimy suburb of Botley. It was only after walking a mile *away* from the centre of

Oxford that he realised the dull shops and terraced houses he had passed could not possibly be the ancient heart of the city. He turned, and there ahead of him in all its ageless beauty stood the sandstone spires and medieval splendour he had dreamed about. And so began a lifelong love affair with this city. Apart from a few years towards the end of his life when he held a professorship at Cambridge, Lewis never lived anywhere but Oxford, and even before he had become a graduate he considered the place his home.

Oxford in December 1916 was not the city it had been three years earlier, nor indeed the vibrant icon of learning it would become once again when the guns were silenced. There were only 315 students in all the colleges and many of these were either foreign scholars or medical students. More than a third of the total were also in the Officers' Training Corps, making ready for their turn at the Front. Many of the fifteen thousand or more students who were at the university during a normal term had already died in France during the first two and a half years of the war, and those still alive were now mired in mud in some godforsaken trench or lying wounded in hospital.

To a visitor transported back in time to Oxford then, the place would seem utterly different from the busy, sprawling city it is today. Oxford has retained much of its beauty and serenity, but this is now concentrated in the tiny lanes and the college quadrangles, the traffic-free squares and the few high-walled gardens in the centre of the city. Here it is still possible to lose oneself and, with a little imagination, picture the place that Shelley or Edmund Halley once saw. But step beyond this idyll and the High Street suffers the same traffic jams and pollution as any other urban area in the early twenty-first century. A McDonald's may be found just off The High and tacky souvenir shops jostle for space with the numerous bookshops lining Broad Street and The Turl.

In 1916 the ancient buildings were exposed and uncluttered and the place would have been very much quieter and cleaner than today. Along the High Street, few cars would have passed Lewis as he headed from his room to the examination hall at Oriel College on

5 December, trudging through the first snow of winter, which had fallen the night before. It was stunningly beautiful. The spires stood bedecked with snow and the low winter sun cast a pale orange light on the glistening crystals. Young girls hurried past him through the chill, rushing to work in shops along The High or in the factories clustered together in Jericho, half a mile to the north-west of the city centre.

In sitting for this scholarship, Lewis was following in illustrious footsteps. It was a trial endured by almost all prospective students wishing to gain entry to Oxford. Some of the men Lewis was later to work with and drink beer with in Oxford's pubs also sat in the hall of Oriel that day or had gone through the same exhausting series of examinations a few years earlier. Tolkien had sat the exam twice: once in December 1909, when he had failed, and again in December 1910, when he gained the lesser award of an Exhibition.

Lewis found the scholarship exams hard going and after finishing them he was utterly convinced he had failed. Returning home to Belfast straight after five days in Oxford, he immediately warned his father to expect the worst. The only thing that tempered his nerves was the fact that, whatever the outcome, he would almost certainly be required to take up a commission in the Army. The first years of the war spent in scholastic isolation in the Surrey countryside had been for him a mere reprieve. His turn would come soon and, like many of his contemporaries, scholarship or no scholarship, he might not live to study at Oxford anyway. Even so, when, on the morning of 23 December, after more than two weeks of anxious waiting, a letter arrived at Little Lea offering Jack Lewis a highly prized scholarship at 'Univ', University College, he was naturally overjoyed.

Jack had genuinely believed he would not be accepted by Oxford, and this illustrates just how much he had changed during his years with the Great Knock. At fourteen and fifteen he had been quite intolerably arrogant and self-opinionated. 'Priggish' was the word he later used to describe himself as a young teenager and it was an accurate one, meaning a person with precise morals but no sense of proportion.

In December 1916 Jack had just turned eighteen. He was relatively fit, troublesome childhood diseases had been left behind, and his liking for long country walks had built up his stamina. He was about average height, broad-shouldered and well built. A photograph of Lewis senior taken around 1881 could, at first glance, be mistaken for one of Jack around 1918. In an age before young people made it their business to dress and to fashion their hair in any way that would mark them out as different from their parents, Lewis junior could easily have passed for his father at the same age. They each wore their hair swept to one side and greased down, each displayed the same scruffiness, even when in a smart suit, each possessed (in youth at least) the same long, slender, elegant nose and each had the same dark, probing eyes. Jack was aware of these astonishing similarities and once declared: 'My father and I were physical counterparts.'[1] Today he might have used the word 'clone'.

And what of Lewis's mind at this time? His most outstanding qualities were his powerful memory and his unquenchable thirst for knowledge. He had not yet shown any unique literary talent but he had a burning desire to be 'a poet'. Of course such a desire was not at all uncommon in 1916. Many young men of Lewis's background and with his intellectual leanings yearned to be poets and there were some of his generation who, in their short lives, did demonstrate their prodigious skills: middle-class intellectuals who fought in the trenches and did not survive the war, such as Rupert Brooke and Wilfred Owen; or Siegfried Sassoon, who lived to resume his literary career after the conflict.

Lewis showed no particular talent for the literary form that immortalised these contemporaries. Many of his early poems are embarrassingly bad – a fact he was all too willing to admit to in later years – and he never did acquire any great gift for pure poetic expression. Indeed it was to be many years before he found his own, unique path to literary greatness, a path that incorporated the spirit of poetry but used it within the confines of a very different genre more suited to his type of intellect.

His intellectual powers were finely tuned but rather narrow. Like many great achievers, his abilities were unfocused when he was a boy, but were later concentrated on a small range of targets. As a young man he was already a good essayist and a gifted critic, and he possessed a natural understanding of language. A boyhood fascination with the arcane, with myth and legend, had remained, and 'Northernness' was still his muse, as it would ever be. The life of the scholar, the writer, the emulsifier of dreams, was one to which he was naturally suited. But before he could even start on the road to becoming an academic and a writer, in 1917 he had to confront the same horror as almost all men of his generation – the war.

By the beginning of the year the fighting was going badly. On many fronts the conflict had reached a bloody stalemate, each side periodically gaining a few hundred feet of blanched soil for the price of thousands of young men. At this time it seemed the war (which a few had claimed would be over by Christmas 1914) might go on for ever, and Lewis knew he would have to join the fighting at some point.

After Christmas 1916 he returned to Great Bookham to prepare for his first examination at Oxford. Known as Responsions, this would test his mathematics, an aspect of the curriculum that he had always hated and which was, in spite of the fact his mother was a brilliant mathematician, one of his weakest subjects. The Great Knock spent two months preparing Lewis for the exam and in March he returned to Oxford to sit it. He failed, but was told he could resit Responsions later in the year. However, he would have to pass it on his second attempt if he wished to continue his undergraduate studies at the university.

It was a glorious, warm summer in Oxford, a world away from death in Flanders fields. The sun shone bright on the River Cherwell and cherry trees spread their vibrant colour against a perfect blue sky. During that summer of 1917 there were even fewer students at Oxford than there had been during the previous winter, and all around the city there were signs of war. One of the University College quads had been set aside as a camp for wounded soldiers, and the dean of the college refused to produce a set course of studies for the students because their work was sure to be interrupted by military service. The only exceptions to this rule were those officially certified as unfit for duty, foreign students and, according to Lewis's memory, one Sinn-Feiner who refused to fight for England. These students were fortunate enough to stay on at Oxford throughout the war as if nothing was happening in mainland Europe.

The upside of all this was that the relatively small number of undergraduates were treated especially well. Indeed Lewis had never known such luxury. He was provided with a vast set of rooms to call his own which came with a grand piano and expensive furnishings. On the polished oak floorboards lay ancient Persian rugs and at one end a huge fireplace stood beneath a carved stone mantelpiece. On his arrival a 'scout', or servant, made him a cup of tea and helped him unpack.

Lectures were delivered in a small hall close to his rooms. Meals were held in college and although the food was not quite up to pre-war standards, it was infinitely better than he had been used to at home or at the Kirkpatricks' house. Nor were beer and wine yet rationed. This was a sacred bubble of civilisation and it could only be enjoyed in full if one was able, for a short time at least, to keep out of mind that very different world not so far away across the English Channel, a world that would be intruding all too soon.

While Lewis was finding his feet in Oxford and cramming for his second attempt at Responsions, he had begun training with the OTC (Officers' Training Corps). He described this in formal, factual letters to his father and in a more honest and revealing correspondence with Arthur Greeves, with whom he had now been in constant touch for well over a year. 'The Corps proves very much more agreeable than the Malvern one — everyone is so friendly and reasonable,' he told his father.[2]

Albert was quite naturally growing worried about Jack joining the action in France. 'It is the beginning of his military career and the prospect covers me like a pall,' he confided in a letter to Warnie about Jack's involvement with the OTC. 'It is almost certain that he will be rushed into the Infantry, either with a commission or in the ranks.'[3]

In his letters to Arthur, Jack told a similar story – of how he was enjoying life in Oxford and finding officer training far from dull – but he could also share news of more risqué pursuits. Greeves quickly learned of his friend's new taste for swimming naked at Parson's Pleasure, a cordoned-off section of the river where gentlemen could 'bathe without the encumbrance of clothes'.

These activities were innocent enough but there were other new, often dark inner drives that were starting to preoccupy Lewis and about which he could tell only Arthur. He continued to write to him of his masturbatory fantasies, and he was beginning to demonstrate a strong interest in sadism, which he described with relish. In a letter written in January 1917 Lewis begins to explain that he is writing the letter on his knee and this seemingly innocent comment leads him on to a discourse on whipping and spanking. He declares: 'Across my knee ... of course makes one think of positions for whipping: or rather not for whipping (you couldn't get any swing) but for that torture with brushes ... very humiliating for the victim.' Soon he was signing his letters to Greeves 'Philomastrix' ('lover of the whip') and detailing gruesome fantasies involving Arthur's younger sister, in which he whipped her 'for the good of her soul'. In other letters he described a particularly beautiful girl he had seen in Oxford and what pain she would have suffered if she had received only half the torment he had inflicted on her in his imagination.[4]

It is difficult to know what to make of all this. Many years later, when Lewis had become a famous Christian apologist, he was naturally rather ashamed of these adolescent speculations. Since then many of his friends (men who only knew him as an adult) have argued forcefully that Lewis's fascination with sadism was a fleeting thing, a by-product of hormonal confusion. This is a possibility, but why did he have these fantasies in the first place? His interest in pain and physical torture indicates a troubled adolescent mind. It is conceivable that his attraction to such practices came from suppressed but understandable fears: of the war, of his own imminent death. Perhaps it was simply a way in which he could deal with living in such a dangerous time, living with the knowledge that his life might soon be cut short.

Another explanation comes from a consideration of his own past rather than any imagined future. His taste for punishment and the infliction of pain might well have stemmed from his inner anger, his resentment and bitterness. Jack, we must remember, bottled everything up, and he had been doing so for many years. There must always have been the possibility that his pent-up emotions would break out in some unusual way.

As far as anyone knows, Jack's attraction to sadism never strayed beyond his own imagination, but no one will ever know what went on behind closed doors later in his life. For the eighteen-year-old at least, these sadistic musings went no further than that: onanistic fantasies and bravura to impress Arthur.

By June 1917 Lewis's first wonderful term at Oxford was over and the long summer vacation was on him. This time, though, the holiday would be different. Because of the war there was no official college 'vac' and he was required to stay in England. He was now in limbo between academia and life as a soldier, for he could be called on to fight at any time. Indeed he was quite sure he would not be returning to lectures in October, and on 10 June he was obliged to leave his rooms in college to barrack in Keble College, which had been set up as a temporary Army camp. 'It is a great change to leave my own snug room at Univ for a carpetless room, with beds without sheets or pillows, kept miserably tidy and shared with another cadet at Keble,' he complained to Greeves.[5]

Lewis placed the soldiers he met there into three categories. The first, the 'rankers', were men who had already fought at the Front and were home on leave or had been wounded in action. For the most part he liked and respected these men, although even then he tarnished his assessment of them with the elitism that still surfaced in him on occasion, reporting that they had: 'naïve conceptions of how gentlemen behave among themselves' and that this led them into 'impossible politeness that is really very pathetic'. The second group were 'cads and fools', a company that consisted of men who were itching for violence or were escaping from some intractable problem in civilian life; they were uniformly vulgar, unruly and best avoided. The third group, in which he placed himself, were public school and university men, officer material and the sort with whom he chose to spend most of his time.[6]

Much of the time life was rather dull for Lewis and he did not like existing in such a limbo. He could not study and he soon became bored with drill and training. The one bright light in his life was a new friend, Edward Moore, always known as Paddy, a cadet the same age as him who had just left Clifton College in Bristol. Paddy was Jack's new room-mate at Keble, and they had been brought together because their names were adjacent in the alphabetical list of cadets. Lewis's first impression of Paddy was that he was rather young and immature, but this changed within days and he was soon writing home about him as a 'very decent sort of man'.[7]

Paddy and Jack were to know each other for only a short time, but the pervading atmosphere of anxiety and impermanence that affected everyone, even before they were to take their turn at the Front, made the two men's friendship unusually intense. Late in the summer, after Lewis had been commissioned as a second lieutenant in the Somerset Light Infantry, he was given a month's leave before his active service was due to begin. Before returning home to Belfast for two weeks, he decided to spend the first half of his leave in Bristol, where he met for the first time Paddy's mother, Janie, and his sister, Maureen.

As we shall see in the next chapter, this encounter was a momentous one for Lewis, a meeting charged with the tense mood of summer 1917. For him, as for so many thousands of young men, the near future was now clearly mapped out. He would soon be in the trenches. But what life then held for him was quite uncertain and this was a thought at once terrifying and exciting.

For others, such as Albert Lewis, this period held no element of excitement, but was simply terrifying. After a brief stay at Little Lea, Jack left on 28 October 1917 to travel to an Army camp at Crown

Hill, near Plymouth, where he was to receive training before embarking for France. Albert, once more alone and depressed in Belfast, chose to spend each evening with a fresh bottle of whisky.

By 15 November Lewis had his papers and knew he would be shipped across the Channel within days. Given forty-eight hours' leave, he decided he would not return to Belfast but instead he boarded a train for Bristol to spend some time with the Moores. Before leaving Plymouth he sent a telegram to his father that read: 'Report Southampton Saturday. Can you come Bristol. If so meet at Station. Reply Mrs Moore's address.'

Albert Lewis had no idea what his son meant and telegraphed back: 'Don't understand telegram. Please write.' But by the time this message reached Bristol it was too late for father and son to meet, for Jack was already under military orders and confined to camp. Clearly anxious to reassure his father, he replied with a long telegram in which he explained that he had only a short period of leave and that he was sorry about the wording of the first telegram. He then told his father not to worry and lied that it would probably be some time before he was to be shipped to France because he had only completed a short period of training. By the time Albert received this message, however, Jack was on his way to Southampton.

This was a crucial moment in the lives of both men, and there are two ways to view this unfortunate exchange of telegrams. One explanation, giving Albert the benefit of the doubt, supposes that his reaction stemmed from a simple misunderstanding. Perhaps Albert, living in Ireland and rather isolated from events, was not altogether aware of what was happening in the war. Indeed, a letter Albert wrote to Warnie some two weeks later makes it clear that he had only just heard that his younger son was then in France and he expressed his horror that an eighteen-year-old boy could be sent to the Front after receiving only basic training. This letter implies that Albert had not realised how soon after he had seen him in October Jack would be sent into the battlefield.

An alternative view casts Albert in a less flattering light. It might be argued that after three years of all-out war with Germany he must have known what was happening. He and Jack must have discussed the gravity of the situation and how young men were being transported into battle in their millions. If indeed he did know what to expect, then he should have responded very differently to Jack's message and gone to see him off.

For us now to apportion blame is a pointless exercise, but that was the reaction of those involved. Albert blamed himself for not responding to Jack's call and he began to drink still more, wallowing in guilt and hurt by the fact that his son had chosen to share what he must have known to be his final leave with another family, the Moores. For Jack, who was then preparing to start the slow, painful journey to the killing fields of the front line, there was at first neither time nor emotional space to think about it. It was only later that he added this incident to what he saw as a catalogue of reasons to feel resentful towards his father.

It is a striking fact that in his autobiography, written three decades after the First World War, Lewis devoted no fewer than eleven chapters to his early childhood and education but only half a short chapter to his war experiences. This tells us a great deal about the man. Lewis had a lifelong fixation with his own childhood, and for him his most important years were not those spent as an academic, a successful writer and Christian populariser, nor indeed a soldier, but the period that shaped his imagination and provided the material from which he later fashioned his literary creations.

Lewis was aware that he had spared very little ink describing his time in the trenches, short though this was. In *Surprised by Joy* he explains this omission by saying that, viewed from many years on, his experiences seemed simply to be those of someone else, not the younger version of himself. Remarkably, his war was less real to him than the images of childhood and the fantastic worlds he read about and manufactured in his own mind. In considering the lives of most men who have had first-hand experience of war, it would be easy to say that the anguish and suffering they endured was too painful to recall, that for them such memories were best compartmentalised and shut away. This may also have been the case with Lewis, but when we consider how meticulously he regurgitated his schoolboy agonies and the loss of his mother, we can see that he was not too squeamish to put other painful recollections on the page.

In his own mind at least, Second Lieutenant C. S. Lewis was an entirely different man from the one who sat at his desk in Oxford and wrote *Surprised by Joy*. As a soldier, he had adopted an alien and quite temporary 'survival persona', and unlike many of those who survived the war and later became writers, he had no wish to draw on what he saw and felt in France and to write about it directly. Lewis's creative wellspring lay in an altogether different place, a more distant land in terms of both his own life and human experience. He had little interest in the work of the war poets and, except for a short experiment with war poetry, he never made mental links between the experiences of late 1917 and early 1918 and his own literary imaginings.[8]

Lewis arrived at the Front on his nineteenth birthday, 29 November 1917. In carefully worded letters to his worried father he gave the impression that things were not as bad as press reports made them out to be. His commanding officer, Lieutenant Colonel Majendie, Lewis described as 'a splendid fellow', and he gave the impression that it was all a rather exciting, *Boy's Own* adventure.[9]

The last Christmas of the war came and went in 1917 and Jack saw action in quick, violent, horrifying bursts that punctuated long periods of relative calm back at camp a few miles behind the lines. Nothing had prepared him for the ghastly sights and the sheer terror of what he was now living through, and, of course, nothing could have. This was as far removed as one could get from the gentility of Oxford and the sweet summer smells of Great Bookham. At the Front all was death and destruction. The trenches often ran thigh deep with filthy, muddy, rat-infested water. Rotting corpses lay everywhere and there was always the chance that a sniper's bullet or a piece of shrapnel could kill you in an instant.

Like the soldiers under his command, Lewis slept, ate and defecated in the stinking corridors of mud that had become his vista, his landscape. During those blessed reprieves at the camp, things were a little better. Clothes could be washed and officers slept on makeshift beds thrown together from anything soft that came to hand. Here there were books, there was tea, even a chair to sit in. But at no time could you escape the noise, the racket of machine guns, the roar of howitzers, the explosions and the screams of pain. Each moment was either an eternity of anxious boredom or as nightmarish as anything from the mind of Hieronymus Bosch. After a few long, agonising weeks in France, Lewis could no longer leave out the painful details in letters to his father. He gave descriptions of the shells whistling overhead and the loss of men whom he had come to know and admire. Only with a huge effort could he leaven this intense horror with tall stories of surprisingly comfortable dugouts fitted with braziers and bunks.

Some time in January Lewis had what he later called 'the good luck' to fall prey to trench fever.[10] This was an extremely common disease in the trenches, spread by lice. In many cases it presented itself merely as flu-like symptoms, but more often than not it proved debilitating, weakening soldiers so much they could hardly stand, let alone fight. The field hospitals of both sides treated more men with trench fever than men wounded in action, and Lewis became another hospital statistic when he was taken to Étaples to recover.

A letter reporting this news reached Albert Lewis a few weeks later, but Warren had learned the whereabouts of his brother much sooner. At that time Captain Lewis was billeted at an Army camp a little over fifty miles from Étaples. At the first opportunity he borrowed a bicycle from a fellow officer and cycled to the hospital to visit Jack before returning to camp that same evening. Many soldiers died from the symptoms of trench fever and it is an indication of just how worried Warnie must have been that he undertook a round trip of over a hundred miles in one day on a bicycle, close to enemy lines, so that he could check up on his younger brother.

Lewis actually had a relatively mild dose of trench fever and, much to his dismay, he was back at the Front a few weeks after being admitted to hospital.

Late in March 1918 the Germans began what was to be the last great push of the war, a desperate and doomed counter-offensive intended to break the armies ranked against them (including the Americans, who had joined the war the previous year). Every man who could stand with a gun in his hand was needed at the Front.

But this time Jack saw little in the way of battle before receiving a wound that ended his career as a serving officer. On 15 April 1918 he took part in the battle of Arras. He was standing on Mount Bernenchon when a stray English shell landed close by. It killed instantly a man with whom he had recently become very friendly, Sergeant Ayres, and pieces of shrapnel from the blast hit Lewis in the leg, hand and chest.

Lewis thought he had died. In this state he visualised himself floating, numb. He felt no fear, no pain; it was, he recalled, a rather dull, uninteresting state of being, a boring nowhere land without markers. His injuries turned out to be exactly the sort most desired by reluctant soldiers, wounds that could get you out of the war for a time but were not permanently debilitating. He quickly found himself back in hospital, and this time he stayed under the care of field nurses until his wounds were bandaged and arrangements were made for his transportation back to England.

He did not know it at first, but for him the war was over. Six months later the Germans surrendered. Lewis could think of the future once more, and if he had learned only one thing from the war it was to make the most of any new chances he was to be given. After the darkness of the past few years, in November 1918, still not quite twenty years old and bursting with energy and a desire to prove himself as an intellectual heavyweight, he must have seen the future as a cloudless horizon.

4

'Mother'

Lewis had arrived back in England on 25 May 1918 and was transported straight to the Endsleigh Place Hospital in London to recover from his wounds. Almost at once he fell into a depression that was almost certainly triggered by post-traumatic stress.

In such a frail mood he turned first to his father for comfort, asking him in letter after letter to visit him in hospital. 'You will be able to come over, will you not, if only for a few days?' he wrote, adding wistfully: 'we must get Kirk up to meet you and have a famous crack.'[1] A few weeks later, after Lewis had paid a quick visit to Great Bookham on a day out from hospital and in a rather sorry state, he wrote again to his father, confessing: 'I know I have often been far from what I should . . . but please God, I shall do better in the future. Come and see me. I am home-sick, that is the long and the short of it.'[2] But Albert Lewis stayed in Belfast and did not once make the relatively easy trip to London to see his son so recently returned from the war.

This behaviour raises questions about the mental state of Albert Lewis as well as the complex relationship between father and son. It is possible that Albert was still smarting from the fact that Jack had not spent all his final leave with him immediately before departing for France. It is also possible that he resented not seeing his son just prior to his heading for Southampton and the trenches the previous November. Maybe he believed Jack had caused confusion deliberately to avoid meeting up. All these thoughts may have gone through Albert's head, but whatever his reasons, it is difficult to excuse his neglect of his son at this time.

Apologists for Lewis senior have pointed out that his work placed great demands on him and that he could not simply drop everything and leave for a few days in England. Warnie himself provided this very excuse in letters to his brother, each of which was written in an effort to smooth over the brewing emotional crisis; but even he hardly seems to have been convinced by his own argument.

It is certainly true that Albert hated travelling and had not left Ireland since 1912, when he had taken a short holiday in France. But this was a superficial barrier. The crucial factor in his decision-making at this period was his growing alcoholism. By 1918 things had become so bad that he was drinking at least a bottle of whisky a night and it is hard to imagine just how he continued working. Jack was only partially aware of his father's condition and it seems that those in the know expended considerable effort in covering for Albert. Warnie, the older, more worldly-wise brother, certainly knew about his father's drinking, and doubtless he sympathised. But Arthur Greeves was also aware of what was happening. On one occasion during the time Jack was in hospital in London, Arthur called round to Little Lea unannounced, to find Albert slumped in a chair unable to focus and looking nauseous. 'I'm in great trouble, you'd better go away,' Albert told the young man.[3] Arthur mentioned nothing of this incident in the letters he was still writing to Jack and only told his friend many years later, long after Albert had died.

The reason why Albert again failed his son when he needed his emotional support may not be clear, but the wounds this rejection caused ran very deep and added to the growing pool of resentment Jack felt towards his father. The rebuff also came at a crucial moment in the young man's emotional life, for he had just found someone who could replace both his disturbed father and his dead mother.

During those dreamlike few weeks before leaving for France Jack had forged a close bond with Janie Moore, the mother of his soldier friend Paddy. Throughout the war they had remained in touch, each writing the other several letters a week, and during the course of this correspondence they had each strengthened the emotional link first formed in September 1917.

It has been claimed that, by keeping in contact with Janie, Lewis was merely fulfilling a promise. According to Maureen Moore, who overheard a conversation between him and her brother Paddy in the garden of the family home in Bristol, just before leaving for France the two young men had formed a solemn pact. Each had promised that if he were to die he wanted the other to look after the parent left behind. Obviously Jack had made this commitment without even considering how Paddy might have helped Albert, but fate was to intervene and this never became an issue. During the early summer of 1919, as Jack lay recovering in hospital, Paddy was reported missing in action some miles away from where Lewis had last been in the midst of combat. Paddy never returned from France, so it was his mother who was to be offered help.

But neither Jack nor Janie Moore needed any excuses. Forty-six-year-old Janie, separated from her husband and as lonely as Jack, was at the young soldier's bedside within days of his return to England, offering comforting words and the companionship neither Warnie (who was still at the Front) nor his father could provide. She knew it was almost certain that her only son had died in France and so she was herself emotionally frail and in need of love. For Jack, Janie was the perfect mother substitute, who had come along at the most felicitous moment. From this emotional need came a special but quite unorthodox relationship that was soon to begin to shape Jack's life and to last until Janie's death more than thirty years later.

Swept up by the disparity in their ages, many commentators have exaggerated the differences between these two people while ignoring the many things they had in common. Brought up in County

Armagh, Janie had lost both of her parents soon after she left school. She had little formal education but she was extremely well read and loved books, so that when she and Jack first met each was able to offer learning to the other and Jack gained greatly from the reading list his new partner gave him in return for his own suggestions. Where, apart from their ages, they were different was that Janie had had responsibility thrust on her when she was young and she had been forced to grow up very quickly. As the eldest of five children when her parents died, she raised the other four, and this had moulded her into an often severe, rather bossy woman. Lewis loved this aspect of Janie's personality; it was what he wanted most in a woman. The young man in whose psyche the nostalgia of the nursery ran deep needed more than anything to be mothered, and the sadism he had flirted with in adolescence was probably an inner rebellion against this, his strongest inner drive.

There are no surviving photographs of Janie taken around the time she first met Jack, but we know that she was blonde and that she was said to be a modestly handsome woman. A rare picture of her taken some ten years after they met offers a few meagre clues. In this image of a slender, fashionably dressed woman with a contemporary bobbed hairstyle, who looks at the camera seriously, she appears relaxed and contented, happy with her unconventional lot.

By 1918 Janie had been estranged for several years from her husband, Courtney Edward Moore, and it appears that he was not entirely reliable with maintenance payments for Maureen, who was twelve when her mother first met Jack. (Janie and Courtney Moore were never divorced, and to the astonishment of Jack and Maureen, some years after Janie's death it was revealed that Moore had been heir to the baronetcy of Dunbar of Hempriggs in Caithness, Scotland, a title that passed to Maureen. See Appendix 3.) Janie dubbed her husband 'the Beast' and the name stuck. His very existence was kept a secret and not revealed to Albert and Warnie until a few months after Jack and Janie started living together in Oxford in 1919. Before this revelation Albert had assumed that Janie was a widow.

The relationship between Janie and Jack was, for the time, unconventional. It brought Jack happiness, but it also endangered his career; it gave him a 'family', but it estranged him from his father; it provided a structure to his life, but it almost wrecked his early development as a writer. Because his love for Janie brought these negative effects, many have criticised the woman unfairly. She has been branded a gold-digger, a manipulative schemer and a woman who placed so many burdens on Lewis that a weaker man would have crumbled and been unable to give us the outpourings of his imagination in the way he managed to do.

Yet, in times of relative peace, it is easy to forget just how much war and its aftermath may influence the emotions and the actions of individuals. Although by 1918 the First World War was won, the cost of victory had been monstrous. Millions of young men had died in the fighting and a huge gap had appeared in the demographic structure of the nations involved that would take a generation to heal. The influenza pandemic of 1918–19 took the lives of millions more, and this time the fallen were not just soldiers defending their country, but women and children, the young and the old. The world was in political and social turmoil. Communism, a new, unpredictable force, had become a poorly understood addition to the vocabulary, and the traditions and customs that had sustained a thousand years of European history were fading or transmogrifying with a speed that alarmed many. The simple fact is that, just like millions of other couples, Janie and Jack found something in each other that held at bay the horrors of their lives and dispelled the shadows that hung around them even in the midst of a new peace. They fell in love.

However, for them this proved to be a complicated matter. First there was the age difference. At the time they met Janie had just turned forty-five and Jack was not quite nineteen. Moreover, Janie was married with two children, and although she was separated from her husband, in 1918 a stigma still clung to liaisons such as Jack and Janie's.

Even more difficult to deal with was the fact that Jack intended to return to Oxford as an undergraduate in order to complete the degree course that had been interrupted by the war. However, he could not do this if he was known to be engaged in a serious romantic relationship with a married woman. The only way they could maintain their relationship was to make it a clandestine one, known only to a few close family and intimate friends.

Janie first visited Jack within days of his return to England and she could hardly bring herself to leave his side thereafter, making the long journey from Bristol to London more than half a dozen times during the two months he was in hospital.

Towards the end of July, with the war entering its final phase, Jack was transferred to a convalescent home. He was able to choose the location and – a sure sign that by this time he had given up on his father and become emotionally dependent on Janie – he picked Ashton Court in Clifton. It was a short bus ride from 6 Ravenswood Road, in the nearby suburb of Redlands where Janie and Maureen lived. He was there until October 1918 and it was during this period that the couple really grew close. In late September, when Janie learned that Paddy had indeed died several months earlier, Jack was there to comfort her, strengthening further the bonds growing between them.

During the final months of the war Lewis was moved from one Army institution to another. Each posting kept him relatively close to Bristol and, in spite of the fact that any form of travel was difficult during wartime, Janie still managed to visit each of his bases whenever she could. Although Lewis was unfit for active service, like many thousands of others he was required to work in clerical positions for the Army. The first of these postings took him for a short time to a command depot on Perham Down, near Andover, and from there he was moved to an officers' training depot in Eastbourne.

Lewis's military obligations were to continue even after the war was over, and at Christmas 1918 he could not get leave. When he was finally granted a few days away from the training depot he returned to Little Lea, where he knew Warren would be spending his first family Christmas since 1913. In spite of the fact that throughout the summer and autumn just passed Albert had failed to visit his ill and depressed son, for all three men the reunion was a happy and emotional one. 'We had lunch and then all three of us went for a walk,' Warren recounted in his diary for 27 December. 'It was as if an evil dream of four years had passed away and we were still in the year 1913.'[4]

Almost from the beginning Jack called Janie 'Mother' and he clearly had few qualms or misgivings about the foundations of his love for her. For her part, Janie never seemed to mind this endearment and she was happy to become a surrogate mother, often referring to him as 'Boysie'. However, although it is easy to see what attracted them to each other, the form in which their relationship expressed itself is harder to understand.

Much has been written on the subject of Jack Lewis and Janie Moore, but almost none of it came from Lewis's own pen. In the early days of their relationship he was forced into secrecy. He could not share the nature of his love with his father, nor with Warnie, who always disliked the woman that his brother had chosen to become involved with. Indeed Warren harboured towards Janie a certain odd, if rarely voiced, resentment based on a misguided belief that she had 'stolen away' his brother. Later the clandestine nature of the partnership had to be maintained if Jack was to keep his academic career. Even after he had become a Fellow of Magdalen, he could never allow anyone to make clear assumptions about his eccentric private life. He maintained this secrecy not so much by deceit or pretence but simply through silence. Lewis almost never discussed Janie, even with his closest friends.

The way the couple's relationship is considered by observers and commentators is largely shaped by their own moral outlook. Many of Lewis's disciples are also evangelical Christians, and for these people it was a purely platonic affair. They refute all suggestion that Jack and Janie engaged in any form of sexual relationship and discard any rational attempts to place it in a realistic context. The reason for this stance is simple. Some fifteen years after meeting

Janie, Lewis became a devout Christian and a religious propagandist. A central tenet of his faith was that sex before marriage was a sin, and so those who wish to canonise Lewis have been required to rewrite history.

In *Surprised by Joy* Lewis skims over the entire subject of Janie, devoting only a few pages to his common-law wife of thirty-odd years. On the matter of their sexual relationship he declared: 'One huge and complex episode will be omitted. I have no choice about this reticence. All I can or need say is that my earlier hostility to the emotions was very fully and variously avenged.'[5]

For many of Lewis's devoted readership this was enough on the subject, but why the reticence? By the time Lewis was writing his autobiography, Janie had been in her grave for more than four years and her only surviving child, Maureen, was then a married woman of fifty and could hardly have been surprised that Jack and her mother had once enjoyed a sexual relationship.

We must, of course, remember that, apart from his brilliance, Jack Lewis was a man like any other. He was also very much a man of his time, tainted by the fashions and moralistic foibles of his age. He found sex an uncomfortable subject to talk or to write about and felt (perhaps with some justification) that what he and Janie did in private was not for public consumption. This is perfectly fair, even admirable, in our time of overexposure to all and everything; but, sadly, it has also allowed misguided devotees to argue that Lewis was a man who led a quite unnatural existence. (We shall see in Chapter 9 that in fact he had another reason for secrecy that was connected with neither his image nor his career.)

Some of those who knew Lewis well have tried to convince the author's devoted fans that they really saw nothing odd about the dynamic of the Lewis–Moore relationship, which they witnessed first-hand. One such friend, George Sayer, a former pupil who wrote a biography of Lewis entitled *Jack*, looked on the couple with a strangely twisted vision. In a passage in his book Sayer assumes the couple had never shared a bedroom simply because when he knew them (by which time Lewis was middle-aged and Janie an elderly woman) they slept in different rooms. Sayer insists he saw nothing at all odd about what he claims was an entirely platonic relationship. 'There she was, a rather stately woman, sitting at the tea table,' he recalled. '"Mother, may I introduce Mr Sayer, a pupil of mine?" is what he would say. Like his other pupils, I thought it completely normal in those days that a woman, probably a widow, would make a home for a young bachelor.'[6]

Perhaps a more realistic view was that expressed by Lewis's close friend from their undergraduate days, Owen Barfield, who, when asked whether he thought Jack and Janie had a sexual relationship, hedged his bets and declared that the likelihood was 'fifty-fifty'.

With the exception of Barfield, most of those who feel convinced Janie was only ever a housekeeper or mother replacement only knew the couple when they were growing old. By this time they may well have settled into a faux mother–child relationship, in which any passion they may once have shared had long since burned out. We can never know the true nature of the intimacy shared by Jack and Janie; and perhaps it is anyway quite irrelevant.

When he was finally decommissioned during the first days of 1919, Lewis, along with many thousands of other former students at universities throughout Britain, was able to return to his interrupted studies one term into the academic year. After a brief stay in Belfast over Christmas and New Year, he returned to Bristol to spend a few days with Janie and he then travelled on to Oxford.

The city had been transformed by peace. In January 1919 it was hard to imagine the ghostly silence and the heavy sense of dread and death that had hung over the university during Lewis's last stay there, eighteen months earlier. But, according to legend, some university administrators had feared the return of the students and imagined that they would bring rough, soldierly ways to this great seat of learning, that military service would have destroyed their respect for tradition and regulations. Such a ridiculous idea was the very reverse of the truth. The survivors of the trenches who returned to their studies became some of the most able and dedicated students in the history of the university. These men and women were bursting with life, determined to prove their intellectual mettle as well as their courage and stamina. They embraced everything college life could offer.

Lewis was no exception. Like any of the others returning to academia, he was relieved, excited and expectant. But in one respect his return to Oxford was very different from that of his peers. Just a few days after arriving in the city, his middle-aged lover and her school-age daughter were installed in a rented house in the rather down-at-heel east Oxford, and Jack began a bizarre double life that would continue for the best part of six years.

To all outward appearances Lewis was a model student and, like most of his contemporaries, he was eager to prove himself. He attended his lectures faithfully and thought many of his tutors were exceptionally good. He joined all the right clubs and student societies, including a debating society called the Martlets that had been in existence for over three hundred years. Lewis took particular pleasure from this society and became so involved that he was quickly elected as its secretary.

Given his old rooms once again, he distempered the walls in a greyish blue, hung a set of framed Dürer prints he had bought and swapped some of the furniture with a few, well-chosen pieces, including a handsome dark oak bookcase. He loved the beamed ceiling, the huge fireplace and the deep-set windows with seats cut into the bay, and he revelled in the comforts of college life. After the war dinner was served in hall again and the JCR (Junior Common Room) was restored to its pre-war glory: the dust sheets had been removed, the ornaments polished and the furniture and rugs cleaned.

Because he had served in the Army for more than six months Lewis was relieved of the need to resit Responsions, which came as a great relief and allowed him to get straight on with his undergraduate studies. The first stage of these was Honour Moderations, a course in Greek and Latin texts. 'Honour Mods' was followed by a degree in Greats (Honours School of Literae Humaniores), Greek and Latin Language and Literature combined with Ancient Philosophy and Ancient History.

All of this Jack described to his father in detailed letters, and, returning to the routine he had established before the war, he continued to bare his soul and expose his inner feelings to Arthur Greeves, who was still living in Belfast with his parents. But even in these, little mention is made of Janie, and most of those that survive are concerned with Jack's thoughts on religion and philosophy.

Like many young intellectuals of the time, in the immediate aftermath of the war Lewis found himself in a spiritual vacuum. Some men had actually found God in the trenches, but a great many others had lost any orthodox faith they may once have possessed. Lewis was in the second category. By the time he returned to Oxford after the war, any religious feelings he had harboured had withered away to absolutely nothing. In 1919 he was able to tell Greeves that he did not believe in a God, and, most poignantly, he never could accept a God that punished men for 'sins of the flesh'. He conceded that there may be some sort of intangible spirit at work in all sentient beings, but he considered this to have precious little connection with any form of traditional Christian deity. Greeves, who at this time held orthodox religious views, and, most crucially, had never served in the war, was saddened by Lewis's thoroughly atheistic stance and did his best to argue against it. It was an endeavour in which he failed singularly.

Jack fitted in easily at Oxford. This was a place far removed from the suffocating atmosphere of public school, it had the vibrancy and excitement missing at Great Bookham, and in this relatively small city he encountered many of the finest minds of his generation. He enjoyed drinking and made good company, he formed friendships quickly and easily, and a few of these lasted and grew to become very important to him.

One such was his friendship with Owen Barfield, an undergraduate at Wadham College. Barfield came from a similar, vaguely middle-class background to Lewis. His father was a lawyer and both parents had little interest in orthodox religion, which had influenced their son to develop a similar liberal mindset. Barfield was a brilliant student, who went on to became a freelance writer before financial strictures forced him to practise Law. Becoming a peripheral member of the Inklings, he continued to keep close ties with Lewis, who thought very highly of him. Lewis believed that the 'First Friend', someone like Arthur Greeves, became an alter ego who shared one's views and proclivities, while the 'Second Friend' (in his case, Owen Barfield) disagreed with you about everything, a quality he always cherished.

But although to outsiders Lewis was leading the life of a typical student, his life outside college, unknown at first to even his closest friends, was anything but typical for a twenty-year-old undergraduate. Whereas most students had only their work and their pleasures to attend to, almost from the moment he arrived at the university Lewis was obliged to stretch his father's meagre allowance to feed and house Janie and Maureen.

His finances were helped a little by a single payment of £145 (roughly equivalent to £8000 today) that he had received from the British government early in 1919 as compensation for his war wound. His scholarship provided a further £100, but from the very start of his time at Oxford Lewis was forever in a state of financial embarrassment that many times approached crisis point. But such financial difficulty was only one of the major problems he faced; three other aspects of his new, unorthodox life were to prove increasingly troublesome.

The first was the quite unexpected burden of domestic responsibility. While most students at Oxford could find the time for hard work as well as play, Lewis, who was also committed to both of these, had to fit a third element into his daily life. At Janie's house he was in constant demand as a handyman, a shopper and a kitchen help. He was expected to clean and cook, tend the garden, escort Maureen to and from the private school (where he paid the fees) and to spend time with his new 'family'.

More painful still was the second problem, the disapproval of his family. Although he was never privy to the details nor the seriousness of their relationship, Albert, by the spring of 1919, had come to learn at least a little of what Jack was up to, and he was not at all happy about it.

Albert's confidant in this matter was Warren, to whom he wrote letter after letter expressing his mounting concern for his younger son. He was becoming depressed over what he referred to as 'Jack's affair' and was worried about Mrs Moore's character. He had not met the woman, but had (perhaps understandably) assumed the worst, reporting to Warren (who also had not met her) that she was old enough to be Jack's mother, that she was in poor financial straits and seemed to have a worrying power over Jack.

Warren wrote back expressing his own rather confused concerns. 'Is she an intellectual?' he wondered, before expressing anger and irritation over what he defined as 'the freakishness' of the arrangement. Albert responded with more fears, commenting on the fact that Jack had apparently written out cheques for Mrs Moore (although how he knew this is intriguing). Eventually he also learned of the existence of Janie's estranged husband and pondered the idea that the man 'might try a little blackmailing'.[7]

In letters to his father Jack glossed over all details of his domestic life, safe in the knowledge that he was most unlikely to pay a visit. He also appears to have kept Warren at arm's length during this time, fearing perhaps that personal information might leak out.

As a consequence, Jack began to write home less and less frequently and found any reason he could to avoid visiting Little Lea, calling on the excuse of work pressures to escape a trip to Belfast during the Easter vacation of 1919. Meanwhile Warren refused to visit Jack in Oxford, and in letters to him he made a point of refusing to acknowledge Janie's very existence.

This impasse could not go on unaddressed without a build-up of conflict in Jack, and by the time the long vac came, in June, he was finding it impossible to refuse the invitation to pay a brief visit to Belfast. Feeling torn between his new life and his responsibilities towards his blood relatives, he left an irritated Janie at Oxford station and set off to play the role of dutiful son.

The trip was a disaster. Jack had hardly been home a few hours when he and his father began to argue. Albert was infuriated that his son was spending his allowance on Janie and her daughter. He did not approve of the affair and he openly expressed his suspicions. But, with both men boiling with resentment, the argument strayed into deeper problems and things were said that had been bottled up for years. Albert felt that both his sons had turned out unfavourably. He considered Warren a baby dressed up in an officer's uniform, and he could see his own weakness for alcohol appearing in his elder son. Jack he viewed as a snob with an inflated sense of self-importance. And, it must be admitted, Albert was not wrong in either judgement.

Jack had his own axe to grind. He saw his father as a meddler who could not accept his boys growing up. But at the same time he was hugely frustrated and emotionally confused. He loved Janie but was dependent on his father, a dilemma that had the effect of intensifying his raw emotions. Lewis later described this period as 'the blackest chapter of my life'.[8] It is easy to see why. After each man realised there was nothing to be gained from Jack's presence at Little Lea, the visit was cut short. Jack left Ireland under an intense black cloud and returned to Oxford to face the washing up and the interminable college work, while Albert hit the bottle with increasing vigour and spent night after night alone with only memories for comfort.

But if all this was not difficult enough, in maintaining his relationship with Janie Jack faced one other major problem. This was the continuing delicate matter of keeping their liaison absolutely secret. Jack had retained his rooms in college throughout his first year, but, along with most university students, at the start of his second year he was expected to move into one of the thousands of rented rooms scattered across Oxford. Here again Lewis decided to break with convention. Instead of renting simple, cheap rooms, he moved into a house which he shared with Janie and Maureen. This was convenient for the women, but it made Jack's Janus existence much more difficult to sustain and to disguise.

Lewis had good reasons for keeping his relationship strictly private. In 1919 some Fellows of Oxford's colleges still held faith with a self-imposed vow of celibacy, and very few dons were married. Only two generations earlier, celibacy had been mandatory for all Fellows and many within the upper echelons of the university administration still deeply regretted and resented the relaxation of the old rules. Genuine sexual freedom only arrived in Oxford during the late 1960s as society in general became more liberal. Oxford in 1919 was closer to the Victorian model, which itself had changed little since medieval times. Students could be 'gated' (forbidden to leave the college for a decreed period) simply for missing breakfast, and a scholar known to be engaged in any form of sexual relationship could face being 'rusticated' – barred from attending the university for a term or more. Within this draconian environment it is easy to see why Lewis, under pressure from both his father and brother, desperate to succeed as a scholar and in love with Janie, had no choice but to lead a double life and to trust very few with his dangerous secret.

These dilemmas were certainly stressful for Jack and have led some commentators to denounce Janie as selfish and calculating. Some claim that she was little more than a burden, that she placed unfair demands on him and put his career at risk simply for her own satisfaction.

Such ideas are quite unfair to both Janie and Jack and stem from the conviction that their relationship was not a sexual, romantic or even a truly loving one. Instead, those who wish to paint Lewis as something other than a normal human being propose that the couple's life together was initiated and sustained purely because Jack made his pledge to his dead friend Paddy Moore, Janie's son.

But how realistic is this notion? Lewis was certainly an honourable man who had been brought up to believe that promises must be kept. But to suggest that this twenty-year-old would antagonise his own family, risk the ruin of his academic career, work all the hours in the day to keep things going and offer himself up to poverty out of nothing other than a sense of duty is, at best, naïve.

This supposition derives solely from a need to believe that Lewis had never committed what he later held to be the sin of sex outside of marriage.

Lewis himself promoted this illusion and wanted to reinforce the impression that he had never 'sinned' in this way. This is one of the primary reasons why, in his autobiography, he did not even hint at a sexual relationship with Janie. Further evidence to support this theory comes from the fact that, as he approached death in November 1963, he gave his brother the explicit instruction that after the funeral he was to destroy a huge bundle of papers that he had kept for many years. Most of these were of little importance or interest, but we do know that the cache included a vast collection of correspondence, along with some unfinished manuscripts and drafts of books. The letters almost certainly included those exchanged between Jack and Janie during the First World War, as well as some of the more intimate exchanges with Arthur Greeves. Why Lewis was so keen to have these papers destroyed is puzzling, although his request to Warren suggests that he did not wish his fans and fellow Christians to be privy to some of the things he thought and wrote about earlier in his life.

Warren did partly fulfil his brother's wishes and he prepared a bonfire in the garden of Jack and Janie's home, The Kilns. However, one of Jack's most prolific literary disciples, the American writer Walter Hooper, says he happened to turn up just as the burning was beginning and talked Warren into letting him take away some of the huge pile destined for the fire. In this way he salvaged a fragment of a novel that was only partly finished by Lewis, published in 1977 as *The Dark Tower*. What else was burned that day remains a mystery, but this incident adds weight to the suggestion that Jack deliberately ordered any incriminating evidence destroyed.

By the time Lewis had been at the university for two years, life had begun to settle into something of a routine. This came as a huge relief to Janie and Maureen, who had moved house some eight times in that period. By 1920 the house they shared with Jack had taken on a vaguely Bohemian air; it was a place filled with music and good books, where the 'family' and their guests ate simple food supplemented with vegetables grown in the small back garden. At dinner parties and weekend lunches conversation covered a vast range of subjects and the mix of characters was eclectic, even eccentric at times.

Owen Barfield was always a delight, and after a few drinks he loved nothing more than dancing wildly to the gramophone. Another frequent guest was Maureen's violin teacher, Mary Wibelin, who taught her in exchange for Latin lessons from Jack. On one occasion they were joined by an old friend of Janie's, a lady of eighty-five who had cycled sixty miles from London to join them in time for lunch.

Conspicuously missing from this set was Warren. From the moment he first heard of it, he had hated the very idea of his brother's relationship with Janie and made no secret of his disapproval. He refused to enter their house and whenever he visited Jack he stayed in a hotel and only met his brother without his partner and on neutral territory, often a pub or restaurant close to the college.

This was probably the lowest point in the brothers' relationship. Many years later Warren called Jack's life with Janie 'restricting and distracting servitude', and in his diaries, written over a period of thirty years, he could barely find a single kind word for the woman, variously describing her as selfish, possessive and demanding.[9] But, aside from Warren's feelings about Janie, the brothers had drawn apart in other ways. Warnie was now a confirmed alcoholic. Booze was dominating his life so much that when he travelled anywhere he could not bring himself to stay in a house where alcohol was not freely available. At the same time his Christian faith was becoming more and more orthodox and devotional, just as his brother's opinions were moving in precisely the opposite direction.

Warren was exclusively a man's man. A career soldier, he loved the company of like-minded men and the exclusive world of masculine interests. He had very little time for women and never had a relationship with one in his entire life. And yet he had no homosexual leanings whatsoever. He seems simply to have been asexual, a compulsive character who relied on the crutches of alcohol and religion, a man most at home in a distorted *Boy's Own* world that was heavily influenced by nostalgia for a lost and treasured childhood. But, with Janie Moore becoming increasingly important to Jack, Warren secretly realised that he must either let his brother fade from his life or come to terms with the relationship. The first choice was something he could never even contemplate, while the second was to take him a long time to accept.

During the summer of 1920 Jack obtained the highest First in Honour Mods (for which he was awarded a prize of £5 to spend on books) and he began studying for Greats. This he completed two years later, gaining another First. Between these two triumphs, in June 1921 he had also won the Chancellor's English Essay Prize with an impressive study of 'Optimism', and as the winner of this he was required to read the essay before the gathered dignitaries of the entire university. Writing this essay was one of his greatest academic achievements and it had clearly inspired him. 'I have almost lived with my pen to the paper,' he told Greeves just after receiving the prize. 'It has been one of those rare periods . . . when everything becomes clear and we see the way before us.'[10]

But if the Chancellor's Prize had come from a clear vision of the way ahead, by the time he had sat the examinations for Greats and achieved his First, Lewis still had no idea what to do next. He had set his sights on a fellowship, or at least a lectureship at the university, but even with the excellent academic credentials he had worked so hard to obtain, this was to prove no easy task, and it took him into the most impoverished period of his life.

By the summer of 1922 his most urgent task was to find an academic position. All he had to sustain himself, Janie and Maureen now was his allowance, which Albert had volunteered to continue paying until Jack found a suitable job. The situation was made worse by the fact that just as the money from Lewis's scholarship dried up, Janie's husband became particularly unreliable over his maintenance payments for Maureen.

Jack's first step was to apply for a fellowship that had come up at Magdalen College. But even he realised quickly that he had little chance of success and that the college would certainly find a man with far greater experience. He was tempted by an offer of a one-year fellowship at Cornell University in the United States, but apart from the fact that Cornell was unwilling to pay for his travel costs, he could not bring himself to leave Janie; nor, one might imagine, would she have tolerated such a thing. This was a factor made abundantly clear in his decision to turn down another possible position, relatively nearby at Reading University. The post was a lectureship in Philosophy that came with a reasonable salary, but he knew he would have to either travel to and from work each day or else take rooms in Reading, neither of which options was compatible with his domestic life.

Nineteen twenty-two had turned from a year of accomplishment and hope into one of poverty and worry. The fact that his father was supporting him continued to exaggerate Lewis's frustration and feelings of humiliation. Rather than taking this help in good spirit, he could only see it as a symbol of thraldom and it made him hungry to succeed and gain complete independence.

Taking the advice of his former tutors at University College, in the autumn of 1922 Lewis decided to suspend his efforts to find a placement and to take a further degree, this time in English so that he could broaden his c.v. and give himself the chance to acquire an English fellowship should one come up. Again he performed amazingly well under stress and in just one year acquired another First Class degree.

But even though he was successful academically, Lewis was finding it almost impossible to shoulder the burdens he had taken on himself. Financial concerns grew rather than diminished, and at one point things became so bad he was forced to borrow £5 from his brother to pay for groceries.

Then, in the summer of 1924, Lewis's gamble of taking another degree finally paid off when he was offered a temporary lectureship at Magdalen to replace the regular tutor, Edgar Carritt, who had accepted a one-year posting in America. The job was poorly paid (a mere £200 for the year, or about £10,000 today) but it came with little responsibility; it was close to home, it was not too demanding and he had been assured that if he was to be offered a fellowship from any college during the academic year, he would be free to accept it.

As often happens in life, just as one of Lewis's problems resolved itself, another difficulty began to fade away. For his own reasons, by 1924 Warnie had finally begun to show a limited acceptance of the relationship between Janie and his brother. He still refused to stay at their home, but he clearly wanted to rekindle the spark of love the brothers had once shared. During the summer of that year, just before Jack was required to begin preparing for his first teaching position, he and Warren went on a motorcycling tour; Warnie at the handlebars and Jack in the sidecar. They stayed in cheap inns or with Warnie's Army friends and they tarried in Colchester for a few days, staying at the base where Warnie was then stationed. It served to help them bond again, to resolve their differences and to place their relationship on a new footing, one from which they never looked back.

Lewis's first experiences as a tutor were not entirely satisfying. He often lectured to no more than three or four students and he was not particularly interested in the philosophy course he was entrusted with. He referred to his time as lecturer at Univ as being 'in bond', but it did offer him two essentials. It almost certainly saved him from a severe financial crisis and it provided him with invaluable teaching experience.

No one could deny Lewis's academic prowess, for he had proven his mettle with three successive examination Firsts. He was also a winner of a prestigious prize and his essay on 'Optimism' had been heard by everyone who mattered at the university. All he lacked was experience.

Between 1922 and 1925 he had gone for two fellowships and

failed in both attempts. First there was his rather naïve attempt to gain a fellowship at Magdalen immediately after passing Greats. A second effort in 1923, in which he had applied for the position of Fellow in Philosophy at Trinity College, Cambridge, worth £500 a year, also came to nothing. Both of these rejections were dispiriting, and so when, in early 1925, he applied to become a Fellow in English Language and Literature, again at Magdalen College, he harboured such little hope of success, he did not bother telling anyone about it other than Janie.

But Lewis's luck was changing and he was now being taken seriously by the university authorities. Much to his surprise, in May of that year, after attending a succession of interviews and a crucial invitation to dine in hall with some of the Magdalen Fellows, he was offered the position he so craved.

On 22 May *The Times* announced the new appointment, declaring: 'The President and Fellows of Magdalen College have elected to an official Fellowship in the College as Tutor in English Language and Literature, for five years as from next June 25th, Mr Clive Staples Lewis M.A. (University College).'

The condition of a five-year tenure was a mere formality, and at last his long apprenticeship was over. This was an occasion to celebrate and to reflect. It marked the end of one era and the start of the next. Lewis may not have realised it as he wrote to thank the Master of Magdalen and accept the appointment, but many things were about to change in his life. There could be no better moment to embrace change, and embrace it he did.

5

Fellowship

Magdalen College is arguably the most beautiful in Oxford. (The name retains the fifteenth-century pronunciation 'Maudlin', as does Magdalene College, Cambridge, with which Lewis was later also associated.) Founded in 1458 by a Provost of Eton, William of Waynflete, Magdalen is also one of the oldest and most prestigious colleges of Oxford University. If you walk along The High, away from the centre of Oxford, you will find Magdalen on the left, immediately beyond the old city wall. The entrance to the college is almost concealed, a tiny stone arch that leads into a lodge; but beyond stands one of the most spectacular groups of buildings in the city. To the east the grounds of the college are bordered by the River Cherwell, and this is one of the most popular stretches for punting. To the north there is a splendid deer park, the only one in Oxford, from which fallow deer wander into the college grounds, where they may be fed from the windows of students' rooms.

The immense wealth of Magdalen College and its centuries-old international reputation as one of the most important seats of learning have endowed it with many splendours. The Cloisters, which circumscribe a tiny quad on which the dons play bowls, are among the few authentic medieval cloisters in Britain and the dining hall, where the students and Fellows attend High Table, is lined with linen panelling, believed to have once adorned the walls of Reading Abbey and dating from the dissolution of the monasteries in the 1530s.

Magdalen Tower dominates the main buildings and stands at one end of a bridge which spans the Cherwell. The roads leading east from Magdalen Bridge cut through a hinterland of student bedsits and terraced houses which since the 1980s have been highly sought after by young professionals. Each May Day morning the choir of Magdalen School sings from the top of the tower as tens of thousands gather on the bridge and in the streets beneath the tower to watch the sun rise.

When Lewis arrived as a Fellow of Magdalen in 1925 he was appointed a set of rooms in the New Building, a splendid structure dating from 1733 that lies to the north of the main part of the college and borders the deer park. His rooms, number 3.4, comprised two large spaces, a sitting-room and a bedroom. The windows of the sitting-room face north, and from them Lewis had a view of an expanse of lawn edged by trees whose leaves form the most gorgeous red canopy every autumn. Beyond this he could see the park, the ribbon of Addison's Walk and the private Fellows' Garden. From the south-facing bedroom he had a view of the medieval splendour of the main buildings and the Tower dominating the landscape. His rooms were some of the finest in Oxford and, not surprisingly, Lewis considered Magdalen College 'beautiful beyond compare'.[1]

He was obliged to provide his own furniture, a fact that came as something of a surprise. Furnishing two rooms with tables, chairs, a bed, rugs, paintings and bookcases cost him £90 (about £4000 today). A loan of two mahogany bookcases from the furniture Janie had kept in storage, along with a gift of some money from his father, helped, but it was yet another financial burden that Lewis had not prepared for.

Fellows were (and still are) treated like nobility. Lewis was appointed a scout who helped him with his ablutions and each day cleaned his room. Every morning the servant arrived early with a bowl of steaming hot water which he placed at the sink in one corner, drew the curtains, made ready Lewis's shaving kit, removed the chamber pot (college rooms of the 1920s had absolutely no conveniences) and arranged his master's clothes.

Although Lewis was always meticulously shaved and clean, he was a scruffily dressed man. It was once said of him that he could make a new suit look old on a second wearing; he certainly had little time for fashion or sartorial style. This was a habit he maintained the whole of his life and in later years it belied his wealth and fame. When he was in his fifties and went through a period of frequently travelling first class by train to London and Cambridge, he was once approached by an elderly lady passenger who asked if he had a first-class ticket. 'Yes,' he replied. 'But I'll be needing it myself.'

One's dress sense is an important indicator of who one is, Lewis believed, although in a quite different way from the lady in the first-class compartment. In his time, college men fell broadly into two groups. There were the 'hearties', sporty types who preferred plainness of dress. They decorated their rooms formally and in simple fashion, and wore nondescript clothes, such as baggy grey flannel trousers, tweed jackets, plain shirts and club ties. The second group were the 'aesthetes', who wore corduroy trousers, colourful silk shirts and velvet ties. Some of the more adventurous grew their hair long (by the standards of the day) and a few experimented with make-up; a good number of aesthetes were homosexual.

Although Jack was not a genuine hearty – he hated all forms of sport or physical exercise save walking – he had little time for aesthetes and wore his drab clothes as a badge of honour. He made no great show of expressing distaste for homosexuals, but equally, along with the vast majority of heterosexuals of the period, he was far from liberal-minded on the subject. In his characteristic fashion, he mocked rather than criticised. One example of this was remembered by a friend many years after the event. Jack was standing at his window with Warnie, looking out towards the main buildings of Magdalen when they spotted two aesthetes walking along holding hands. Warnie pointed them out and remarked that they were incredibly ugly specimens, to which Jack retorted, 'Well, buggers can't be choosers!'[2]

By 1925 Lewis had begun to age quite noticeably. Still only in his late twenties, he was losing his hair and, like Warnie, had started to put on weight. The face that looked back at him from the shaving mirror each morning was considerably flabbier than the one he had seen in the trenches. This was in large part a genetic trend – Albert had aged in the same way – but Lewis's new life as an Oxford don did nothing to help.

A typical day would begin in leisurely style and continue so until bedtime. Breakfast was taken in the dining room of the Senior Common Room (SCR). Dons sat at a large round table that dominated the room, helped themselves to food laid out on silver platters and drank tea or coffee brought to them by college servants. It was Lewis's favourite meal of the day and he was always at the table as soon as breakfast began, at 8 a.m. This was a time during which he could converse with the other Fellows and, if the mood took him, flick through *The Times*, although he was never very interested in newspapers. After breakfast he would take a walk in the college grounds and then return to his rooms for his first tutorial, which began at 9 a.m. The usual routine was two tutorials, but occasionally three, before lunch, with a break of thirty minutes between them. Lunch was served at one o'clock precisely.

Some afternoons were taken up with lectures. These were normally held in rooms in college, but sometimes elsewhere, and on afternoons when there were no scheduled lectures or seminars, Lewis was free to prepare work, appraise essays, deal with any administration for which he was responsible, and read. The evening meal, or High Table, was served in the college hall. Diners were required to dress smartly but wore black tie only for special events or on the infrequent occasions when the college president was in attendance.

In Lewis's day High Table was already a wonderful anachronism. Droves of college servants carrying silver trays paced between the tables that ran the length of the hall. At one end of the room stood a screen dating from the seventeenth century and depicting scenes from the life of St Mary Magdalen. At the other was a dais spanning the width of the hall on which the High Table stood. Here the president, vice-president and the college dons ate, each positioned at the table according to their seniority, with the president at the centre. Other college officials, scholars and students ate at tables set out on the floor of the hall.

High Table consisted of five courses, along with wine, vintage port and Madeira, followed, after the dessert, by Lewis's favourite after-dinner tipple, brown sherry. Fellows could order any drinks they wished for themselves and any guests they had invited by using a device called a 'buzz', which drew the attention of a college servant who would dutifully bring a new decanter of a chosen wine or spirit. After the meal the Fellows retired to the Senior Common Room to enjoy what was referred to as 'wines', where they imbibed some more.

Not surprisingly, 'wines' was the favourite time of the day for many dons, who not only took understandable pleasure in the fare offered but also enjoyed the witty and stimulating conversation that came from keeping company with some of the finest minds of their generation. During the early years of his fellowship Lewis enjoyed these evenings immensely. The life of a don brought him respect and an air of authority, and he relished SCR conversation and cherished the society of men as brilliant as himself. Only later, after leading this life for some years, did he begin to find that many of his colleagues irritated him and he attended these evenings with less enthusiasm.

However, from the start Lewis was not so fond of the workload he was expected to shoulder. The tutorial system used at Oxford dates back to the early nineteenth century and is part of the unique character of degree courses in the Arts at the university. Until the nineteenth century Oxford had a rather poor academic record and was easily surpassed by other centres of learning. It was only after the reforms of 1803–7, when examinations became better regulated and the duties of tutors and other academic staff were rationalised, that academic standards began to improve. Part of these reforms involved the creation of a tutorial system in which a tutor spent time with individual students going over set work and discussing the finer points of a topic forming part of the curriculum.

Tutorials continue to be an essential component of an Arts degree at Oxford and are used to complement lectures. In lectures students gather information *en masse*, take notes and follow a strict course of learning. The tutorial, usually held in the tutor's rooms and lasting one hour, gives the student time to read aloud a prepared essay and then to discuss it with the tutor.

Many of those taught by Lewis during his early years as a tutor have complained that they found him harsh and uncompromising. He loved rhetoric and argument, but there is no doubt that for a first-year undergraduate Lewis's verbal onslaughts were unnerving. In his early days as a tutor Lewis expected too much of his young charges. He had himself been a brilliant student, but not many came close to his intellectual level, and he was unfair and unsympathetic to many students. One former pupil recalled that 'the more the pupil showed a capacity for self-defence the better'.[3]

This harshness softened later in Lewis's career and he used humour as a way to bypass his irritation with less bright students. This made him far more popular and also happier in his role. According to one of his former students, Professor John Lawlor, Lewis later 'tended to accept them [his students] with ironic resignation'.[4] Elsewhere he has said that within Lewis 'maddening obstinacies and sword-sharp disclaimers co-existed with an untroubled awareness of the highest order'.[5]

Lewis had a very distinctive lecturing style, quite different from that of most of the dons teaching at the university in the 1920s and '30s. He invariably arrived five minutes late and began talking as soon as he entered the room. As well as packing a huge amount of information into a short space of time, he had a gift for keeping his young audience interested with jokes and anecdotes, and he was very good at relating his erudite subject to modern life by using allegory and simple illustrations that made his points clearer. He possessed the great talent of being able to put into his lectures the same warmth and attractiveness as he displayed in his writing.

Another way in which Lewis made himself popular after he had settled into the job was through his creation of what became known as 'English Binges'. A form of end-of-year party for the department, they were paid for entirely by Lewis, who supplied the alcohol and hired a private room at Magdalen for the function. The highlight of the evening came when everyone had drunk far more beer than was good for them and Lewis stood on a table reciting bawdy Old English verse.

Very bright students and those who, like their teacher, thought little of Oxford's aesthetes, fared better than the many narcissistic dandies he was also obliged to teach. Lewis was particularly considerate towards hard-working types, even if they were not terribly clever, and for many years he took great pleasure in pushing a student to a first-class degree when he or she was clearly second-class material. Later, though, he began to wonder about the ethics of this and questioned the value of turning mediocre students into academic high-flyers. This was perhaps an odd overreaction and suggests that he dismissed the very idea that he might have initially misjudged his students' abilities or that he had merely given them the opportunity to shine through hard work coupled with average ability.

Two of Lewis's students became very famous and respected figures in the world of the Arts: John Betjeman, who later became Poet Laureate, and the writer and critic Kenneth Tynan. Lewis disliked both of them, although all three men made light of the fact publicly later in life.

The young Betjeman was in almost every way the sort of man Lewis disapproved of instinctively. He had enjoyed a highly privileged education, first at the Dragon School in Oxford and then as a pupil at Marlborough School, and he was the very embodiment of the aesthete who enjoyed creating at least the impression of sexual ambivalence. He often held wild parties in his rooms to which he invited the most eccentric figures at the university, and he did very little work.

Arriving at Magdalen in 1925, Betjeman was one of Lewis's first students and the two men quickly assumed a brittle relationship. Betjeman rarely completed essays on time and when he did deliver them Lewis quickly realised they were plagiarised almost wholesale from secondary sources. As a result, he grew to consider his student an 'idle prig' and 'ignorant and stupid'.[6] But then occasionally Betjeman would produce a startlingly accomplished and original essay that would temporarily soften Lewis's judgement.

Betjeman liked to tease Lewis. Knowing that by college statutes, he was entitled to be tutored for his 'special subject' in any area of language he wished, Betjeman chose medieval Welsh. He was aware that Lewis was not proficient enough in this arcane language to teach it to degree level and would be obliged to find a specialist from outside the university. As a result, the college had to pay for an expert to travel by train from Wales to Oxford each week for one sixty-minute tutorial.

Anecdotes about Lewis and his wayward student give the impression that although Lewis rather distrusted him, the younger man wanted to form a closer bond with his tutor. Betjeman tried to interest Jack in the modern poets and lent him books. He even went as far as to invite him to his rather colourful parties. Lewis did attend one such tea-party but disliked what he considered the 'pansyism' of it all. He found he had little in common with the other guests, who were almost all aesthetes in flamboyant dress. According to his recollections later in life, all these people talked about were 'lace curtains, arts and crafts (which they all disliked), china ornaments, architecture and the strange habits of "hearties"'.

Betjeman introduced Lewis to Louis MacNeice, whom he described as a 'great poet'. But all Lewis could recall of the encounter was that MacNeice had not only been 'absolutely silent' but was also 'astonishingly ugly'.[7] Yet, on this occasion, Betjeman's judgement was spot on: MacNeice was soon to become the most admired poet in England after W.H. Auden. At the time of his one meeting with MacNeice, Lewis was still far from finding his own literary voice and his own efforts as a poet had gone largely unnoticed.

Betjeman did not last long at Oxford. At the end of his first year he failed his Divinity examination. This could have been glossed over as a relatively minor setback. If he had chosen to, Lewis could have easily argued the case for letting the young man resit the exam, and if he had passed, he could have returned to his studies in October 1926. Such a thing had happened many times before with other tutors and their charges. But Lewis chose not to help Betjeman and simply stood back as he was cast out of the university; an act the future Poet Laureate never forgave.

Some two decades after Betjeman's brief spell at Magdalen, Kenneth Tynan produced a similarly negative reaction in Lewis. Tynan, who became famous for his brilliant and acerbic theatre criticism, his extreme left-wing politics and his anti-establishment work, such as the nude revue *Oh Calcutta!*, was a flamboyant character at Oxford who adored flaunting the rules and challenging convention. He dressed outrageously, and, like Betjeman and many others before and after him, he entertained extravagantly, hosting dinners and events that attracted some of the most creative young people of the day.

In spite of his wild student life, Tynan worked hard and was a natural academic. Also, curiously for a man whose political views became increasingly radical as he grew older, he was always enamoured with Lewis's conservative Christianity, something for which, by the time he began teaching Tynan in 1945, Lewis had become internationally famous. Yet none of this stopped Lewis disliking the man intensely. 'Tynan is a very clever man and knows it,' he once told another student. 'I am tempted to do all I can to prevent him getting a First, but I don't think I should succeed even if I tried my hardest. All I can do is try to knock some of the conceit out of him.'[8]

What saved Lewis's reputation as a tutor and left fond memories in the minds of many of his pupils was his wit and capacity for humour. The consensus seems to be that, although he could be a tough combatant in an argument and found it hard to conceal his irritation with having to attend to the needs of undergraduates at all, this was more than made up for by the fact that he was a good listener and tempered his rapier mind with considerable levity. He never liked lazy students nor those who believed they could cruise through university either because of superior intellect or a wealthy background. For those who treated Jack with respect and showed a genuine thirst for knowledge, he was an ideal tutor.

Lewis could be unfair and even ruthless, as exemplified by the way he mistreated John Betjeman, but he had a compassionate side too. He often displayed unexpected acts of kindness towards those less fortunate than him. One particularly amusing anecdote tells of a time he was walking along The High with a friend. A beggar came up to them and asked for money. Lewis immediately emptied the contents of his pockets into the beggar's hands. Then, as they continued on their way, Lewis's friend said, 'You know, Jack, that beggar is only going to go and spend that money on booze.' To which Lewis replied, 'Well, you may be right, but if I had kept the money I would only have spent it on booze.'

During his first few years at Magdalen Lewis was popular with the other dons and quickly made close friends with a few like-minded men. He formed a close friendship with a colleague named Paul Victor Mendelssohn Benecke, with whom he shared breakfast each morning. Benecke, who was some thirty years older than Lewis, was the grandson of the composer Felix Mendelssohn and had followed a similar academic path to Lewis, gaining Firsts in Honour Mods and Greats. He was an extremely unconventional scholar, a vegetarian, who rarely drank and never smoked. When food rationing was at its worst soon after the end of the Second World War, Benecke attempted to live only on foods that were not rationed. He fasted once a week, wore tatty old clothes and never put the heating on in his study even on the coldest of days. Instead he simply wore an extra sweater or cardigan and students often attended tutorials in overcoats, scarves and gloves, all of which they kept on throughout their time in Benecke's rooms.

To Lewis, Benecke was a model of human purity, and he had

enormous respect for the man. On several occasions he leapt to his colleague's defence if he was taunted by students or criticised by another don. Although Lewis claimed that Tolkien provided the model for one of his most carefully constructed characters, Arthur Ransom, the hero of his famous space trilogy, Benecke surely provided the template for the older Ransom, the spiritually enlightened Pendragon figure of the last of the three books, *That Hideous Strength*.

As much as Lewis revelled in the exquisite lifestyle offered to a Fellow of Magdalen and enjoyed the company of some of his colleagues, he found the state of clubs and societies at the college quite lamentable. Always a highly clubbable man, since his earliest undergraduate days Lewis was naturally drawn to the society of like-minded men willing to partake in intellectual discussion, preferably while consuming large quantities of alcohol. The sorts of clubs Lewis found on arriving at Magdalen specialised in the latter but had practically no interest in the former. Most were linked to some form of sporting activity or acted as vehicles for the politically active of all shades, neither of which appealed to Lewis, who detested politics almost as much as he despised any form of sport.

Even though he had been educated at a succession of private schools, Lewis had never come to terms with the education system as it was in England in the first decades of the twentieth century. Throughout his life he retained a deep-rooted contempt for many of those who emerged from what he considered to be institutions that distorted young minds and spirits. Magdalen's clubs were designed by and for the very sort of people Lewis disliked most, those he referred to as 'the idiot bloods of Eton and Charterhouse'.[9]

To rectify the situation, after only one term at Magdalen Lewis decided to form his own club, centred on what he called 'Beer and Beowulf' evenings for his pupils. These were held each week in his rooms. As the name he gave the occasions suggests, meetings consisted of much talk of Old English, including Lewis's efforts to teach his students mnemonics to help them learn passages from Beowulf and other arcane texts, while they all drank liberal quantities of beer. One can only imagine what the young Betjeman thought of the proceedings.

In May 1926 Lewis met J.R.R. Tolkien. The occasion was a meeting of the faculty of English at Merton College, where Tolkien had been Professor of Anglo-Saxon for little more than two terms. At first they seemed rather wary of each other, and Lewis confided to his diary: 'Tolkien managed to get the discussion round to the proposed English Prelim. I had a talk with him afterwards. He is a smooth, pale, fluent little chap . . . thinks all literature is written for the amusement of *men* between thirty and forty . . . No harm in him: only needs a good smack or two.'[10]

This is a rather strange recollection of their first encounter and sadly we have nothing from Tolkien with which to compare it. If we ignore Lewis's rather pompous tone, it says much about Tolkien at the time. Clearly, he was forthright, confident and good at steering a conversation in a direction he wanted. The fact that he was a good talker and proselytiser immediately endeared him to Lewis.

The other odd comment concerns Tolkien's feelings about the uses of literature. Very much like Lewis, Tolkien was a rather old-fashioned man and had strong views about the correct roles of men and women in society, but Lewis's assertion that his colleague regarded literature as being 'written for the amusement of *men* between thirty and forty' does not really fit with Tolkien's character. Perhaps Lewis put words into his mouth, or maybe Tolkien had made a statement to that effect out of mere bravado, for he had some experience of intellectual women. Within his own family, his Aunt Jane, with whom he had lived for a short while in 1904, was one of the first English women to obtain a science degree and he considered her a quite remarkable woman.

At the time Lewis and Tolkien met, they had much in common. Tolkien was older by almost seven years, but both men had fought in the trenches and both adored language. Tolkien was an expert in the study of ancient tongues (including Icelandic and Finnish as well as Anglo-Saxon), while Lewis was fascinated with the arcane intricacies of Norse mythology and with Old English literature. It was this confection of interests that originally gelled their relationship.

However, their backgrounds were very different. John Ronald Reuel Tolkien was born in South Africa in 1892. He never really knew his father, who died in 1896, and his beloved mother died from diabetes in 1904, when he was twelve. He lived with a variety of relatives in many different houses, but was lucky enough to enjoy a good education at a small public school in Birmingham. He went up to Exeter College, Oxford, in 1911, and after serving in the Army in France and lecturing at Leeds University for a brief period, in 1925 he acquired the prestigious Chair of Anglo-Saxon at Oxford, the same year that Lewis was made a Fellow of Magdalen.

Tolkien came across as less urbane than Lewis. His interests were narrower, and in many ways he was a far more conventional character. While Lewis shared his life with a fifty-three-year-old married woman and spent his weekends with her in the house he rented in east Oxford, Tolkien was a husband and a father of three (his fourth child, Priscilla, was born in 1929). But the two men were intellectual equals, both extremely clever and with impeccable academic credentials. Each was rather outmoded in his perception of the world, each heartily eschewed almost all contemporary culture, from modern poetry to Hollywood, and each was rather distrustful of politics and politicians. Indeed, neither man much liked the twentieth century; neither could drive a car (although Tolkien did teach himself and drove infrequently and terribly for a few years during the 1930s); they ignored the radio and showed only marginal interest in current affairs. In fact their strongest bond was an almost total absorption with cerebral concerns, to the exclusion of most other things. Each of them maintained a powerful link with childhood, admired fantasy literature and, from an early age, had set his sights on becoming a writer.

The close friendship that grew between Tolkien and Lewis was inevitable. Many of the other dons they were to encounter at their respective colleges were intelligent men, but with the exception of rare individuals such as Benecke, most demonstrated little imagination and simply lived for their work. In one of his earliest books, *The Pilgrim's Regress* (1933), Lewis lampooned the type as 'Mr Sensible', defining them as witty and intelligent but narrow-minded and shallow.

Lewis was keen to write fiction and poetry and had grand plans for his career. In this respect he found a kindred spirit in Tolkien. Also, both men were attracted to a form of camaraderie into which they had been immersed since schooldays, a man's world which had gained greater significance for them during the war. But their friendship also developed because of their shared intellectual background and through their measured criticism of each other's literary efforts. Within a few months of being introduced, the two men took to meeting regularly in Lewis's rooms in Magdalen, where they would often sit by the fire late into the night discussing literature and history and reviewing each other's manuscripts.

By the summer of 1926 Tolkien had loaned Lewis a draft of a long poem he had written called *The Gest of Beren and Lúthien* (which later became *The Lay of Beren and Lúthien*, a story in *The Silmarillion*) and Lewis filled the margins with constructive comments. He realised quickly that Tolkien was sensitive to criticism, and so instead of offering a blunt commentary he mocked his own criticisms of the work by adopting the guise of the fictitious critics 'Schick', 'Peabody' and 'Pumpernickel', each of whom had a few well-chosen words to say.

But if literature had been one of the major spurs, the friendship soon developed in other directions too, for both Lewis and Tolkien liked good conversation with other men, strong beer and reading aloud to a small group from ancient texts and their own writings. Only a few weeks before their first meeting, during Tolkien's second term as Professor of Anglo-Saxon, he had formed an Icelandic reading group called the Coalbiters. The name derived from the Icelandic word *Kolbíter*, which means 'those who in winter get so close to the fire they bite the coal', and the group's purpose was to bring together those interested in the traditional Icelandic sagas, which were then read aloud by the members.

In the autumn of 1926 Tolkien invited Lewis to join the Coalbiters and although Jack knew almost no Icelandic, he was keen to learn and gradually took on more and more ambitious passages to read to the group. Among the Coalbiters there were linguistic experts such as G.E.K. Braunholtz, the Oxford Professor of Comparative Philology, and R.M. Dawkins, the Professor of Byzantine and Modern Greek, but Lewis was not the only novice scholar of Icelandic. An English don from Exeter College, the aristocratic Nevill Coghill, knew no Icelandic at all, and George Gordon, Tolkien's former boss at Leeds and now Professor of English Literature at University College, Oxford, was also just a keen beginner.

For those lucky enough to live the life of an Oxford don it has always been very easy to seal oneself off from the world, to ascend the clichéd ivory tower. Many of those who become dons are by nature uninterested in most mundane matters and prefer the realm of pure intellect to the prosaic world of what most people would consider normal life. Lewis and Tolkien were very much of this type. Jack split his time between his work, his early literary efforts and his domestic life with Janie. Tolkien had a family, but although he was a loving father, he was preoccupied with his academic work and his writing, spending most evenings either in college or in pubs talking and drinking with Lewis. Both men showed little interest in the affairs of the world; flicking through *The Times* at breakfast was about the limit of their connection with it. And yet the year in which they met was a dramatic one and even scholars like Lewis and Tolkien would have been aware of news from the world beyond the Cloisters and the quads.

Nineteen twenty-six began with John Logie Baird transmitting the first television signals and ended with the death of Monet. It was a year of great aviation feats, in which pilots flew to the Cape of Good Hope and made the first round trips from England to Australia, a journey of fifty-eight days. But the biggest news story of the year was unfolding the very week Tolkien and Lewis first met over sherry in the Senior Common Room of Merton College. During the General Strike, the greatest civil disturbance in Britain since the English Civil War, the vast majority of workers downed tools and left their factories, shops, warehouses and yards for nine days from 5 to 13 May. On the very day the two scholars met at Merton, students and white-collar professionals were realising their boyhood dreams by manning buses and lorries in The High and climbing on to the footplates of strike-bound trains pulling out of Oxford station.

As much as Lewis was removed from the general flow of modern life, there were still things that anchored him, that broke through his self-imposed isolation from the mundane comings and goings of the world. The most important of these was his relationship with his father. Albert Lewis retired in May 1928, when he was sixty-five, and almost immediately went into a rapid and irreversible decline. He lived in the rambling house, Little Lea, in which Jack and Warnie had grown up and he employed a single servant to cook for him and tend to his domestic needs. Warnie had taken a posting in Shanghai in April 1927 and Jack visited his father rarely, so that by the time Albert left his legal work he was more lonely than he had ever been. By 1927 he had become a hopeless drunk.

Jack's problems with his father had been aggravated over many years through carelessness and inconsiderate behaviour on both sides, and his years at Oxford had been particularly difficult because of the unconventional decisions he had made and his commitment to Janie. At the same time he felt extremely frustrated that he still had to rely on his father for financial support. A part of him was grateful, but a larger part felt resentment. Quite aware how clever he was, he could hardly contain his bitterness over the fact that he was incapable of sustaining himself and his common-law wife unaided and was therefore forced to accept his father's charity.

However, in May 1925, with Jack's elevation to a fellowship at Magdalen, much of the pressure that had created such bad feeling between him and Albert was lifted. The position came with an annual salary of £500, whereas his father had provided £210 each year. Jack was at last his own man and this shift did much to improve communication between father and son.

Immediately after receiving his fellowship Jack wrote to his father thanking him for all his support over the years and declaring that without him he could never have achieved this accolade. Soon afterwards Jack began to make more frequent visits to Belfast and during one long vac he spent four weeks with his father, during which they began to revitalise their relationship and find some new common ground. And, although Jack could never admit it, this visit also gave him a break from domestic commitments in Oxford, among them Janie's ceaseless demands. He took full advantage of this time and spent each morning writing before embarking on a long walk, often in Albert's company.

From letters from Albert and news passed on by Warnie, during the early summer of 1929, while Jack was finishing the academic year at Oxford, he learned that his father was unwell. However, it was not until he arrived at Little Lea on 12 August that he realised quite how serious this illness was.

A few days after Jack's arrival, Albert was examined by the family doctor and received the dread news that he had cancer of the bowel. In depressed and doom-laden mood, Jack wrote a letter to Warnie in China, reporting on their father's condition and implying that he should try his utmost to get leave. A few days later, Albert was installed in a nursing home in Belfast in preparation for surgery.

Jack had been quick to realise that for Albert the end was close. Indeed, he wrote later that he had sensed it almost immediately on arriving from England and he could recall the air of finality hanging over the family home and clinging to poor Albert. However, the end did not come quite so soon as Jack had anticipated; and after the operation Albert's doctors were surprised by what appeared to be a marked improvement in his condition. Jack visited him for several hours each day and the two men got on better than they ever had before. Jack kept his father entertained with humorous stories about the dons at Magdalen and with well-worn favourite anecdotes about Oxford, while Albert recalled some of his favourite 'wheezes', the practical jokes and funny stories he had been so fond of all his life.

In late September Jack was forced to return to Oxford to prepare for the new term. He took some assurance from his father's doctors, who believed that Albert might well live for a few more years, and it was clear the staff at the nursing home were looking after him well. Even so, it was with a heavy heart that on Saturday 22 September he took the boat back across the Irish Sea and caught the train to Oxford. Three days later Jack received a telegram saying that his father had taken a turn for the worse and was in a critical condition. After catching a train an hour later, he arrived back at the nursing home only to find that Albert had died the previous afternoon.

Jack was slow to react to his father's death. On 29 September he wrote calmly to Warren explaining what had happened. Perhaps he felt little urgency in imparting the news because he knew his brother would probably not receive the letter for at least a month and could in any case do little about leaving his posting. It was only a few days later, after spending a little time on his own or with Arthur Greeves, walking through the rooms in which he had grown up, now empty and silent, that Jack began to fully realise his loss. Now, with the passing of his father, the man he and Warren had mocked so ruthlessly, all tangible links to his youth had started to dissolve. The brothers would be obliged to sell the house and to scatter its contents. With each book and every piece of furniture sold to a dealer or passed on to a distant relative, another element of child-hood and bitter-sweet memories would be chipped away. It was a thought that filled him with horror.

Lewis reacted by displacing his concerns. For six months he sub-merged himself in everyday life in Oxford, for it was not until April 1930 that Warren was able to return to England and the brothers made a final journey to Little Lea and set about dealing with their father's estate.

Jack's plan was to buy another house with the proceeds of the sale of the family home. In December 1929 he and Janie had found a large, expensive property just outside Oxford and had set their hearts on it. The Kilns was a sprawling, rather ugly house, but it was idyllically situated in several acres of woodland on the edge of Headington Quarry, about three miles south-east of the centre of Oxford. It offered Jack isolation and peace yet was not far from the university.

In correspondence and discussion with Warren it was decided that when his posting in China ended he should live with Jack, Janie and Maureen. Little Lea took almost a year to sell and fetched less than hoped for, a little over £2000. So each of the four, excluding Maureen, helped raise a set of mortgages to cover the asking price for The Kilns of £3300, most of which was paid off after the house in Belfast was auctioned in the autumn of 1930. From his salary and an annual £190 he and Warren received from Albert's investments, Jack was able to raise £1000. Janie had a trust fund which enabled her to take out a mortgage for £1500, while Warren had savings of £300 and obtained a mortgage for £500.

The decision to buy the house and for all four to live under the same roof was a risky one, but each of them was convinced that The Kilns would make the perfect home. There was a study for Jack, a large vegetable garden, a homely kitchen where the 'family' spent most of its time, and the Oxford bus stopped almost at the end of the drive. The house was also big enough to entertain and to accommodate visitors, a luxury that Janie had craved when they lived in more modest homes in the city itself. For Warren, who was about to retire on an Army pension, the move meant he never needed to work again. Jack was aware that his brother had never really cared for Janie and that at best the two most important people in his life could never do more than tolerate each other, but this new arrangement offered each of them far more advantages than disadvantages.

Jack was not naïve about the challenge of the move. Writing to Arthur Greeves, he confessed that he was concerned that Janie and Warren would not get on. He hoped, however, that as Warnie slowly adapted to domestic life he would begin to like the woman, although he admitted that 'in the interval there is a ticklish time ahead'.[11]

Before they could settle into The Kilns it was necessary to empty Little Lea ready for auction, a job that Jack and Warren had been dreading. When the brothers set off for Belfast in the spring of 1930, they left Janie behind to arrange details concerning the new house. For them this final visit was an emotional one. Even so, it might be expected that men in their thirties would have long since grown used to the empty nursery and might hear only as a distant echo the laughter and tears of childhood. But not Jack, and even less so Warren. The biggest concern for the elder brother, a thirty-five-year-old Army officer, was what to do with their old toys.

From Shanghai, Warren had written to Jack about their toys and on several occasions he had expressed great concern about what would happen to them. He hated the thought of other children playing with them because it would destroy the meaning they had for him. He had even suggested that they build a Little End Room at the new house where they could preserve the memories of childhood by installing the objects that had meant so much to them.

Jack was quick to quash any such notion, even though a part of him was tempted to go along with the plan. He at least realised that the idea of creating a shrine to their lost childhood came close to delusional behaviour and was a desire amplified in his brother's mind by his dependence on alcohol. It was clearly a dangerous emotional road to head down and Jack knew he had to stop himself following and at the same time hold back his brother.

At Little Lea Jack took charge of sorting out the possessions and ordered a distraught Warnie to select a few items to keep, while he piled up the rest for distribution to relatives and auctioneers. During a final tour of the house they came across, in the dusty and malodorous wine cellar, hundreds of empty wine and whisky bottles, piled up to ceiling. It was a testament to Albert's loneliness every bit as symbolic as the empty Little End Room now stripped bare and silent.

Jack probably felt the same pain as his brother as he shut the front door of Little Lea for the last time and handed in the key to the family's solicitor. But, unlike Warren, he had everything to live for and could smother the pain with creativity. Albert's death finally gave him the resources he needed to blossom. He now had a stable domestic life and a secure career. The two decades that were to follow would be the most creative of his whole life, a time during which he was able to distil his learning and all he had experienced and felt since childhood. Henceforth he would direct his creative energies towards producing a body of work that would elevate him from successful college tutor to world-famous writer.

6

Fantasy

As a writer, C. S. Lewis was a late bloomer. He really only got into his stride around the age of forty. In his earliest attempts to find his voice as an author, he, like most other writers before and after him, suffered the usual dispiriting failures. Some have believed that Lewis's late development stemmed from his complicated lifestyle, in particular the strictures placed on him by his job as a full-time scholar and his responsibilities towards Janie and Maureen. Indeed Jack and Janie both fretted about this during their early years together. They shared the conviction that Jack was destined to be a great poet and were concerned that the need to find work and the move towards an academic career would distract him and stifle his creative energies. Even as they were compelled by their circumstances to accept the need for Jack to earn money, they believed sincerely that it was only a matter of time before he would be recognised as the most important poet of his generation, and that his poetry would be his life's work.

Jack was certainly tied to both domestic and college duties. On the one hand he was constantly called on to cook, repair, wash up, shop and clean, while on the other he was required to advise, research and administer. However, these distractions were not the primary reason for his slowness in producing successful literature. Real writers are born, albeit in unrefined and unsophisticated form, and in this sense, at least, Lewis had always been a writer. If they are lucky, young writers receive guidance, find confidence and direction and then grow. But, in Jack's case, the influences, intellectual energies and circumstances that together turned him into a published author did not coalesce for some time. When they did, it was with a force amplified by years of suppression.

At the age of thirty-seven he had published only two works of poetry, an allegorical work of Christian apologetics (*The Pilgrim's Regress*) and a single work of scholarship, *The Allegory of Love: A Study in Medieval Tradition*. The last of these was published in 1936. During the remaining twenty-seven years of his life Lewis saw published no fewer than thirty-eight books, including, between 1942 and 1946, two novels – *Perelandra* (later retitled *Voyage to Venus*, although Lewis preferred the original title) and *That Hideous Strength* – and four works of non-fiction. In addition, many collections, incomplete manuscripts and anthologies have been published since his death in 1963.

The factors that drove Lewis to write came together in the late 1930s. It was a complex chemistry that opened up the author in him, but it consisted of three crucial ingredients. The first was his conversion to Christianity. This resulted in his non-fiction works dealing with religion that started to appear soon after he returned to the faith in 1931. Allegorical pieces, such as *Perelandra* and the seven-volume *The Chronicles of Narnia*, and fictionalised religious commentary, such as *The Screwtape Letters*, soon followed. The second factor, one that fell into place somewhat later, was an ability to tap into the nostalgia for childhood that was ever present in his mind and to employ it to create great fiction. The third was an interest in fantasy that had been germinated in the Little End Room and nurtured throughout adolescence and early adulthood.

The first of these influences will be considered in the next chapter, and the second has been discussed already, but before looking at his own work we should pause to consider the third major shaping force in Lewis's literary development: his deep and abiding interest in fantasy literature.

As we have seen, during their early childhood Jack and Warnie were surrounded by books. Both of their parents were well read and enjoyed a wide range of literature, which inevitably had an influence on the boys' own early tastes. Jack's first literary efforts, the stories linked by the creation of the alternative universe of Boxen, were precocious but rather lifeless. However, at the time the young Lewis was pleased with them and from a relatively early age this personal satisfaction encouraged him to think of himself as a writer.

We have seen already the importance to Jack of Beatrix Potter and E. Nesbit, but during his teenage years he acquired a voracious appetite for reading and one author or set of books led to another, each drawing him further into the great tradition of fantasy writing.

In terms of global popularity, the genre of fantasy is today one of the most important, but when Lewis was a boy 'fantastic fiction' (or 'romantic epic literature', as it was called by some), lay at the very margins of popular literature and was often lumped together with works of science fiction.

Yet fantasy has a long and distinguished pedigree of its own. There are many and varied arguments about who was the first writer in this genre, just as there is still debate about what constitutes fantasy and how it is distinguished from science fiction. Lucian of Samosata, a Greek who lived during the second century AD, may well have been the first; his *Lucianic Satires* are probably the oldest surviving examples of fantasy and acted as templates for many more modern works. Later, during the fifteenth century, the English intellectual and statesman Thomas More revived the style of Lucian and composed his classic *Utopia*, a work imitated by many, including the Italian heretic Tommaso Campanella, who was persecuted and tortured by the Inquisition for what he wrote in his book *The City of the Sun*.

One of the most famous fantasies, Jonathan Swift's *Gulliver's Travels*, follows the eponymous hero on his travels to lands far from the reality of the author's own rather genteel existence in seventeenth-century England and Ireland. Swift's talent was quite unique, and because of its complexity his most famous tale had many imitators, though few successful ones. Yet the eighteenth and early nineteenth centuries produced a wealth of significant fictions that could be classed as fantasy, among them *A Journey to the World Underground* (1741) by Ludwig Holberg, *Micromégas* (1752), by no less a figure than Voltaire, and Mary Shelley's seminal work *Frankenstein*, which appeared in 1818.

Another writer who greatly influenced future fantasy writers was Walter Scott, whose novels, which began to appear at the start of the nineteenth century, blended historical realism with fantasy. Today Scott is best known for his chivalric tales, especially *Ivanhoe*, published in 1819, and his 'Waverley' novels, which appeared over several decades. Scott was an accomplished scholar and researched his novels with meticulous care, creating gripping heroic narratives which made his writing an important influence on later generations of fantasy writers, many of whom set their stories in what might be called an alternative medieval landscape.

A century later, at the advent of the technological age, science fiction and some rare fantasy fiction began to grab the interest of the reading public. The works of Jules Verne and H.G. Wells are perhaps the best examples of the genre from that time, although their books, most notably Verne's *Twenty Thousand Leagues Under the Sea* (1870) and Wells's *The Time Machine* (1895), were quite distinct from fantasy or romantic fiction because they dealt with *possible* worlds, a recognisable 'reality' in which scientific and technological innovation played a pivotal role in the plot. Fantasy diverged from science fiction around this time because, instead of working with futuristic scientific ideas, writers in the genre chose instead to set their stories in alternative worlds that could be as far removed from reality as they wished.

One of the most important fantasy writers at the turn of the nineteenth century was the Irish peer Lord Dunsany. Born Edward John Moreton Drax Plunkett, the 18th Baron Dunsany, in 1878, he was educated at Eton, became a close friend of fellow Irishman the poet W.B. Yeats and wrote some seventy books during a career spanning half a century. Like Lewis and Tolkien, Dunsany was an academic, and he held the position of Byron Professor of English Literature at Athens University, writing fiction in his spare time. His first book, published in 1905, was a collection of short fantasy stories called *The Gods of Pegana* and he went on to write others, including *The Sword of Welleran*. He coined the evocative phrase 'beyond the fields we know' to describe the genre in which he wrote, the depiction of worlds in which almost anything could happen and the regular rules of our earthly realm did not necessarily apply.

Lewis was captivated by Dunsany's novels and collections of stories, in particular *The Hoard of the Gibbelins*, *The Distressing Tale of Thangobrind the Jeweller* and one of his most successful stories, *The King of Elfland's Daughter*. But a far greater influence was a writer who had also acted as an inspiration for Dunsany, William Morris.

Morris was born in 1834. His parents were wealthy Evangelists who indulged their son so much that he became something of a loner. From the age of seven he was fascinated by the Middle Ages and all things linked with chivalry, knights errant and heroic deeds. This interest was nourished by his great love for the works of Walter Scott, particularly the Waverley novels. Young William's fascination became almost an obsession, to the extent that when he was nine his doting father presented him with a pony and a tiny suit of armour so that he could live out his fantasies in the depths of Epping Forest, close to the family home.

Academic and highly creative, Morris was interested in art, books and history, and as he grew older he began to divert his energies from role playing to creative work. He did well at school and went on to study at Exeter College, Oxford, going up in 1853. His original intention was to study for the Church, but he was soon smitten by the artist's life. When his father died he inherited an annual income of £900, which was more than enough to live on without a conventional job.

Influenced by Chaucer, Keats and Tennyson, Morris's fiction is drenched in medieval imagery but blended with an alternative world entirely of his own creation. He became a leading figure in the Pre-Raphaelite movement of artists and was close to Dante Gabriel Rossetti, Edward Burne-Jones and the poet Swinburne. His first published work was a long poem entitled *The Earthly Paradise* (1868–70). During the late 1860s he became deeply interested in Icelandic mythology and went on to publish a translation from the Icelandic of two ancient tales, *The Saga of Gunnlaug Worm-tongue* and *The Story of Grettir the Strong.*

By the middle of the 1870s Morris was blending his lifelong devotion to medievalism and the English chivalric tradition with his understanding of ancient myth to create novels such as *Sigurd the Volsung* and *The Fall of the Niblungs.* These were followed by his most famous narratives, *The House of the Wolfings* (1888) and *The Wood Beyond the World* (1894). Two years later came *The Well at the World's End,* which, at over a thousand pages, was, until Tolkien's *The Lord of the Rings,* the longest work of fantasy ever published. This work bears some of the marks of heroic fiction that would later be integrated into Tolkien's epic saga.

These later books by Morris were extremely important to Lewis and they played an influential role in the development of his fictional worlds, but there were other popular writers of the time who did just as much to establish the genre of fantasy and were read and absorbed by Lewis as a young man.

Henry Rider Haggard, best remembered for his stunning novel *King Solomon's Mines* (1885), and Edgar Rice Burroughs, who blended fantasy with science fiction, were becoming popular early in the twentieth century. Another was James Branch Cabell, whose multi-volume fictional work *The Biography of the Life of Manuel* was set in an alternative United States. Like Morris, Cabell created a world in which magic and a mythical tradition replaced conventional religion. His books caused outrage and one of them, *Jurgen: A Comedy of Justice* (1919), was banned for many years.

Another significant influence on Lewis was the English writer Eric Rucker Eddison, who in 1922 had published a novel entitled *The Worm Ouroboros.* In this tale the central character, Lessingham, is transported to an alternative world called Mercurius where he is drawn into an epic struggle in his efforts to mediate in a conflict between warring tribes.

Eddison was not the first to create an alternative world like this – we need only consider Swift – but in some ways the world of Mercurius can be seen as a darker version of Lewis's Narnia and it offered a template for the creation of a self-consistent, imagined reality in which to set a story. However, it is interesting to note that, like Lewis, and indeed William Morris and Tolkien, Eddison was fascinated with Nordic mythology. In 1926 he published a Viking novel, *Styrbiorn the Strong*, and, like Morris before him, went on to translate an ancient Icelandic epic tale, *Egil's Saga Skallagrimssonar*.

Lewis met Eddison many times and invited him to attend meetings of the Inklings whenever he was in Oxford. Eddison was a rather brash character who never stood on ceremony and said what he thought, with little consideration for the feelings of others. He cared little for Tolkien's work, thinking it 'soft', and pulled no punches in making this clear to the other Inklings when they met. For his part, Tolkien had always been a great fan of Eddison's novels and even after this blunt rebuff he was magnanimous enough to continue expressing the belief that Eddison was probably the best fantasy writer of his generation.

Lewis corresponded regularly with Eddison and sometimes asked his advice on a variety of subjects that he wanted to cover accurately in his novels. On one occasion he sought the older writer's comments on bears and their domestication, information he needed to help him with the creation of his character Mr Bultitude, the bear in *That Hideous Strength*.

Although the importance of all these literary figures on Lewis was considerable, the single writer most influential in moulding his fiction was the Scottish author George MacDonald. Born in 1824, MacDonald was a preacher and Christian apologist who wrote some thirty novels, numerous fairy tales, books of poetry and collections of essays in a career spanning some fifty years and he is considered by some to have been one of the most original of nineteenth-century thinkers. Like his contemporary William Morris, MacDonald was very much part of the Victorian literary scene and his friends included many of the English Pre-Raphaelites, social reformers such as Octavia Hill, and, in America, Ralph Waldo Emerson and Mark Twain.

At the age of sixteen Lewis discovered the writings of MacDonald by chance when he picked up a paperback of his most famous adult novel, *Phantastes*, at a bookstand on the platform of Bookham railway station while he was on his way to the house of his tutor William Kirkpatrick. MacDonald was not a very good writer and Lewis knew this, but what captivated him about the man's work was his amazingly flexible imagination. Reading MacDonald is rather hard work, as his writing does not flow well (which is one of the main reasons for his falling into relative obscurity soon after his death in 1905), but for some readers his ability to conjure believable alternative realities is more than enough compensation. After enjoying a brief period of success during the late nineteenth and early twentieth centuries MacDonald's books began to sell in ever-decreasing numbers. However, his influence was considerable and, apart from providing inspiration for Lewis, he was important to writers as diverse as G.K. Chesterton, W.H. Auden and Madeleine L'Engle.

Lewis enjoyed many of MacDonald's books, including his fairy tales for children, *Back of the North Wind*, *The Princess and the Goblin* and *The Princess and Curdie* (perhaps his most lasting achievements), but *Phantastes* remained Lewis's favourite and he returned to it time and again throughout his life. For him, MacDonald's adult fiction pointed the way towards a style of writing which, after many abortive attempts, he eventually adopted himself.

The essence of MacDonald's skill is his great ability to portray complex ideas in the form of a story, and this provided Lewis with the valuable lesson that no concept was too difficult to portray as fiction, and that in fact, if handled skilfully, fiction is a wonderful medium through which a readership may be educated.

But Lewis was a man whose literary interests were far broader than just one genre could satisfy, no matter how free the form might be. It must not be forgotten that he had studied English to degree level, obtained a First at Oxford in the subject and, by the time he began to write fiction, he was teaching English literature at the university.

And yet he had very particular dislikes and prejudices. Although the literary critic William Empson once professed the belief that Lewis was 'the best-read man of his generation', this must be considered in the light of the fact that there were whole areas of literature that Lewis completely ignored and even considered unworthy of his attention.[1] Lewis was not quite so entrenched as Tolkien, who believed sincerely that nothing written after AD 1100 was worth reading, but he despised what both men habitually referred to dismissively as 'modern literature', a ridiculously mixed bag of writers from Dickens to Joyce. The poetry of T.S. Eliot did nothing for Lewis, nor did the prose of Lawrence. But he was a great fan of William Morris, he liked Walter Scott and Lord Dunsany and his tastes stretched from Edmund Spenser and William Blake to Kenneth Grahame and E. Nesbit via G.K. Chesterton. Also, like Tolkien, Lewis was steeped in the mythical traditions of the Nordic and Germanic peoples. Oddly, perhaps, he was a man who could read *Beowulf* any number of times but struggled with a few chapters of Hemingway or Fitzgerald. His literary imagination was driven primarily by an ancient world vision of romance and a love of fairy stories.

As a child Jack had created fantasy realms populated by weird and wonderful creatures, his alternative world of Boxen being the best example. He had written narratives and verse and illustrated them with fanciful drawings and paintings, but there was no hint in those early years that he would wish to become a poet. The belief that his true vocation, and his destiny, lay in poetry only came to him in late adolescence. And when it did it was a conviction based on sincerity but also something of a fashionable fantasy.

His first attempts appeared in a collection of notebooks he carried around with him from about 1915. He took them with him to the trenches of France and returned with them when he was sent home wounded. He did not realise it at the time, but in doing this he was following the same path taken by many other creative young men of his generation. Indeed in 1918, as Jack began to perfect the growing collection of poems in his notebooks, another young man, one he would not meet for another eight years, J.R.R. Tolkien, had found himself sick with trench fever and was convalescing in England while his mind was already formulating the original verse form of *The Silmarillion*.

At first all went well for Lewis the poet. In September 1918, while he was recovering from his wounds at Ashton Court in Bristol, a thrilling letter arrived from the publisher Heinemann in London in which they expressed the wish to publish the collection of work he had recently posted to them. Lewis was particularly impressed by the fact that Heinemann published many of the most famous poets of the day, including Robert Graves and Siegfried Sassoon. Furthermore, the house had close links with John Galsworthy, one of the most popular authors of the time, who, Lewis was informed, would do his utmost to publicise the collection, including publishing one of Lewis's poems in his widely read journal *Reveille*.

But the excitement was to be short-lived. Jack's book *Spirits in Bondage*, written under the pseudonym Clive Hamilton, was published in 1919 into a complete vacuum and went quite unnoticed by all but friends and family. Galsworthy did not publish Lewis's poem until the summer of that year, some four months after the book appeared, and so this did little to promote the collection. Consequently the tiny print run of some 750 copies went largely unsold.

For Lewis, though, part of the thrill was simply seeing his work in print. He was stoical enough to realise that few writers find success with their first endeavours, and he was buoyed up by the enthusiastic comments of his father, who thought his son's contribution to *Reveille* was the best poem in the issue and infinitely superior to offerings from more famous figures such as Hilaire Belloc and Siegfried Sassoon. As might be expected, Janie was also full of praise for the book. She loyally expressed the belief that Jack was a truly great poet and that the fact that he had sold so few copies of his first collection meant absolutely nothing.

Ironically, because Lewis's first book was totally ignored by every newspaper and magazine and did not receive a single review anywhere, the only adverse comments about *Spirits in Bondage* came from the author's own brother. Warren, it seems, took offence over what he perceived as Jack's clear poetic depiction of atheism. Jack was confused by this. He considered his work to be humanist and starkly realist rather than atheistic and had tried deliberately to avoid any significant religious slant. In poems such as 'Victory', which is one of the best of the collection, he expresses anger about the insanity of war and a belief that the indomitable human spirit reigns triumphant over pain, but it is not the attack on God it could so easily have become.

Warren harboured rather simplistic ideas about Christianity, but the most likely reason for his reaction to *Spirits in Bondage* is jealousy. This assumption is supported by a very complacent letter he sent to his father a few days after reading the book, in which he declared: 'Jack's Atheism is, I am sure, purely academic, but even so, no useful purpose is served by endeavouring to advertise oneself as an Atheist. Setting aside the higher problems involved, it is obvious that a profession of a Christian belief is as necessary a part of a man's mental make-up as a belief in the King, the Regular Army, and the Public Schools.'[2]

Another eight years were to pass before Lewis saw another piece of his work in print, but this is not to say he was idle during that time. These were the years during which he lived a settled life in Oxford with Janie and obtained his fellowship at Magdalen. When he was not teaching or keeping Janie happy by completing his household chores and running errands, he spent any free time he could find writing a long poem he had begun during the summer of 1918, a work he entitled *Dymer*.

In spite of the fact that Lewis's friends at Oxford loved the poem and he was fired up by Nevill Coghill's conviction that *Dymer* was a considerable poem by a great new poet, when it was eventually published by Dent in 1926 (thanks to Coghill passing on the manuscript to the publisher) it went the same way as *Spirits in Bondage* and was ignored by all.

Lewis's first book, as emotionally charged as it had been for him, might, at a pinch, have been considered a work of juvenilia, but the failure of *Dymer*, the product of eight years' effort and completed after he had become a Tutor of English Literature at Oxford, brought down the curtain on his attempts to become a poet.

Between the two books Lewis had also started a diary and he kept up the writing of this fairly consistently from 1922 until 1927, when he suddenly decided that the process was after all a rather futile exercise because he was merely recording the minutiae of his life. He had begun the effort with the enthusiastic conviction that it would, on future reading, cast some light on ideas and thoughts that had passed through his mind in the past. But, by 1927, he had come to realise that he looked back on his thoughts so rarely that writing them down was actually a worthless occupation.

Although this decision is galling for the biographer, even a superficial appraisal of Lewis's diaries (published in 1991) leads one to agree with him. His assertion that writing a diary was futile was, in his case, indeed quite correct. Part of the reason is that Lewis could not really express his own feelings and deepest concerns because the diary was open to Janie. He either read her extracts on request or felt compelled to leave the diary on show for his partner to read at her leisure. As a result, what could have been revealing, intimate and honest became merely an act.

Even so, it is unfortunate for the historian that the period in which Lewis was dealing with the emotional impact of failing in his second full-scale attempt to become a poet produced no surviving personal account of his feelings. Between July 1926 and January 1927 Lewis took a break from writing in his journal and so we do not even have a sanitised version of his emotional life during what must have been one of the most frustrating and deflating periods of his career. However, one thing is clear: this failure affected him deeply, because Lewis rarely attempted to write any serious poetry after *Dymer* and a further six years were to pass before he again published anything at all.

This long break came to an end soon after Lewis went through the life-changing experience of religious conversion, an awakening that was to have a most profound effect on his world view and with it the way in which he expressed himself creatively. The first fruit of this conversion was *The Pilgrim's Regress: An Allegorical Apology for Christianity, Reason and Romanticism.*

The Pilgrim's Regress was written during a two-week burst of creativity in August 1932, while Jack was visiting Arthur Greeves and his family in Belfast, and it was a complete departure from anything he had done before. Eschewing verse for a simple prose narrative form, *The Pilgrim's Regress* is Lewis's first serious attempt to combine his two most powerful obsessions, myth and Christianity. In form it is a simple retelling of John Bunyan's story of 1678 and, in deference to the original, Lewis named his main character John.

It is almost certainly no coincidence that Lewis wrote this book while staying close to his childhood home, by then occupied by the family who had bought Little Lea a year after his father's death in 1929. He had told Warnie in January 1932 that he wanted to write a long allegorical poem on the subject of a man's search for 'Joy', a concept that had been a preoccupation of his since childhood. But this story describing a man's route to enlightenment was first and foremost a straightforward allegory of his own recent awakening, which had been brought to the surface by an emotionally charged return to the home of his childhood.

In terms of construction and readability, *The Pilgrim's Regress* was the most successful of the three books Lewis had written up to this point. Fleeting glimpses of the power of his later writing are revealed and there are hints of ideas that were to be recycled more successfully. The best example of this is a witch John encounters on his journey who tries to seduce and ensnare him.

The major weakness of *The Pilgrim's Regress* lies not in the ideas or the form but in some aspects of Lewis's writing style. Throughout the book he attacks people and objects that represented real-life targets of his disapproval. During his journey John encounters such tempters as modernist writers, occultists and Broad-Churchmen. In the more subtle passages Lewis uses the often amusing trick of filling his imaginary world with barely disguised real-life contemporaries. This works well with some caricatures, such as Victorian ones, a thinly veiled John Betjeman, and the character Glugly, modelled on the less-than-beautiful socialite poet Edith Sitwell. But from the perspective of a modern reader, the use of fantasy creatures such as the Marxomanni, Mussolimini and Swastici is less successful and serves only to cheapen and date the tale.

The Pilgrim's Regress was another book enjoyed by Lewis's friends – he read it aloud to Tolkien, who greatly approved of it – but his publisher, Dent, found little success with it when they launched the book in May 1933, and struggled to sell 650 of a first print run of 1000.

Ironically, the book had a second and indeed a third lease of life. Lewis's second chance with it came soon after publication of the original Dent edition and from an entirely unexpected source. A few reviewer of *The Pilgrim's Regress* had made the erroneous assumption that Lewis was a Roman Catholic and this prompted a specialist publisher, the Catholic firm of Sheed and Ward, to gain permission from Dent to issue a new edition. This appeared two years later, in 1935, and sold some 1500 copies.

Lewis was not happy about having what he bluntly dubbed 'a Papist publisher' handling the book, but after realising that this house would do better than Dent, his commercial sense quickly overrode any religious prejudice. However, he was, as he later put it in a letter to Arthur Greeves, 'well punished' for his acquisitiveness because, unknown to him at the time of going to press, his new Catholic publisher added a blurb to the dust jacket which included the comment: 'This story begins in Puritania (Mr Lewis was brought up in Ulster).' This implied that the author was attacking his Northern Irish roots and it played well to the partisan readership Sheed and Ward were targeting. Jack called the statement 'a damnable lie told to try to make the Dublin riffraff buy the book'.[3]

But perhaps the most surprising aspect of this publishing story concerns the third and most successful incarnation of the book. In spite of the way Sheed and Ward had treated him in proselytising their Catholic agenda, in 1944 Lewis granted them permission to publish an entirely new edition of *The Pilgrim's Regress*, without the offensive blurb. The reason for this was not purely financial but was based on his conviction that he might inspire Catholics to question and think about certain aspects of their creed. He even quietly hoped he might win over some papists to his own brand of High Church Protestantism.

One of the things for which Lewis deserves great credit is his tenacity and determination as a young writer. Many hopefuls would have given up after three successive failures, but he knew that he was hitting his stride even if the commercial aspects of his career were underwhelming. After each failure he simply moved on and tried something new, for it was becoming quite apparent to him and his close circle of admirers that he was nothing if not an extremely versatile writer.

The last book Lewis wrote before finding a broad readership and fame beyond the confines of academic life in Oxford was again entirely different from its predecessors. *The Allegory of Love* was Lewis's first truly academic work, a critique of love literature from the early Middle Ages to the late sixteenth century, and from the late 1920s, when he first began to plan out the book, until its completion in 1935, he considered it to be his most important work-in-progress.

The Allegory of Love was, in every way, Lewis's most accomplished book to date. In it he succeeded in finding the non-fiction voice that would become the distinctive trademark employed in every book of religious commentary and academic study he wrote during the most successful years of his career. It is a friendly, warm and inviting voice that not only makes you want to read on, but, in the case of *The Allegory of Love*, compels the reader to find out more about the poetic works Lewis dissects with such fondness and authority.

The book received a raft of favourable reviews from the academic community and beyond and it established Lewis's name as a scholar. Furthermore, it not only sold well for this type of book, but actually boosted the sales of the poets Lewis wrote about, many of whom had been almost forgotten and were in great need of rehabilitation. The most significant example is Edmund Spenser's *The Faerie Queene*, first published in 1596, which, in part thanks to the success of Lewis's book, was re-established as one of the most important works of late sixteenth-century literature.

Today *The Allegory of Love* is still regarded by specialists as the most important book on the subject of love literature from the sixth to the sixteenth century and it made Lewis's name in Oxford. But, to widen the perspective, its importance lies in the fact that it was the first book in which Lewis employed the authorial voice that would make him a household name. He used this voice in the writing of other non-fiction, but he also employed a version of it to bring to life the fictional characters who populated his fantasy worlds. From the 1930s onwards this voice never let him down.

Lewis's first major success came with his next book, which once again was a piece of work derived from an entirely different genre from its predecessors. Realising that the type of success he had enjoyed with *The Allegory of Love*, as satisfying as it was, would for ever encase his work in an academic environment, Lewis was beginning, by 1937, to consider branching out into fantasy fiction as a way in which he could express his moralistic and religious concerns.

This idea had sprung, like many of Lewis's most important decisions, from a conversation with Tolkien. The two men were, in middle age, still avid readers of fantasy literature, but neither felt satisfied with many of the books published at the time. They agreed that the best way to remedy the situation was to write their own fiction, of a kind that would reflect their personal tastes. After briefly toying with the idea of writing something together they realised this would not suit them and instead decided that Lewis should attempt a story about space travel and Tolkien should begin work on one about time travel.

Lewis and Tolkien were wise to quickly dispense with the idea of a collaboration, for this would certainly have ended in disaster. Although in many ways they were very similar, as writers they were utterly different. Tolkien was a slow, meticulous developer of stories, a man who cared deeply about the details and the historical backdrop to even the most trivial aspects of a story. He wrote and he rewrote, he agonised over every tiny element and he built an image from the bottom up to create a world of startling realism and intricacy. Lewis, by contrast, savoured the overall picture, sketched out the overall vision and then coloured in the details. But whereas Tolkien moved with snail-like speed and a watchmaker's precision, Lewis sped through his work, usually content with a first draft and only occasionally rewriting a passage. If he could not get something right on the second attempt, he would discard it.

For Tolkien, the idea of writing a science-fiction fantasy led quickly to a dead end. All that remains of his time-travel story is a set of notes and an outline for a book that was to be entitled *The Lost Road*. The reason for this is that around the time he and Lewis agreed to undertake their twinned books, *The Hobbit* was receiving critical acclaim and had established Tolkien as a writer of children's fiction. Therefore, during 1937 and 1938 he was preoccupied with attempting to repeat his success with a book he originally called 'the New Hobbit', the book that slowly developed into *The Lord of the Rings*. This effort was, in the end, to occupy him for almost twelve years, and so *The Lost Road* was discarded and forgotten. Lewis, however, had been inspired by the idea of writing a story of space travel, and to Tolkien's astonishment he produced, within just a few months, a complete novel, which he entitled *Out of the Silent Planet*.

At the heart of *Out of the Silent Planet* is the battle between good and evil. There are no grey characters – they are either pure and good or corrupt and evil – and by the end of the story Lewis has established a 'hierarchy of being'. At the top of the pyramid is the one God, Maleldil. Below him we find creatures called eldila, ethereal beings that resemble angels and are invisible to most humans.

These powerful figures live in a parallel universe but may incarnate into our reality at will. Each of the planets of the solar system is watched over and supervised by eldila. Mars (or Malacandra, as it is called by its inhabitants) is presided over by an eldila named Oyarsa. A similar being oversees Venus (Perelandra), but the earth has long since 'fallen' and is viewed as a corrupted planet, where 'bent eldila' reign. These are led by a figure who equates to the Devil.

The hero of the piece is an 'everyman', an Oxford philologist named Ransom who finds himself embroiled in the schemes of an obsessive and violent scientist, Professor Weston, and his friend Devine, an upper-class chancer who is involved with Weston simply to make money. At the start of the story we learn that Weston has built a spacecraft and already made one trip to Mars. He plans to return on the night that Ransom appears at his and Devine's head-quarters, a remote country house that Ransom is drawn to while on a walking holiday. Weston harbours dreams of dominating the new world of Mars and talks of human colonisation and endless advancement. Devine is simply after gold and other resources he believes are to be found aplenty on the red planet.

The story starts as a simple, rather clichéd tale and the descriptions of the journey to Mars are closer to the writing of Jules Verne from half a century earlier than anything the reader of today would expect from science fiction. But the plot quickly broadens to become a blend of sci-fi, mysticism and religious allegory and to encompass Lewis's unique cosmic vision. Indeed, it is clear even from this first book in the Ransom trilogy that Lewis was not really writing sci-ence fiction at all. Unlike his contemporaries, writers such as Isaac Asimov and Robert Heinlein, Lewis brings almost no science into his books, so that they might better be described as 'space fiction'.

Although he did not realise it at the time, with this early foray into fiction Lewis had begun what was to be only the first part of a larger project. Although *Out of the Silent Planet* may be considered as a self-contained story, it really sets the stage for a more complex overarching tale. As this first novel unfolds, Ransom becomes the agent of the good forces, the pure, uncorrupted eldila who are engaged in an age-old spiritual battle with the evil beings who have established their nerve centre on earth. By engineering this development, Lewis managed to open up vistas he could not have contemplated when he started the book in 1937. With *Out of the Silent Planet* he had established the beginnings of a mythology. He had described a 'cosmic religion', a broad canvas on which the narrow vision of Christianity on earth constitutes but a tiny part.

In a literary sense it is easy to see the influence of Verne and H.G. Wells in *Out of the Silent Planet*. Lewis was also influenced by a book called *A Voyage to Arcturus*, written by David Lindsay and published in 1920, in which the author had likewise added a 'spiritual' dimension to an otherwise quite orthodox space yarn set in an alien world. But what makes Lewis's novel unique is the grand mystical sweep, the occult panorama that provides far more than a backdrop to a simple science-fiction tale. The mystical and religious aspects of the story, rather than science, act as primary drivers. It is this element that gives *Out of the Silent Planet* an enduring quality and lifts it above the mundane.

Almost before he had finished the final draft of the manuscript, Lewis was keen to have his book in the shops, but, ironically, he found that it took longer to find a willing publisher than it had to write the book. On Lewis' behalf Tolkien approached Stanley Unwin, who had published *The Hobbit* only a year earlier, and encouraged him to read his friend's manuscript. Unwin passed it on to an in-house reader, but he found little to recommend in Lewis's book and submitted a negative report.

In the meantime Lewis had approached Dent, who had published *Dymer* more than a decade earlier, but they too turned it down. Fortunately for Lewis, Unwin, although he decided against taking the book himself, had passed it on to a friend at a small fledgling house called the Bodley Head. This editor liked it enough to publish the book in the late summer of 1938.

Although it did not enjoy massive sales until after Lewis gained international fame during the 1940s, *Out of the Silent Planet* sold much better than any of his books published up to this time and it did much to establish him in the genre. Within a year of publication it had received over fifty reviews on both sides of the Atlantic, the majority of them full of praise, while the worst conveyed misgivings softened with words of support. In the *New York Times Book Review*, Horace Williams wrote: 'Everyone says a new world is just around the corner, but everyone is pretty vague about just what it is to be. The plain truth of the matter is that Man has to imagine this new order before it can be realised. Mr Lewis's romance is one step forward in the preliminary dreaming, the discovery of the Mystery.'[4] In London the *Times Literary Supplement*'s reviewer was disappointed and seemed quite uninspired by Lewis's spirituality. 'Alas! And alas,' he wrote, 'a capable writer with an excellent basic notion did not attend longer upon and learn more from his evident teacher . . . it lacks too much of Mr Wells's special gift of dramatic sharpening, and above all of running characterisation, other-worldly exposition and vivid incident in triple harness.'[5]

As he was finishing the manuscript of *Out of the Silent Planet* Lewis realised that he had only just started describing a bigger picture, but he appears to have been quite confused about how he would deal with it. In a short section tacked on after the story draws to a close, he decided to include a letter from his hero Ransom relating his astonishing adventure. At the end of this letter Ransom implies that he may take another journey but that next time it will almost certainly be a journey through time rather than space.

This has undoubtedly confused readers who have discovered the Ransom trilogy many years after it was written, because the second book, *Perelandra*, has absolutely nothing to do with time travel.

This confusion was only clarified for the reading public when, in 1977, fourteen years after Lewis's death, a fragment of a book Lewis called *The Dark Tower* was published by Collins. This fragment, a proposed sequel to *Out of the Silent Planet*, picks up the story immediately after the conclusion of the first book and presents the first section of a time-travel adventure involving some of the characters Lewis had already created. Lewis began it in early 1939 but gave up on it a few months later after writing only sixty pages, some 30,000 words.

The Dark Tower possesses an entirely different mood from *Out of the Silent Planet*. It is much darker and more disturbing, but it also has little spiritual or religious allegorical content. It may be unfair to judge a book by a fragmentary first draft, but what has survived offers a rather confused plot built around a machine called a Chronoscope that allows observers to view scenes from other times. Ransom appears as one of a group who use the machine to view the dark tower of the title. Here strange 'Stinging men' stab and inoculate victims in the lower spine with a unicorn's horn protruding from their foreheads.

It is unclear why Lewis abandoned *The Dark Tower*, because he was enthused enough by it to read this fragment to the Inklings. The most likely reason is that he simply lost the thread of what he was trying to convey, and being the kind of author who felt uncomfortable with plans and plot programming, he felt compelled to put it aside. However, another possibility is that one of his fellow Inklings may have pointed out the dangers of such obvious Freudian symbolism in the story, a matter Lewis had obviously overlooked.

The book that did eventually become the sequel to *Out of the Silent Planet*, *Perelandra*, was in almost every way different from *The Dark Tower*. Part of the reason for this is that Lewis did not go straight back to writing a new adventure for his hero Ransom. He took a break from the series and it was not finished and published until 1943, some time after he had found fame as the author of *The Screwtape Letters*.

Like its predecessor in the trilogy, *Perelandra* was written very quickly. Although it was dashed off during the first four months of 1942, it was based on an idea that had been germinating as early as 1937, and Lewis moulded it so that it could become a new story to illuminate further the 'cosmic religion' he had begun to describe in *Out of the Silent Planet*.

The plot was inspired by *Paradise Lost* and came to fruition in Lewis's mind during a period in which he was lecturing and writing on the subject of Milton's great work. The book of these lectures was *A Preface to Paradise Lost* (1943), in which Lewis analyses the sources of and influences on Milton's masterpiece, as well as its impact on future generations of writers. It is a stunning piece of scholarship delivered with warmth and confidence, and it may be considered the non-fiction equivalent of the theme that runs through *Perelandra*.

At the start of the novel Ransom is called to Venus/Perelandra, a young, virginal planet, a world before the Fall. Here he meets the Green Lady (who equates to Eve), an innocent, free spirit, whom he is to educate. However, the 'bent eldila' are also there to corrupt the Green Lady and turn her to their purposes.

A substantial chunk of the book is taken up with verbal battles between the good forces represented by Ransom and the evil powers in the form of Weston, the amoral scientist of *Out of the Silent Planet*, a man who is now entirely possessed by the Devil.

Perelandra was Lewis's favourite of the three Ransom books, a fact that should immediately set alarm bells ringing, for it is often the case that an author's personal favourite is their most self-indulgent and subjective work. This is certainly true with *Perelandra*, and the alarm bells ring for good reason, for the book is only really satisfying or inspiring to those who are spiritually in tune with the author and his personal vision of the universe. The plot only wholly carries you if are a Christian. For non-believers the story comes across as trite, even irritating. The problem stems from the fact that the novel contains almost nothing but religious allegory. It is the story of Genesis wrapped up as pseudo space fiction, a thoroughly partisan work, which, although cleverly written and ingeniously developed, is little more than a religious argument. To sceptics, atheists and agnostics this is quite meaningless, and because its plot is wafer-thin, the book is not even redeemed by being entertaining.

At the same time, in terms of style, *Perelandra* is the work of a master. The substance may be single-focused and uninteresting, but it is dressed up beautifully. Lewis's imaginative descriptions of the new Eden are often exquisite, lush and sometimes wholly original. He wisely steers clear of any of the scientific aspects of Ransom's adventure and instead concentrates on creating a carefully constructed, strikingly vivid world in which he could set his lengthy religious discourse.

With the publication of *Perelandra* the critics were almost entirely unanimous in their praise, but a few made the very good point that as a work of literature it would have been more successful if it had been written as verse rather than as a prose narrative. As true as this might have been in purely artistic terms, such comments were made without a thought for the expectations of the marketplace or the sensibilities of the majority of Lewis's readership. And, beyond this, Lewis could not have failed to see the irony in such a proposition, put as it was to an author who had tried and failed to achieve even the tiniest hint of success with verse, a writer who had given up on it years earlier to turn instead to prose narrative.

Perelandra drew a great deal of attention from reviewers around the world and this time, because Lewis had only recently gained global recognition as a Christian apologist, the book worked commercially. Many science-fiction readers had taken *Out of the Silent Planet* to their hearts (although a large number of aficionados considered it dated and rather arch), but *Perelandra* reached a much wider audience. This success helped to relaunch the first of the Ransom books, which came out in a new edition and sold many times more than the original, and it also laid the ground for a third volume.

That the third book, *That Hideous Strength* (1945), should be set on earth had been implicit from the moment in *Out of the Silent Planet* that Ransom met the eldila of Mars and learned of the tensions and dynamics of the cosmic hierarchy in which all Maleldil's beings exist. Earth was, Ransom learned, the home of the corrupt eldila and so it was inevitable that here the final battle, an Armageddon, would be played out.

With *That Hideous Strength* Lewis managed to pull off the trick of writing a third book which, except for a single common character and the continuation of an overarching theme, bore very little relation to the previous titles in the trilogy. The mood is dark and brooding but in a very different way from the occasional sinister episodes in *Out of the Silent Planet* and *Perelandra*. This mood is intensified by the fact that the setting in twentieth-century England is immediately familiar, and although *That Hideous Strength* is flawed it is by far Lewis's most successful adult science-fiction novel.

The book's faults take several forms. Linguistic anachronisms leap from the page and distract, especially in dialogue that is often creaky. Some of the characters are wooden, clichés from 1940s Britain, extras who have escaped the set of *Brief Encounter* or *The Thirty-Nine Steps*, and Lewis's caricatures of women, as either rather simple types or highly emotional, silly young girls, date the book horribly. There is also a rather clumsy religiosity to contend with, but at least this is a layer of the writing that is kept under control very carefully and only becomes intrusive during the final (and quite unnecessary) scene.

But what, in spite of these failings, makes *That Hideous Strength* so memorable is its brooding atmosphere. Ransom appears as a latter-day incarnation of Pendragon of Arthurian legend and is pitted against the sinister group, the N.I.C.E. (National Institute of Co-ordinated Experiments), who plan to alter human consciousness and install a new regime to rule the earth and to start humanity on the road to cosmic domination. Earth (and indeed the universe) is saved by the interference of the eldila, who resurrect the sleeping figure of Merlin, inducing him to form an alliance with Ransom's motley crew of 'good' men and women.

The character of Merlin is beautifully rendered. Rather than modelling him on a fairy-tale wizard or perhaps the character with which, by 1945, he would have been very familiar, Tolkien's Gandalf, Lewis conjured up a dirty, bedraggled, half-savage sorcerer who is amoral and intellectually unstable. Merlin embodies old magic, ancient, primitive Christianity and brutal self-preservation, a stunning counterpart to his allies, the prim village folk who stand behind Ransom in his defence of God and humanity.

That Hideous Strength, which Lewis subtitled 'A Modern Fairy-tale for Grown-Ups', possesses an ingenious, melodramatic plot. In almost every way the novel is the very opposite of *Perelandra*. Where *Perelandra* is most often as light and delicate as one of the floating

Venusian islands on which much of the story unfolds, *That Hideous Strength* is dense, dark and often macabre. Where *Perelandra* is almost plot-less, with few characters and almost purely cerebral, *That Hideous Strength* is plot-driven and filled with both characters and thrills and spills.

In creating the N.I.C.E. Lewis produced the image of a morally corrupt group of human beings who place too much faith in science and believe that nature can be dominated, broken and eventually beaten into submission by technology. Although well rendered and dramatic, Lewis's attacks on science via his portrayal of the N.I.C.E. were thoroughly naïve, and it is revealing that until he embarked on the first of his fantasy novels he had shown almost no interest in any form of science. The anti-scientific aspect of *That Hideous Strength* is pivotal to the plot, but it lacks any real substance. Based as it was on irrational fear, it does not possess the objectivity required of a novelist. Too often we see through the veil and witness Lewis kicking against something he dislikes emotionally but neither understands nor wishes to understand.

By taking this stance Lewis pinned his colours to the mast. His rather unfocused and uneducated science-bashing is irritating, especially to the scientifically trained, but there is a positive side to this in that he anticipated and examined with remarkable accuracy the public anxiety and distrust of science which runs through modern society. Lewis was probably aware of Aldous Huxley's *Brave New World* (1932) and was certainly very familiar with H.G. Wells's invariably pro-science writing, both of which would have prompted him to feel free to express his feelings about the way science was moulding social evolution. Yet we must remember that in 1944, when Lewis was writing *That Hideous Strength*, the general public was quite unaware of atomic power, genetic manipulation or the possibilities of social engineering. This was an age in which science was by and large still trusted and increasingly relied upon by an ill-informed and often unquestioning public. Lewis should at least be commended for his defence of a principle that concerned him deeply but went against the popular trend of the time.

In the writing of *That Hideous Strength* Lewis was greatly influenced by his friend and fellow Inkling Charles Williams. A master of blending the everyday world with gothic horror, Williams had the unerring ability to create stories in which a very nasty undercurrent counterpointed a prosaic, parochial world. This style and method of perverting a plot had a profound effect on Lewis as his novel was taking shape.

That Hideous Strength also proved highly influential on others. Those of sufficient age reading it today could not fail to recognise it as the prototype for the macabre TV science fiction of *Quatermass*, produced some ten years after Lewis's novel. The early episodes of *Dr Who*, in which the Time Lord was pitted against dark, evil forces on earth, owe so much to Lewis's creation that a television writer could have replaced one of the organisations opposing the Doctor with the N.I.C.E. and the script would have suffered no harm.

The Ransom trilogy was written between 1938 and 1944 and its creation was, as the false start of *The Dark Tower* illustrates, a rather ad hoc, hit-and-miss affair. Lewis stumbled through the writing. He had a clear notion of what he was doing in each of the three books, but he never sat down and planned out the trilogy and the way the stories might link together. This fault shows, and it weakens the collection.

That Hideous Strength received the most uneven reception of the three books, but it has since become Lewis's best-selling novel. (The sales figures for the book were boosted by an abridged version published in the United States as *The Tortured Planet* which has sold in the millions.) Some reviewers found the characters unconvincing and the plot laboured, while others saw it as a perfectly apt parable for the mid-twentieth century. Writing in the London *Evening Standard*, Graham Greene declared: 'Mr Lewis writes admirably and excitingly when he is describing the Institute [N.I.C.E.] with its sinister muffled life under a Deputy Director who talks as a crab walks, but I found Professor Ransom and the "good" characters peculiarly unconvincing. The allegory becomes a little too friendly, like a sermon at a children's service, or perhaps like a whimsical charade organised by a middle-aged bachelor uncle.'[6] By contrast, the *New York Times* compared the novel favourably with *Brave New World*, while *Time* magazine's reviewer, writing less than a year after the horror of Hiroshima and Nagasaki, believed it to be 'a timely allegory for atomic man'.[7]

Lewis was a speedy writer and most of the time he wrote brilliantly, but he was an impatient man and disliked reworking. It is unfair to compare, as some have, his trilogy with *The Lord of the Rings*, which Tolkien was writing contemporaneously. There are three main reasons why such a comparison is unjustifiable. First, as we have seen, Tolkien and Lewis were quite different types of writer. Tolkien prided himself on his meticulous approach whereas Lewis placed speed and spontaneity high on his list of priorities. Secondly, Lewis was working to an agenda. For him the themes of his stories came first, while plot (especially in the middle book of the three, *Perelandra*) came a very poor second. In complete contrast, Tolkien was a story-teller first and everything else followed. Thirdly, Lewis wrote his books as separate entities loosely amalgamated after the event, whereas Tolkien wrote *The Lord of the Rings* as a single book. Only later, and much against his wishes, was Tolkien's masterpiece divided into three volumes for popular consumption.

The trilogy was the only space-fantasy novels Lewis wrote. The books remain extremely popular and are rediscovered by new generations of readers who find in them a rather warped and discordant beauty that is both seductive and memorable. They were successful in their own right but were not the books that made Lewis a household name. Much to the author's irritation, such recognition came instead from a short collection of fictional letters he had composed for a British newspaper and later put together as a single, rather flimsy volume entitled *The Screwtape Letters*.

With *The Screwtape Letters* Lewis succeeded in encapsulating many of his intellectual preoccupations. The core idea of the book, a correspondence between two devils, came to him in July 1940 during an early-morning service at Holy Trinity Church in Headington. Lewis often claimed that *Confessions of a Well-Meaning Woman* by Stephen McKenna, published in 1922, had given him the conceptual paradigm for his book. Another influence may have been *Letters from Hell* by Valdemar Thisted, which he read while living in Great Bookham before gaining a scholarship to Oxford. Furthermore, this inspiration occurred only a matter of weeks before he began attending confessionals at the Society of St John the Evangelist in the Oxford suburb of Cowley, a move he had been mulling over for many months and a step that took him beyond the conventional limits of Protestant orthodoxy and into semi-Catholicism.

During the summer of 1940 Lewis was greatly concerned with the concepts of guilt, temptation, seduction, sin and the nature of heaven and hell, subjects given extra gravitas by the oppressive mood of the times. England had been at war for almost a year, but that June the British Expeditionary Force had been evacuated from Dunkirk. Late the following month Lewis recounted in a letter to his brother Warren, who had been one of the soldiers brought home from the coast of northern France, how the previous night he had felt momentarily seduced by the voice of Adolf Hitler in a BBC broadcast he had heard in his college rooms. 'I don't know if I'm weaker than other people,' he wrote, 'but it is a positive revelation to me how *while the speech lasts* it is impossible not to waver just a little. I should be useless as a schoolmaster or a policeman. Statements which I *know* to be untrue all but convince me, at any rate for the moment, if only the man says them unflinchingly.'[8]

This is a surprisingly candid confession and it illustrates just how thoughts of seduction by the forces of evil and the guilt of mortal man were very much at the forefront of Lewis's mind at the time. Such preoccupations laid the groundwork for the book that was, in terms of ingenuity and originality, his most successful literary adventure.

The Screwtape Letters consists of thirty-one letters exchanged between two devils, one named Wormwood, a young trainee demon out in the field, the other his Uncle Screwtape, who works in Hell's Civil Service, where he is an Undersecretary for the Infernal Lowerarchy and Wormwood's supervisor. The letters follow

Wormwood's ultimately unsuccessful attempts to corrupt the soul of a rather ordinary young Englishman and the devilish advice given to the trainee by Screwtape.

The pivotal aspect of the book is the notion of temptation, the need for Christian faith to overcome it and the ever-present fear of failure leading to sin. This was also a core idea in *Perelandra*, but with *The Screwtape Letters* Lewis succeeded in writing a story that could be enjoyed by non-believers as well as Christian devotees. Essentially, he achieves this success through the lightness of his writing. *The Screwtape Letters* is not only clever and perfectly poised, it is also extremely funny; any theological objections (or even the simple lack of interest) of non-believers are overwhelmed because the reader is constantly entertained and made to appreciate the sheer ingenuity of Lewis's writing.

Much of this power revealed in *The Screwtape Letters* derives from the fact that the book is modelled on personal experience in that it is directly linked to his religious conversion, the most important event in his life up to this time. The unnamed hero, a straightforward, level-headed ordinary man, is an alter ego of Lewis himself, while the older devil, Screwtape, is the product of cross-breeding a contemporary demon, Hitler, with traditional images of the Devil which Lewis had absorbed from his reading, from Dante to Milton.

But perhaps the most striking link to reality comes from the character of our hero's mother. The life of the young man being tempted by Wormwood is rather dull and uneventful except for two things. The first is his war work as an air-raid warden. This was the very duty in which Lewis was engaged during the autumn of 1940 as he was writing *The Screwtape Letters* and it offers a useful opportunity for the young man to ponder his role in the war and to question his Christian responsibility. The other, more important aspect of the character's life is his relationship with his mother, a fussy, demanding, vexing woman. Wormwood tries hard to exploit the power of minor resentment and daily accrued irritations to corrupt the son's soul, but eventually he fails. The personality of Janie Moore, the woman Lewis habitually called 'Mother', is never far

from descriptions of our hero's mother passed on in Wormwood's
letters. Whether or not Lewis was consciously aware of what he was
writing is uncertain, but there is much here that reflects the state of
Lewis's own life when he was himself a young man. Indeed it holds
up a mirror to his life as he was first returning to God in the early
1930s, when he was struggling to forge a career while constantly distracted by domestic chores.

In typical Lewis style, *The Screwtape Letters* was written very quickly.
From the original germ of an idea seeded in July 1940 it took little
more than six months to complete the 30,000 words covering the
thirty-one letters, and Lewis often wrote a letter in a single sitting
of just a few hours. However, the speed with which he wrote the
book belies the fact that it was for him a rather painful experience.
The central premise of the book is the correspondence between the
two devils. All that they think and say is an inversion of the thought
processes, feelings and instincts of a good Christian. So, for
Screwtape and Wormwood, God is 'the enemy', 'Our Father' is the
Devil and their great mission is to defeat God, pervert His ambitions and sow the seeds of havoc and destruction. Not surprisingly,
Lewis, who at times brings his characters frighteningly close to
home, felt sullied by the experience, his mind contaminated by dab-
bling in devilry and corruption, albeit only on the handwritten
page.

Shortly before Lewis had started writing *The Screwtape Letters* he
had taken out a subscription to a Church of England weekly called
The Guardian, and when his collection was complete he offered it
to the editor as a serialisation. The magazine took all the letters
for an agreed fee of £62 (about £2000 today, which Lewis asked
to be forwarded to a charity for the widows of Church of England
clergymen) and they were published weekly between February and
August 1941. From about this time Lewis gave to charity all his
earnings from his writing on the subject of religion.

After only a few weeks the letters had begun to draw attention
from readers of *The Guardian* and Lewis started receiving a large
quantity of fan mail. This quickly became an overwhelming torrent

and prompted him to offer Warnie the job of 'personal assistant', a task his brother took to with relish. Indeed Warnie often replied to readers in a witty and engaging style which they assumed was Jack's but much of the time the younger Lewis was so busy he had not even seen the original fan letter.

One of the responses to *The Screwtape Letters* came from a very earnest country clergyman who unwittingly delighted Lewis, as well as his new associates at *The Guardian*. 'Much of the advice given in these letters,' the reader declared without a trace of irony, 'seems to me not only erroneous but positively diabolical.' Outraged, the poor deluded man withdrew his subscription to the magazine forthwith.

Among the piles of letters relating to Lewis's satirical pieces was a request from an editor named Ashley Sampson, working for the publisher Geoffrey Bles, asking if the author would be interested in seeing the letters collected together and published as a book. Geoffrey Bles had already published a book by Lewis the previous year, a non-fiction religious tract called *The Problem of Pain*, and Lewis had enjoyed working with the company. (Although this book had been generally well received on its publication in 1940, one Oxford wit and critic of the author was said to have remarked: 'The problem of pain is bad enough without Lewis making it worse.')

But, even as *The Screwtape Letters* was being made ready for the presses, the publisher had no idea he had bought an instant hit. The first print run of 2000 copies was sold out before publication in February 1942, and by the end of that year the book had gone to no fewer than eight reprints. *The Screwtape Letters* still sells extremely well today. Having been translated into fifteen languages, it has notched up sales in excess of two million copies.

The Screwtape Letters was also an instant hit with the critics. The *Saturday Review of Literature*'s Leonard Bacon called it 'this admirable, diverting, and remarkably original work ... There is a spectacular and satisfactory nova in the bleak sky of satire.'[9] The critic in *The Times Literary Supplement* wrote of Lewis's work: 'A reviewer's task is not to be a prophet, and time alone can show whether it is or is not an enduring piece of satirical writing. In any case that is a minor matter. It is much more to the point that in so readable a fashion Mr Lewis has contrived to say much that a distracted world greatly requires to hear.'[10]

In *Time and Tide* Lewis's friend and fellow author Charles Williams wrote a review in the style of *The Screwtape Letters*, using two other devils of his own creation, Snigsozzle and Scorpuscle, who are greatly irritated by Lewis's 'cursedly clever letters'. In their correspondence it is suggested that 'they make the infernal text a primer in our Training College'. And Snigsozzle adds as a postscript: 'You will send someone to see after Lewis? – some very clever fiend?'[11]

The reason *The Screwtape Letters* works whereas much of Lewis's earlier allegorical writing failed or mattered only to a tiny academic readership is that it is a straightforward story told in an engaging, direct way. Of course, the central conceit is clever and Lewis sustains it brilliantly, but it is the writing (possibly his finest) that carries it through. One of Lewis's great strengths as a writer was his ability to connect with the reader. From the time when he hit his stride, around the late 1930s, his directness of style was rarely off target and his warm authorial voice attracted an increasingly large readership.

With *The Screwtape Letters* more than with any other book he wrote, Lewis performed his favourite trick of setting up targets and knocking them down. He attacks scientists, sociologists, Low Church advocates and politicians, and in the one-off short sequel, *Screwtape Proposes a Toast* (1965), he drags educators and supporters of egalitarianism centre stage and publicly disembowels them. Yet, it is all done with such finesse and grace, such ready wit and endearing confidence, it is impossible to feel the author is being sanctimonious, elitist or puritanical: three failings which sometimes emerged in his other writings.

However, while Lewis's book shows off his talents perfectly, he let one of the least attractive aspects of his character mar the enjoyment of success. Quite soon after its publication he began to consider *The Screwtape Letters* to be a rather scrappy collection of ideas and concluded that he had oversimplified and over-popularised key, complex religious ideas. This is a shame because he had been struggling for years to reach a wider audience and was keen to be noticed. In his books for a general readership (and indeed in his academic writing) he never deliberately obfuscated. He believed strongly in the power of clarity and clear expression. Yet an inherent and powerful resistance to the idea of mass appeal, and what would in later decades be called 'pop culture', caused him confusion and inner conflict over this book. While most authors would have been delighted with global recognition, the young literary snob of Great Bookham days was still there not far beneath the veneer of urbanity and the carefully manicured image of 'Jack, the relaxed everyman'. Consequently, Lewis would have strongly disagreed with many readers (myself included) who believe that, for sheer cleverness and stylish delivery, *The Screwtape Letters* is by far his best book.

The Screwtape Letters brought Jack great commercial success, yet in terms of popular appeal he had still to peak. By virtue of the book's success, Lewis's space-fiction works that followed, *Perelandra* and *That Hideous Strength*, were both automatically elevated to the status of best-sellers. But then, in 1950, eight years after *The Screwtape Letters* appeared, Geoffrey Bles published what was to become Lewis's most famous, and for many, his most important and enduring book.

Some of the original inspiration for *The Lion, the Witch and the Wardrobe* had come to Lewis as early as 1914, when he was sixteen. These seeds of ideas appeared in the form of dreams and what Lewis sometimes referred to as 'mental pictures'. The most striking of these images and one that appears almost unaltered in the book is that of a faun carrying some parcels and an umbrella in a snowy wood. This became the character Mr Tumnus, who appears near the start of *The Lion, the Witch and the Wardrobe*. It was only later when he was already a good way into the book that Lewis created the character of Aslan (Turkish for 'lion'), who, he claimed, 'came bounding into it'.[12]

In the autumn of 1939, soon after the outbreak of the Second World War, the threat of bombing raids on London prompted the evacuation of the capital's children to the countryside or rural towns. The Kilns was a semi-rural idyll with plenty of room to spare and so a small group from London was invited to stay there soon after the evacuation began. Because of his commitments at college and his regular sessions with the Inklings, Lewis rarely encountered the children staying in his house, but one day he saw them sitting around bored and began to write a story to entertain them.

One of the children had been interested in an old wardrobe in a bedroom of the house and had asked Lewis what was behind it. This, it appears, acted as another spark in the creation of the story. Lewis began a tale about a family of children who had been evacuated to a large old house in the country owned by a mysterious professor. But it seems the story then went off on a different tangent and was never written down and eventually forgotten. Lewis only returned to the theme a decade later when he began an entirely new story built around the wardrobe and the thought of what could be behind it and linked it with the mental images from his own childhood.

Serious writing of *The Lion, the Witch and the Wardrobe* began during the summer of 1948 and, once Lewis began to write, most of the seven books that make up *The Chronicles of Narnia* flowed from his pen easily and quickly. By Christmas *The Lion, the Witch and the Wardrobe* was finished and ready for his publisher, and before he had even heard back from Geoffrey Bles, he had started work on a second book, an early version of what became *The Magician's Nephew*. This effort was abandoned in the spring of 1949 and Lewis started to write the book that was published second in the series, *Prince Caspian*.

However, as Lewis was racing on with his children's story, his editors at Geoffrey Bles were confused and sceptical about the manuscript of *The Lion, the Witch and the Wardrobe*. This, they knew, was his first attempt at fiction for children and, irrespective of the quality of the writing, they were quite unconvinced that he would be capable of crossing over into that market. There were even some at the company who feared that Lewis's career as a 'serious author' might be damaged in some way by the publication of this rather simplistic children's fairy story.

But Lewis was too important to Geoffrey Bles to be ignored, and *The Lion, the Witch and the Wardrobe* was duly published in the autumn of 1950. By the time it appeared in the shops three more books had been completed, *Prince Caspian* (originally *Drawn Into Narnia*), *The Voyage of the Dawn Treader* and *The Horse and His Boy* (originally *Narnia and the North*). Each of these took between three and six months to write and the fifth book in the series, *The Silver Chair*, was completed by March 1951, just a few months after the publication of *The Lion, the Witch and the Wardrobe*. The final two books, *The Magician's Nephew* and *The Last Battle*, came a little more slowly but were finished by the end of 1953.

The seven Narnia books appeared in print at the rate of approximately one per year between 1950 and 1956, and although they were not well received by many reviewers, young readers quickly took them to their hearts and word spread. In spite of adverse criticism and the initial doubts of Lewis's publisher, within a year of its publication *The Lion, the Witch and the Wardrobe* had become a slow-burning best-seller on both sides of the Atlantic and the others in the collection repeated this success. By the time the final book, *The Last Battle*, was published in 1956, *The Chronicles of Narnia* had become one of the most successful children's literary series ever published, with millions of sales globally. That year Lewis was awarded the highest honour in the world of children's literature, the Carnegie Medal for the best children's book of the year, an award that was really in recognition of the entire collection of seven titles.

In many ways *The Chronicles of Narnia* is Lewis's most personal work. Although at first this statement may seem confusing and others may point to books such as *A Grief Observed* (which deals with Jack's feelings after the death of his wife, Joy, in 1960) or *Surprised by Joy* (the account of his religious conversion), the essence of the Narnia stories is dredged directly from Lewis's personal memories. Extracted from his own childhood imaginings, the stories are almost a wish fulfilment, the recounting of a dreamed-of childhood.

In *A Grief Observed* Lewis dealt with a single issue, a tragedy that came to him late in life and his reaction to it. In the book that comes closest to an orthodox autobiography, *Surprised by Joy*, he constantly shied away from any deep, honest truths, skirting any mention of his relationship with Janie Moore, glossing over many aspects of his relationship with his father and obfuscating his sexual development. Even in the pages of his personal diaries Lewis could not bare his soul. But with *The Chronicles of Narnia* he was able to create a fantasy world that provided him with a mechanism through which he could reveal his inner drives, dreams and personal feelings otherwise completely hidden.

The powerful presence of Jack Lewis the boy is ubiquitous in the Narnia stories. Most obvious is the way in which the children who travel to Narnia – Edmund, Peter, Susan and Lucy – are, even by the standards of the time in which Lewis created them, very old-fashioned characters. In many ways they are clones of Jack and Warnie Lewis. They speak and act anachronistically and seem like children from an earlier age planted in a wartime setting. Indeed, in Lewis's original manuscript the children all spoke and behaved in an even more antiquated way, saying such things as 'Crikey!' and listing bird's-nesting as one of their favourite hobbies. It was only after these idiosyncrasies were pointed out to Lewis by his friend Roger Lancelyn Green that he reworked the book.

For *The Magician's Nephew*, which was the penultimate book to be written and tells of the creation of Narnia, Lewis set the story during the first decade of the twentieth century, precisely the time during which he and Warnie were first fantasising about imaginary worlds at Little Lea. This backdating is necessary because one of the main characters in the book, the young boy Digory, is to grow up to be the Professor in *The Lion, the Witch and the Wardrobe*, but it also serves the purpose of placing Jack and Warnie at the very source of the Narnia mythology.

Commentators on the Narnia books, from Tolkien to modern-day critics, have pointed out the numerous inconsistencies, contradictions and clumsy passages to be found there. These criticisms are certainly justified, and taken as a whole, the collection displays surprising shoddiness, confusion and poor composition, especially when one remembers that Lewis was an English tutor at Oxford. However, his preoccupation with his own childhood is a crucial aspect of the Narnia mythology and adds such enormous power to his writing, imbuing the stories with an aura of sincerity and personal conviction, that many millions of readers still love the story for all its faults.

One of the most famous tags applied to *The Chronicles of Narnia* is that of 'religious allegory'. Interestingly, Lewis himself did not care for the term when applied to his creation. He preferred to call his work a 'supposal'. What he meant by this was that the story of Narnia was not exactly an allegory of the Christian story from Christ's incarnation (*The Lion, the Witch and the Wardrobe*) to the Book of Revelation and Armageddon (*The Last Battle*), but an account of what might happen if God were to save another, completely alien world through the sacrifice of His Son.

Lewis claimed that with each of the seven books in the collection he had set out to write a good story first and the Christian aspects of the tale only came later. This would seem like a contradiction of his idea of a 'supposal', but with respect to the first book in the series the two claims are not in fact incompatible. The writing of *The Lion, the Witch and the Wardrobe* originated with a fantasy sequence, Lewis's mental pictures, and only later did the overwhelmingly powerful images of the author's childhood and the character of Aslan give the story the shape of a 'supposal'. The six books that followed, all of which, we should recall, came in quick succession, were, in their early stages at least, influenced greatly by Lewis's need to integrate them into the larger picture of an 'alternative Christian myth': the myth he had created with the writing of *The Lion, the Witch and the Wardrobe*. It is inconceivable that by the time Lewis wrote *The Last Battle* he was thinking only of a good story; this final instalment rounds off the *Chronicles* perfectly and ties them irredeemably to the concept of a 'supposal'.

Lewis knew very few children and the fact that he was able to write a collection of children's books that became such a stunning success adds substance to the idea that the mythology of Narnia is modelled almost entirely on his own childhood fantasies. It would be a mistake to say that the creation of Narnia derived from the adult Lewis reinterpreting his childhood world of Boxen and the stories he wrote as a young boy. Except for the presence of talking animals, Boxen is a fictional world that is not so far removed from the everyday one in which Lewis grew up. With their political intrigues and their social structures, his animal characters behave more or less like humans. The characters inhabiting Narnia are far from realistic and this entire world is an elemental fantasy, an alternative universe to our own.

Strikingly, most children who have read *The Lion, the Witch and the Wardrobe*, and the books that followed it, read it as a simple fantasy story and do not recognise the allegorical or 'supposal' nature of the plot. Today this might be explained by the fact that many young children coming to the books at the age of seven or eight as a bedtime story read to them by parents have little awareness of the Bible and the beliefs of Christianity. But, even during the 1950s, when Christianity had a stronger social presence, most children only became conscious of the inner meanings and multi-layered nature of the *Chronicles* when the links were pointed out to them. This is probably one of the cleverest aspects of Lewis's creation. He succeeded in writing great stories beloved by generations of children but also placed his intended messages into the Narnia books subtly and without losing clarity of meaning or drama.

As we shall see later, this very 'cleverness' has recently created a backlash led by those who feel that Lewis's writing is little short of deliberate indoctrination and Christian propaganda. Whether or not this is true, the story of Narnia has given a great deal of simple pleasure to many millions of readers without too much observable harm being done.

During the decade between the completion of *The Last Battle* and Lewis's death in 1963, he wrote another ten books. These included some of his most important academic contributions, most especially *English Literature in the Sixteenth Century Excluding Drama*, as well as his last novel and the work of fiction that meant most to him, *Till We*

Have Faces (a modern retelling of the story of Cupid and Psyche). However, none of these titles enjoyed anything like the impact of *The Chronicles of Narnia* and *Till We Have Faces* proved to be his least commercially successful work of fiction since *The Pilgrim's Regress*.

With the writing of *The Chronicles of Narnia* Lewis reached the pinnacle of his public appeal, and with it his commercial success. And, although he would have disagreed, in some ways this was most fitting. Many of Lewis's books were written with greater care and displayed superior dexterity and finesse, many illuminated dark intellectual recesses with charm and wit, but none had the power to engage, entertain and unlock the imagination in quite the way the mythology of Narnia continues to do for many people. In writing the Narnia stories Lewis was able to distil his own childhood fantasies and channel them through a mature mind skilled and trained to preserve the magic of youthful imagination. Herein lies the secret of their enduring success.

7

Friendship

'At my first coming into the world I had been (implicitly) warned never to trust a Papist . . . ,' Lewis once wrote, 'and at my first coming into the English Faculty (explicitly) never to trust a philologist. Tolkien was both.'[1] Yet, in spite of these sentiments, for many years Lewis and Tolkien were the firmest of friends, leading lights of the Inklings, drinking companions, critics of each other's work and mutually inspirational colleagues. Later, in a period during which he was confronting his own demons, Tolkien was moved to say: 'Friendship with Lewis compensates for much.'[2]

By the early 1930s, with the Coalbiters fading, both Lewis and Tolkien were searching for a focus, a means by which they could combine their twinned interests in drinking and serious discussion with like-minded men. It did not take them long to find a substitute for their first club. At University College a weekly literary discussion group calling itself the Inklings had been founded by an undergraduate named Edward Tangye Lean.

Lean was the editor of an important university magazine, *Isis*, which still exists today, and an ambitious young author who had started the club so that members could read to each other their unpublished work. In 1933 Lean left Oxford to begin a career in journalism and broadcasting and his club stopped meeting, but within a term some of the original members, including Tolkien and Lewis, decided to start it up again and kept the old name for informal gatherings in Lewis's rooms at Magdalen. No one really knows why they used the name Inklings, but Lewis and Tolkien liked it because of its ambiguity, the fact that it implied members were grappling with 'big ideas' and that it also suited academics and writers whose lives had been built on large quantities of ink.

The earliest meetings of the new Inklings took place each Thursday evening in Lewis's spacious college rooms, but by 1939 they had also begun to hold regular Tuesday morning meetings at a pub in St Giles called the Eagle and Child (affectionately known as the Bird and Baby). The sign outside the pub depicts the baby Ganymede being carried away by Jove's eagle and it is believed that this acted as the inspiration for Tolkien's illustration of Bilbo in the eagle's eerie used in *The Hobbit*.

The Eagle and Child has been extended considerably since those times and the room in which the Inklings met was once part of the back of the pub. Today it is something of a shrine to the Inklings, with photographs of Tolkien, Lewis and Charles Williams adorning the walls. Those partaking of the 'Inklings Tour' conducted each Wednesday morning during the summer months stop off here to soak up the atmosphere. On the wall by the bar is a large plaque that reads:

C. S. Lewis

His brother W.H.L. Lewis, J.R.R. Tolkien, Charles Williams and other friends met every Tuesday morning between the years 1939–1962 in the back room of this their favourite pub. These men, popularly known as the 'Inklings', met here to drink beer and to discuss, among other things, the books they were writing.

This was not the only pub the Inklings frequented; they also enjoyed the King's Arms near the Bodleian Library, and the White Horse and the Mitre in the centre of Oxford, but, as the plaque says, the Bird and Baby was their favourite. Here Tolkien first read to his friends extracts from what he had long called 'the New Hobbit', *The Lord of the Rings*, and Lewis told them of Narnia, of his cosmic mythology and of one of his most acclaimed creations, Screwtape.

By the mid-1930s the core of the Inklings had been established. This included the founders, Lewis and Tolkien, along with Warren Lewis, Nevill Coghill, a doctor friend named Robert Havard, always known as Humphrey or UQ (the Useless Quack), and Hugo Dyson, Professor of English Literature at Reading University. By 1940 this group had grown to include Charles Williams, who that year joined the Oxford University Press and was the author of a number of critically acclaimed novels.

The Inklings were not all literary men. Humphrey was a Catholic and an Oxford man, which endeared him to Tolkien, but he had no literary leanings other than being thoroughly admiring of the efforts of his friends. By the late 1930s Warnie had begun to try his hand at writing and had become deeply interested in history. In his ample spare time he had also started to collect together what would become known as the Lewis Papers, a collection of letters, diaries and writings that told the history of the Lewis family. Nevill Coghill was a Fellow of Exeter College and a scholar of Middle English who gained academic acclaim for his translation of Chaucer's *Canterbury Tales* and became Professor of English Literature at Oxford in 1957. He was also greatly interested in the theatre and staged many lavish productions in Oxford. Most famous was a spectacular outdoor *Tempest* during the summer of 1949 performed on a stage constructed next to a lake behind Worcester College. Coghill was tutor to W.H. Auden, and during the period in which he attended meetings of the Inklings at the Bird and Baby he also taught Richard Burton, who acted in several of his productions.

It was an exclusive club. The membership changed little except when Lewis encountered someone new and invited them along when they were next visiting Oxford. Any member had to fit several criteria: they had to be a good conversationalist, interested in or involved in writing, they had to enjoy drinking and be a friend of Jack's; but, most crucially, they had to be male.

No women ever gained admittance to this most select of men's clubs. According to legend, in 1943 the wit and respected literary figure Dorothy Sayers turned up at the Bird and Baby expecting to be invited to join the men around the table, but she was politely asked to leave. It was very important to these men that the Inklings remained an exclusively male preserve.

Lewis captured well the atmosphere of Inklings meetings in letters to friends and in his essays. They usually met in the evening, but he, Tolkien and Williams also often read to one another over a morning smoke in Lewis's rooms. 'Picture to yourself,' Lewis wrote, 'an upstairs sitting-room with windows looking north in the "grove" of Magdalen College on a sunshiny Monday morning at about ten o'clock. The Prof [Tolkien] and I, both on the chesterfield, lit our pipes and stretched out our legs. Williams in the arm-chair opposite to us threw his cigarette into the grate, took up the pile of extremely small, loose sheets on which he habitually wrote – they came, I think, from a two-penny pad for memoranda – and began.'[3] Describing a more typical meeting involving at least half a dozen Inklings, Lewis recalled: 'Our fun is often so fast and furious that the company probably thinks we're talking bawdy when in fact we're very likely talking theology.'[4]

It is easy to underestimate the importance of this group and it has been said that: 'The Inklings as an organisation is more our conception after the fact than it ever was in reality.'[5] In other words, this group of individuals who met in Oxford pubs and discussed literature, religion or whatever took their fancy did not think of themselves as a literary group in the way that, say, the Bloomsbury Group did. But this does nothing to detract from the fact that they *were* immensely influential. In 1996 (soon after the first polls naming Tolkien as the most popular author of the century and placing *The Lion, the Witch and the Wardrobe* high in the ratings) journalist Nigel Reynolds commented: '[the poll] suggests that The Inklings, a 1930s Oxford drinking club, has been a more powerful force than the Bloomsbury Group, the Algonquin set in New York, Hemingway's Paris set or the W.H. Auden/Christopher Isherwood group of writers of the 1930s.'[6]

Although the Inklings may not have perceived themselves in entirely the same way as the Bloomsbury Group or other affiliations, they enjoyed a certain mystique that slowly developed during the 1930s and they were not shy to use their influence. The most significant example of this was the role played by Lewis, Tolkien and some of the other Inklings in determining the outcome of an election to find a new Professor of Poetry at Oxford in 1938.

The Chair of Poetry is unusual in that the holder is chosen by the MAs of the university rather than by exclusive consultation among members of the highest echelons of its administration. As a result, those usually elected to the position are Oxford men who have established themselves as either great poets or scholars of poetry and, most importantly, men who have made themselves popular with the other dons.

One morning in the summer of 1938, over breakfast at Magdalen, a good friend of Lewis's, Adam Fox, Dean of the Divinity School, read in the newspaper that a retired scholar, Sir Edmund Chambers, was the leading candidate for the position of Professor of Poetry. According to legend, Fox stood up from the table and declared: 'This is simply shocking, they may as well give me the job.' To which Lewis, who was sitting close by, apparently responded, 'We will, we will.'

The reason for this exchange was that Lewis and his friends felt that Chambers was a rather crusty poetry hobbyist who had no real understanding of the subject. In fact this was a misconception: far from merely dallying with the subject, Chambers was himself an accomplished, published poet and something of an authority on sixteenth-century verse. Lewis almost certainly knew this, but partly out of a sense of misplaced mischief combined perhaps with an element of bloody-mindedness, he decided that he and the other

Inklings should make the election of Adam Fox to the Chair a *cause célèbre*, even though they knew the man was quite unsuited to the job.

Lewis set about organising a campaign in Oxford to get Fox elected. He created slogans, visited all the key voters and held gatherings to support his candidature. This had the predictable effect of greatly upsetting the more conservative dons and others within the literary fraternity of the university who had great respect for Chambers and were outraged by Lewis's bullishness.

What began as a half-serious, impulsive reaction on the part of Fox and Lewis soon degenerated into a farce. The dons who had grown angry over Fox's candidature had also begun to doubt the ability of Chambers to triumph over the popular clergyman and so they decided to put up a third candidate, the English Tutor at New College, Lord David Cecil, who also happened to be a good friend of Lewis and occasionally attended meetings of the Inklings. This decision proved to be a bad move because, although Cecil was a popular figure at the university, his inclusion in the running split the vote within the anti-Inklings camp greatly, aiding Lewis's campaign and playing a major part in Fox's eventual easy victory.

Although on the night of the election win the Inklings celebrated with a toast to Fox and revelled in the belief that they had won an important victory against those they perceived as the crusty old guard of the university, their victory was rather hollow. Fox turned out to be a most unsatisfactory Professor of Poetry who delivered lacklustre lectures and did nothing for the image of Oxford's faculty of English. In later years even Jack had to admit that his effort to elect his friend had been a mistake. More importantly, this rather childish episode caused great harm to Lewis's career. He had acted without consideration for the feelings of others and had not paused for thought about the harm it might do to the reputation of the university or what damage it might cause the aspirations and hopes of the innocent Chambers. It is not surprising that the move was remembered by the powerful of the English faculty, men who later expended as much effort in blocking Jack's career progression at Oxford as he had in interfering in their business.

This rather sorry episode was played out when the Inklings were at their peak, long before the group began to fracture. However, within a decade Tolkien had begun to lose interest and was attending fewer meetings. By the late 1940s the Inklings gathered less frequently in Lewis's rooms and met instead at a pub in Oxford called the Roebuck (now the Oz Bar) in Market Street. This venue was unofficially divided into two. Upstairs was a large room with heavy velvet curtains at the windows, a bar, a piano and a small kitchen where food was served, and it was almost exclusively a university domain. Downstairs was the public bar.

However, although Lewis adopted the new venue readily, sessions upstairs at the Roebuck were not very appealing to Tolkien, for the place had none of the gentility of the Bird and Baby. This meant that the Inklings was not what it had once been and at the Roebuck more drinking than reading was done. An abiding memory of the townsfolk who kept to the public bar was the sound of First World War soldiers' songs sung so loudly they could be heard through the ceiling. Lewis was always the choir leader on these occasions.

Tolkien and Lewis remained close friends for some twenty years from 1926 to about 1946, but then their relationship began to cool until, by the early 1950s, almost none of the old warmth remained. The reasons why the relationship fell apart are as complex as the friendship itself.

For many years Tolkien had been fond of Hugo Dyson and Warren Lewis. He also enjoyed many cordial relationships with other academics at Oxford; but for Tolkien, Jack was a very special friend. With him he could open up his heart, from him he could accept detailed criticism, and of all the Inklings he viewed himself and Jack as being the most like-minded and intellectually equivalent. But Tolkien was also a very jealous man who was unusually possessive of his friends, and easily became resentful of them if they gained recognition and success.

Lewis was aware of Tolkien's insecurities and tendency to be jealous. As early as 1939 he was able to write to Warnie describing how Tolkien's 'trials, besides being frequent and severe are usually of such a complicated nature as to be impenetrable'.[7]

Lewis's feelings for Tolkien were never as intense as those of Tolkien for him. He had unbounded respect for him, enjoyed his company enormously and gained much from their relationship, but he was an altogether more colourful, less orthodox man than Tolkien. Lewis did not have the conventional family lifestyle of his friend and he had many more close associates. Thanks in part to these differences, by the late 1930s cracks began to appear in their relationship. Three things slowly came between the pair. First there was the Christianity Lewis adopted at the start of the decade, which took a quite different form from Tolkien's and, to his irritation, was something Lewis was keen to write about and popularise. Second was Lewis's first hints of commercial success as a writer, which began in the late 1930s. Finally, but perhaps most importantly, Lewis did not consider his close relationship with Tolkien to be exclusive in the way Tolkien did. Lewis was really Tolkien's only intimate friend in Oxford (although he had stayed in close contact with his school friend Christopher Wiseman). Throughout the 1930s Lewis gathered to himself a substantial group of friends and associates and was as close to Owen Barfield, Nevill Coghill (and later Charles Williams) as he was to Tolkien. Coupled with this, he had Warnie as a male companion and their relationship grew much closer after his brother left the Army in 1932.

Of these three factors, Lewis's religious conversion and subsequent proselytising is the most complex and should be considered in some detail. Raised an Ulster Protestant, Lewis had, by the time he reached adulthood, largely discarded all forms of religious faith. Indeed, he was fond of paraphrasing G.K. Chesterton in declaring: 'Christianity was very sensible apart from its Christianity.'[8] Tolkien only became aware of these sentiments gradually, but when he did he quickly began to see it as in some way his duty to enlighten his friend to the mysteries of religious doctrine. As a consequence, they had many long conversations on the subject.

When he was an undergraduate and during his earliest years as a

Fellow, Lewis may have found it hard to define his position on religion. To some he might have described himself as an agnostic, while to others he was an atheist. By the time he was in his early twenties he had given much thought to religion and had reached the conclusion that he could not believe in the Gospels. Furthermore, he found it quite astonishing that intelligent, sophisticated people could suffer what he saw as the mental aberration of being a Christian. This incongruity was apparent to him almost every day because many of those with whom he had become close friends, Arthur Greeves, Nevill Coghill and Tolkien, men whose intellects he respected, were believers.

This fact forced Lewis to think more about religion rather than dismiss it. By the early 1920s he had reached what he called a 'New Look' concerning religious orthodoxy. Lewis's philosophy led him to consider the Christian doctrine as a myth just like any other. But gradually his view began to change, and by the time he met Tolkien in 1926 he was growing confused over some of the deepest questions of faith, and initially at least, Tolkien's orthodoxy added to this confusion.

Among his friends, Lewis found Tolkien's religious commitment the most difficult to fathom. Tolkien shared many of his thoughts on literature, language and history, his new friend was one of the most interesting, intellectual and intelligent men he had ever met and yet he was a devout Christian, and a Catholic to boot. To simply regard such a contradiction as an anomaly was not good enough. Lewis tried to separate intellect from faith, to propose that a person may have a highly developed intellect but that their faith derives from something quite separate and more powerful; but this did not support closer scrutiny.

This struggle to understand was one of the great catalysts in the mental reaction that made Lewis one of the most famous converts of the twentieth century. Although Tolkien could not really be said to have converted Lewis, his eloquent portrayal of religious belief and his capable explanations of subtle nuance and meaning did much to make him reconsider. During the first five years of their friendship, until 1931, Lewis's stance on religion moved a considerable way. By the end of this period he had concluded that there was a God, but his vision of the divine was not an orthodox Christian one. It was more akin perhaps to the God of many Eastern religions, almost a pantheist God, a source of inspiration, a wellspring of Nature, far from any portrayal in the Bible.

The moment Lewis began to believe in God occurred when he was sitting upstairs on a bus travelling up Headington Hill, returning home to the rented house he shared with Janie and Maureen. It was a strangely ill-defined experience but one that nevertheless influenced him greatly. He described it as generating the odd sensation that he was encased in a confining suit, a corset or armour that stifled him. He knew that if he wanted to he could break out and accept the fact that there is a God, or else he could remain held back by the strictures of his own mind. He decided to break the binds and to accept. That night, back in his college rooms, he prayed for the first time in years.

In itself this moment of extreme clarity might not have cemented Lewis's new belief. Many people argue that revelation of this kind comes in an instant and remains indelible, but this may not be true in all cases. For Lewis, although he had no way of knowing it, the timing of this event was extremely significant, for a few weeks later he was to visit Belfast to find his father seriously ill. What followed was a time of emotional pain and stress. Quite naturally, Lewis felt vulnerable and emotionally frail, and although he later went to great pains to deny it, there is no doubt that this was an apposite moment for God to rush in.

And yet Lewis still trod most carefully. The experience on the bus going up Headington Hill was the first step on the road to conversion and the death of his father consolidated his feelings; but although his first move was probably the most profound leap he took, it was another two years before he shifted from a simple belief in God to acceptance of any defined form of Christianity. What pushed him into some semblance of orthodoxy was, like the apparent moment of revelation on the bus, another fairly mundane event, this time a conversation with Tolkien during a late-night walk in Oxford.

It was a Saturday evening, 19 September 1931. Their mutual friend and fellow Inkling Hugo Dyson (who was also a Christian) was making one of his frequent visits to Oxford and had dined with Lewis and Tolkien at Magdalen. He was quite aware of the many conversations his two friends had had on the subject of religion and was keen to join them. After dinner the three went for a stroll and the conversation naturally turned to Christianity. Lewis had become entrenched in his pantheistic vision of God and because of this he could not begin to embrace orthodox Christianity, which at its heart requires a belief in Christ and an unflinching conviction that Jesus was sent to die on the Cross in order to save our souls. Lewis could accept none of this as anything other than myth. Like Tolkien, he was a scholar of ancient mythologies, tales of heroes and of pagan moral salvation. To him the story of Christ was simply just another legend, another myth no more accurate or meaningful to him and the modern world than any other. And at their root, he believed, myths are lies.

Tolkien listened carefully to what his friend said and, when Lewis reached this conclusion, throwing his arms up as if to say: 'So how then can you believe the Christ story to be anything but an ancient legend?' he came back with an argument that changed the course of Lewis's life.

Myths, he declared, are most certainly not lies. Myths derive from a kernel of truth and portray a very specific cultural meaning. Christianity, Lewis thought, is based on the 'myth of Christ'. Very well then, Tolkien argued, call it a myth if you want to, but it was constructed on real events and it was inspired by a deep truth. Ultimately, no myth was a lie, he believed, and the 'myth' that lay at the core of Christianity provided a route to follow for the non-materialistic part of every human being, a road to a deeper, spiritual truth.

Revelation did not come to Lewis instantly, but it is clear that this conversation set him thinking about the problem of faith in a quite different way from the one he was used to. Even so, he never could accept some aspects of Christian orthodoxy; it seemed his intellect sometimes stood in the way of his faith, so that years after becoming a Christian he could write to a friend: 'How could I – I of all people – ever have come to believe this cock and bull story?'[9]

A few days after this talk Jack, Warren and Janie visited Whipsnade Zoo, some twenty-five miles from Oxford. Janie, with Maureen and a family friend, made the journey by car and Jack rode in the sidecar of Warren's motorcycle. It was an unseasonably cold day and a thick fog enveloped them for almost the entire journey, but as he sat in freezing silence Jack's mind was racing, running again over what he had discussed with his friends a few nights earlier and trying to reconcile it all with the years of intense thought he had devoted to religion. The journey was a short stretch of time when his ideas began to gel with a mysterious elemental force that some people call divine inspiration. It was an event that became etched into his mind so that twenty years later he could clearly recall that 'when we set out I did not believe that Jesus Christ is the Son of God, and when we reached the zoo I did'.[10] The day after the journey to Whipsnade, Lewis wrote to Arthur Greeves and reported that he had moved from his long-held convictions to a new position in which he could finally embrace Christ; in other words, he now considered himself 'a Christian'.

Although the intensity of Lewis's spiritual awakening was enough to convince him so thoroughly that he spent the rest of his life a devout believer, it must have been a difficult intellectual shift to accept. Many of his friends were Christians and Warren had been a churchgoer for many years, but Janie Moore was vexed and cynical about the whole thing. When Jack later began to practise Holy Communion, she accused him of attending 'blood feasts', and in his diaries Warnie made several references to Janie's evident irritation at the spiritual course his brother was following.[11]

Although raised an Irish Protestant, Janie Moore had, she claimed, become an atheist after losing her son Paddy, and she was often scathing about the Church. However, her feelings on the subject seemed to be confused because during the 1930s and '40s she often attended church with Jack and she supported Maureen's wish to be confirmed into the Church of England. Almost certainly she did these things simply to make her loved ones happy.

We must consider the possibility that the reason for Janie's disquiet over Jack's conversion stemmed from the fact that it further confused their personal lives. In Lewis's new view the question of sex outside marriage now had a clearly delineated answer: Christian purity and sex without the sanctity of marriage are completely incompatible.

By the time Jack became a Christian, Janie was in her late fifties and so the matter of sex may have been academic; but, because she was an atheist, his new faith became another way in which his life beyond their relationship intruded. She had never been entirely comfortable with his living in college during the week and she disliked his spending evenings with his friends and leading an independent intellectual life. Jack's adoption of what soon became a strict, High Church orthodoxy was an emotional blow for Janie, and it says much for the strength of their relationship that they stayed together and thrived even with this new addition to their already complicated lives.

The conversation between Lewis and Tolkien that September evening in 1931 shows how Tolkien influenced his friend's religious thinking, but it also offers a fascinating insight into the way the two men intellectualised everything in their lives and how this process of analysis fuelled their writing. The idea that Christianity is a true myth lies at the heart of what Lewis went on to spend the rest of his literary career describing. It is the principle behind his *Narnia* books and his science-fiction trilogy. By linking Christ with something cerebral — the meaning of myth — it was as though he first intellectualised religion and only then could let it become emotional, a passion.

His exchange with Tolkien marked a new intensity in their relationship, but ironically it also planted the seeds of their later falling out. Tolkien had hoped sincerely that Lewis would adopt

Clive Staples Lewis as a young boy, with his brother Warren.

Little Lea, Belfast, the house to which the Lewises moved in 1905.

The area around the Belfast docks. From the upper windows of Little Lea, Jack could just about see the shipyards.

Jack with his friend Paddy Moore during the First World War.

Lewis the undergraduate
in 1919, when he
returned to Oxford after
the war.

Magdalen College, Oxford, where, after two failed attempts, he was finally
made a Fellow in 1925.

Lewis with Janie Moore, with whom he lived for over thirty years, and her daughter Maureen, later Maureen Blake, Lady Dunbar of Hempriggs, who died in 1997.

The Kilns – the house in Oxford to which Lewis moved with Janie in 1930.

Charles Williams — playwright, fantasy novelist, poet and leading member of the Inklings, an informal literary group in Oxford of which Lewis was also a member.

John Ronald Reuel Tolkien, with whom Lewis became close friends.

Lewis with Joy Gresham, the American woman he married in 1956 (Dundee University Archives), and (below) with her stepsons Douglas and David.

Jack and Warren
as older men.

C. S. Lewis at his desk.

Anthony Hopkins and Debra Winger in *Shadowlands* — the film of the story of Jack and Joy Gresham's romance.

Catholicism, and even two years later he was able to write in his diary that his friendship with him, 'besides giving constant pleasure and comfort, has done me much good from the contact with a man at once honest, brave, intellectual – a scholar, a poet and a philosopher – and a lover, at least after a long pilgrimage, of Our Lord'.[12] But Tolkien had seriously misjudged his friend. Instead of embracing Catholicism, Lewis returned to his roots, to a form of Irish Protestantism which Tolkien, who was almost a fundamentalist Catholic, loathed. When the man he had helped to find God became 'one of the enemy', and not only that but a renowned Anglican proselytiser, their friendship began to crumble.

For his part, Lewis had no liking for Catholics or Catholicism. He and Warnie often referred to Irish Catholics as 'bog-trotters', and whenever Tolkien mentioned his religious devotions or slipped into talking about what Lewis saw as arcane and ludicrous religious practices, Jack could barely rein in his disgust.

Furthermore, because they were both writers, Lewis's conversion was especially painful for Tolkien. From finding God, finding Christ and becoming a believer, Lewis immediately leapt into the role of Christian apologist, a role that also made him famous far beyond Oxford. The speed with which Lewis began publishing his thoughts on religion, and indeed found an audience, only increased Tolkien's distress. Lewis's *The Pilgrim's Regress* and *The Screwtape Letters* were, to Tolkien's mind, rushed and shoddy. Probably with some justification, he believed that his friend had not given himself time to reach a clear understanding of his religious outlook, that he had been published before he had even begun to refine his ideas.

The stream of commercially successful books Lewis wrote during the 1940s and '50s, all quite different in character and displaying a variety of styles, but each carrying forward the underlying theme of using allegory to portray his religious viewpoint, was anathema to Tolkien, who despised allegorical literature. It is probable that if Lewis had become a Catholic, Tolkien still would have disapproved of his literary output, but Lewis's growing fame as a

Protestant writer incensed him and he cynically dubbed his drive to proselytise 'the Ulsterior Motive'.

At first, though, Lewis seems to have been largely unaware of his friend's asperity. In a genuinely magnanimous gesture, he dedicated *The Screwtape Letters* to Tolkien, and to a personal copy for him he added the inscription 'In token payment of a great debt'. Tolkien, though, cared little for the story and in particular he disliked the way Lewis was mocking some fundamental aspects of Christianity. To friends and associates Tolkien expressed the view that *The Screwtape Letters* was rather trite, but actually he had a more personal reason for disapproving of the book. In his view, devils and demons were very real forces intimately involved in the mechanism of the universe and it was dangerous to play word games on this subject.

Yet Tolkien's greatest scorn was reserved for Lewis's most famous and successful work, *The Chronicles of Narnia*. Lewis began to read these at the Inklings' meetings in the spring of 1949. The other members had been entranced by Tolkien's reading of *The Lord of the Rings* during the decade in which he had taken them from Hobbiton to the borders of Mordor, but now Lewis was working through his own mythology at a staggering pace and presenting lengthy passages which in many cases had been written in a matter of days. Such haste was one cause of annoyance for Tolkien, but he also hated the story and found it filled with contradiction and inconsistency. As one who applied exacting standards to himself, he expected the same quality and integrity from his friends.

In fact Tolkien had heard the first Narnia book, *The Lion, the Witch and the Wardrobe*, before the other Inklings. Towards the end of the Christmas holiday of 1948 Lewis read his story to Tolkien in his rooms at Magdalen. Tolkien disliked it immediately and bluntly expressed his feelings to Lewis. His principal gripe was the fact that, to his mind, Lewis had mixed up his mythologies. He had Father Christmas in the same tale as a Christ-like Aslan the lion, with witches, nymphs and beavers all thrown into the melting pot. It was, Tolkien declared, a meaningless jumble, an unmitigated disaster.

Worse still for their relationship, Tolkien did nothing to hide his feelings at meetings of the Inklings and embarrassed Lewis in front of their friends. Eventually he decided not to turn up when he knew Lewis was going to read anything to do with Narnia. One of Lewis's former students, Roger Lancelyn Green, had begun to join the Inklings occasionally and heard some of Jack's reading from an early draft of the book during meetings which Tolkien refused to attend. Later, when Tolkien bumped into Green in the street and he began to talk about Lewis, Tolkien declared: 'I hear you've been reading Jack's children's story. It really won't do, you know!'[13]

But there was more to this cooling of their relationship than Tolkien's taking offence at Lewis's writing speed. By the mid-1940s Lewis had become a famous writer. His Screwtape books had sold almost a quarter of a million copies and his science-fiction novels were rolling off the press, garnering ever more acclaim and global recognition. *The Hobbit* had done very well for Tolkien, but now its author was struggling with some sort of sequel and he could find no publisher interested in the project that really mattered to him, his masterwork, *The Silmarillion*. Salt was rubbed in Tolkien's wounds when, less than a year after finishing *The Lion, the Witch and the Wardrobe*, Lewis had American and other foreign publishers beating a path to his door in an attempt to acquire rights to the book. There is no coincidence in the fact that by October 1950 the Inklings' Thursday gatherings in Lewis's rooms had ended and the group met less frequently and with less formality and then only in Oxford pubs.

To add another turn to the screw, by the late 1940s Tolkien had begun to suspect that Lewis had 'borrowed' from him. He believed there were echoes of his ideas in Lewis's books and that he had reworked and reused some of his names. An example was Lewis's Tinidril, which was, Tolkien surmised, a combination of his own Idril and Tinúviel. Tolkien's personal copy of Lewis's *Perelandra* contains a rather caustic note in his own hand that reads: 'A bottle of sound vintage (?) I hope!' (This book is now in the Wade Collection at Wheaton College, Illinois. It is interesting to note, however, that Lewis's character Wormwood, the apprentice devil of *The Screwtape*

Letters, predates Tolkien's Wormtongue, Saruman's spy in *The Lord of the Rings*.)

Matters were made more complicated by the emergence of other stresses within the Inklings. One source of tension was the fact that only half of the members of the group were actually writing anything, while the others attended meetings simply for the company and conversation. Initially, those who were not writers were enthralled by the work of their friends and thoroughly enjoyed the readings of Jack, Tolkien and even Warren Lewis, who in 1948 had started work on a book about seventeenth-century French history. But, after a few years, this division began to influence the dynamic of gatherings. On one memorable occasion a small group had gathered in Lewis's rooms and were listening to Tolkien read the latest instalment of *The Lord of the Rings*. They were sitting quietly puffing on pipes and sipping tea when Hugo Dyson, who had been lounging on a sofa and growing increasingly bored with the proceedings, suddenly exclaimed: 'Oh, fuck! Not another elf!'

Lewis had a wide circle of contacts and acquaintances, and once in a while he would encounter a new person about whom he quickly grew very excited, almost to the point of hero worship. He would then try to thrust this person on his long-established friends. This he did many times when the Inklings were still a strong unit, but the most irritating occasion for Tolkien was when Lewis first met the writer Charles Williams. Within days Jack was telling his Oxford friends what an amazing man Williams was. 'If you were going up The High in a bus,' he told a friend, 'and you saw Charles Williams walking along the pavement among a crowd of people, you would immediately single him out because he looked so godlike; rather like an angel.'[14] Elsewhere he described Williams as 'an ugly man with a rather cockney voice. But no one ever thinks of this for five minutes after he has begun speaking. His face becomes almost angelic. Both in public and in private he is, of nearly all the men I have met, the one whose address most overflows with *love*. It is simply irresistible.'[15] These were typically over-the-top comments from Lewis, but Williams was to become more than a passing interest and soon rivalled Tolkien in Jack's affections.

The eldest of the three, Williams was already fifty by the time he first met Lewis in 1936. He had had a rather chequered education which began well enough with a scholarship to St Albans Grammar School and then an award to University College, Oxford, beginning in 1901, some fifteen years before Lewis. By all accounts Williams had been a promising student, but then, after he had spent two years at university, his father hit financial difficulties and the family could no longer contribute to his fees, so he was forced to leave without obtaining his degree. He then worked for the Oxford University Press and wrote in his spare time.

Williams was extremely prolific: by the late 1930s he had published more than twenty books, including novels, non-fiction titles, collections of poems and plays. It was one of his novels, *The Place of the Lion* (1931) that drew him to Lewis's attention a few years after it appeared in print. In 1939, some three years after the two men had first met, Williams moved to Oxford, where he (and later his wife and son) spent the duration of the war. From this time onwards he began to see a great deal of Jack, whose friendship and advice he valued greatly. Writing to his wife in 1939, he said of his new friend: 'I have fled to C. S. Lewis's rooms . . . he is a great tea-drinker at any hour of night or day, and left a tray for me with milk and tea, and an electric kettle at hand.'[16] Much to Tolkien's chagrin, Williams was soon inviting himself to the regular Monday talks at the Eastgate Hotel that Lewis and Tolkien had been enjoying alone each week for more than ten years.

Jack quickly became almost inseparable from Williams and began campaigning to have him accepted as an official lecturer at the university in spite of the fact that he had never been awarded a degree. In the face of opposition from almost all quarters, he succeeded in this (largely thanks to the severe shortage of qualified teaching staff during the war) and he was later instrumental in acquiring for Williams an honorary MA at Oxford. This was another example of

Lewis's campaigning for an unpopular cause and as a result generating great upset within the university establishment.

In spite of, or perhaps because of, Lewis's adulation, Tolkien was never entirely comfortable with Jack's new friend. Williams was viewed by some as a rather arrogant, self-possessed man who, in the company of the Inklings, seemed to need to overcompensate for his fractured education, and Tolkien certainly did not much care for his character. Tolkien also disliked Williams's writing, especially *The Figure of Arthur*, an account of the Arthurian legend. Moreover, he was constantly suspicious of his religious and philosophical ideas, many of which were diametrically opposed to his own. Williams was a mass of contradictions. He was a devout member of the Church of England and yet almost obsessively fascinated with mysticism and the occult. He had joined the mystical group the Order of the Golden Dawn, which counted among its members the notorious Aleister Crowley, 'the Great Beast', but on Sundays he attended church and said his prayers. These two aspects of his philosophical and spiritual interests made for an interesting blend when expressed poetically, but Tolkien, who had harboured little sympathy for Protestants since childhood, had almost nothing in common with a Protestant who was also interested in the Hermetic tradition, devil worship and black magic.

Worse still, Williams appears to have had quite serious sadistic tendencies. Although, as far as anyone knows, these were never expressed physically, he described them vividly in his poetry and novels. In the poem *Antichrist* he wrote:

> *My mind possessed me with delight*
> *To wrack her lovely head*
> *With slow device of subtle pain.*[17]

When combined with his attraction to the occult, such sadistic impulses added an exciting intensity to his writing, but some of his friends felt Williams was only just in control of his emotions, able to rein in his darker side only with a great effort of will.

All of this would have made it difficult for Tolkien and Williams to become friends without the complication of their respective relationships with Lewis, but clearly Tolkien also felt jealous and usurped by Williams. The best that can be said about their relationship is that they tolerated each other, and familiarity changed this little. They spent perhaps two evenings a week together for some six years, but were never able to trust each other, and Tolkien often felt extremely uncomfortable in Williams's presence.

None of this seems to have made any sort of impact on Lewis. He was thrilled by Williams's rather edgy character and adored his mind. It should be remembered that, in his younger days at least, Lewis had nurtured sadistic fantasies and the two men shared an appetite for the darker side of fantasy fiction that influenced both Lewis's *That Hideous Strength* and Williams's *All Hallows' Eve*, published within months of each other in 1945.

Strangely, however, Lewis seems to have laboured under the misunderstanding that all his friends, including Tolkien, felt the same way about Williams. 'By 1939, Williams had already become as dear to all my Oxford friends as he had to me,' he wrote.[18] This appeared in an essay that was part of a memorial collection written by some members of the Inklings and their friends called *Essays Presented to Charles Williams*, published in 1947, two years after Williams's death. This was probably true for some of Lewis's friends, but definitely not Tolkien, who made his feelings perfectly clear in a comment he added to his own copy of the book (to which, ironically, he had also contributed). In the margin he wrote: 'Alas no! In any case I had hardly ever seen him till he came to live in Oxford.'

Lewis not only enjoyed Williams's company, but he was also greatly influenced by his work, and the writing of at least one of his books, *That Hideous Strength*, owed much to his friend's unique imagination. One commentator went so far as to claim that it is 'a Charles Williams novel written by C. S. Lewis'.[19] This is an exaggeration, but the book was undoubtedly inspired by Williams's slightly off-kilter way of thinking and the techniques he employed in constructing his own novels.

This is not entirely surprising. One of Lewis's characteristics as a writer was that he unconsciously soaked up influences from all quarters. Furthermore, the hours of conversation between Williams and Lewis and the latter's deep admiration for Williams's work, especially *All Hallows' Eve* and *The Place of the Lion*, the book that had first drawn him to Williams, must have left its mark.

Tolkien often contradicted or ignored altogether Lewis's enthusiasms, and considered his friend to be a very impressionable man as well as a rather poor judge of character; he was also a stickler for accuracy, especially on the printed page. His comments about Williams were made when he and Lewis were approaching the nadir of their relationship, but the resentment was painfully real. To a journalist many years after Williams and Lewis were both dead, Tolkien remarked of Williams: 'I have read a good many of his books but I don't like them . . . I didn't know Charles Williams very well.'[20]

Interestingly, Tolkien's dislike of Williams was not shared by many in Oxford and some liked him very much. Williams is said to have been enormously attractive to women and to have possessed a certain manicured charm that appealed to some but instinctively repelled men like Tolkien. In remarkably candid mood Auden said of Williams: 'I had met many good people before who made me feel ashamed of my own shortcomings, but in the presence of this man – I did not feel ashamed. I felt transformed into a person who was incapable of doing anything base or unloving.'[21] Unfortunately for the friendship between the two founders of the Inklings, Tolkien shared none of these sentiments.

With the halcyon days of the Inklings passing, Lewis presided over the group pretty much alone. He saw Tolkien from time to time and they were always very civil to each other, but the old fire had died. Lewis continued to praise and encourage Tolkien, and even as late as 1949 he was still pushing his friend to get *The Lord of the Rings* finished and published. When the book did eventually appear, in three volumes in 1954 and 1955, he did everything he could to help the trilogy on its way, offering the sort of public praise that aroused suspicion among cynical critics and journalists.

For the jacket of *The Fellowship of the Ring*, Lewis wrote: 'It would be almost safe to say that no book like this has ever been written.'[22] To this one sceptical reviewer, Edwin Muir, writing in the *Observer*, responded: 'This remarkable book makes its appearance at a disadvantage. Nothing but a great masterpiece could survive the bombardment of praise directed at it from the blurb.'[23] And much to the irritation of both Tolkien and Lewis, Muir went on to become one of the most vociferous critics of the trilogy.

In retrospect, the friendship between Lewis and Tolkien is tinged with sadness. These two very similar men were almost destined to find each other, and each grew from their association. But they also held very different beliefs and opinions about many important issues and approached certain crucial aspects of their lives in very different and mutually exclusive ways. Their relationship ended in quiet bitterness and suppressed resentment. Perhaps the greatest sadness about the loss of their friendship is the fact that while it lasted each was a better man because of it.

8

From War to Joy

Lewis had a good war. In many ways it was the happiest and most productive time of his life. These years were the era when the Inklings were at their most active and mutually inspirational, and it was a period during which Lewis's writing career finally took off. However, when we consider the entire arc of his life it becomes clear that the decade between the outbreak of war and 1950 can, in terms of Lewis's fortunes, be almost precisely divided into two equal halves — a happy time followed by a lacklustre period. As much as the war years were enlivening for Lewis, those that immediately followed them were often both humbling and depressing.

Although greatly disturbed by the British declaration of war against Germany on 3 September 1939, Lewis considered it a necessary evil. His philosophy was pragmatic: he thought harming people was wrong and living in peace was right, but he also believed that it was one's moral duty to work towards the greater good. Therefore, if a war meant hurting many people but that a much larger number would be freed from tyranny and their lives saved or made better, then war was justified. Hitler, Lewis believed, was a force for evil; he was a man who wanted to bring harm to many and therefore he had to be stopped even if that entailed the loss of innocent lives.

For a short time Lewis was fearful that he would be called up, as the age range for eligibility set by the British government in 1939 was eighteen to forty-one, a category into which he just fitted. But there was never any real danger he would be called to serve. He had been a soldier for only a short time during the First World War, so he was not especially experienced; furthermore, he was extremely unfit and quite seriously overweight. However, Warren Lewis had been a professional soldier for many years, and although he had been retired in December 1932, he was called back into active service as soon as war was declared.

During the first year of the war Warren was posted initially at Catterick in Yorkshire and then spent six months in northern France, where he was elevated temporarily to the rank of major before being evacuated back to England from Dunkirk. Throughout the war he was on stand-by for action, but his services on the battlefield were never required, which was fortunate because in 1940 he was forty-five and in even worse shape than his brother.

Warren was very unhappy about returning to the Army and he never spoke about his experiences in France; nor did he record events in his journals. As a result, much of this period of his life is obfuscated. What we do know is that he spent most of his time in and out of military hospitals because of alcohol-related illness. He was also at least three stone overweight, but whereas Jack could spend the war trying to make himself useful without too much physical strain, Warren, the Sandhurst graduate, was expected to behave in a way befitting a senior officer and to command the respect of both those under him and his peers.

Jack was justifiably concerned for his brother, not least because he was all too aware of his weaknesses and vulnerability. Warren was often a danger to himself during peacetime, but in France he was likely to be facing external dangers too, and in Jack's opinion he was entirely unfit for the job.

For his own part Jack wanted to be involved with the war as much as possible just so long as it did not call for anything too physical. His first approach to the military authorities was an offer to train cadets, but he was turned down because of his limited military experience and poor physical fitness. Shortly after this he was offered a position at the Ministry of Information, but he felt compelled to pass this over because it involved the writing of propaganda and the production of what he considered to be, in many cases, thinly veiled lies. This was something he could not contemplate on moral grounds. Finally, like many other middle-aged academics, including Tolkien, he volunteered to serve with the Oxford City Home Guard Battalion.

During a period of great anxiety about a possible invasion of the British Isles, the Home Guard was given the important task of watching for spies or advanced military units. And, for a while at least, Lewis enjoyed playing his part in the effort. He was required to join three other members of the battalion to patrol a pre-designated area of Oxford between one thirty and five-thirty in the morning one day each week. This usually followed a meeting of the Inklings in his rooms, and after his friends had headed home to their families or their bedsits, he would shoulder his rifle, grab a box of sandwiches he had made earlier in the evening, and between sessions having a smoke and a chat at suitable stop-off points, he and his colleagues poked around looking for anything suspicious.

Although it sounds mundane, and Lewis did tire of the exercise after a few months, in the beginning the work was quite an inspiration for him. He loved the early mornings, the silence, and the darkness during the blackout. He considered the others he met in the Home Guard intelligent and engaging men, but he also enjoyed few things as much as sitting in a silent field smoking a cigarette and watching the sunrise. It was during these lengthy spells of solitude with nothing to intrude on his thoughts that he wrote many of the short pieces that later appeared as *The Screwtape Letters*, which had wartime England as its backdrop and an everyday hero who happened to be an air-raid warden.

Lewis was quick to realise that the war would very rapidly alter things for everyone and he readily embraced this change. Less than two weeks after the beginning of the war he wrote to his old Belfast friend Arthur Greeves, telling him that 'for me, personally, it has come in the nick of time: I was just beginning to get too well settled in my profession, too successful, and probably self complacent'.[1] This seems like a rather strange comment to make, because, from our perspective, in 1939 Lewis was not entirely successful. He was certainly an accomplished teacher and academic admired by many, but as a writer he had yet to really make his mark. Admittedly, he had seen publication of his first science-fiction novel, *Out of the Silent Planet*, but this had been only moderately well received. *The Screwtape Letters*, the other two books in the Ransom trilogy, and most importantly in terms of commercial success, *The Chronicles of Narnia*, still lay ahead of him. During that year Lewis was living on a rather meagre academic's salary and earning almost nothing from his writing.

And yet perhaps he had a point. In 1939 life was in most ways rather settled and cosy for him. He had a coterie of friends, he lived in a large house (which was almost completely paid for), he had settled into a commodious, rather safe routine and he enjoyed the reassurance and comfort of religious conviction and devotion. From this comfortable platform another man might easily have allowed to drain away the enthusiasm and energy needed to become a successful writer.

But Lewis did nothing of the sort, and this is why, in terms of his creativity and his career as an author, he may be said to have enjoyed a good war. What he wrote during this period, fiction and non-fiction alike, was, for a great many people, perfectly in tune with the time. This meant that as he developed a style and absorbed himself with his religious sentiments, these just happened to strike a perfect chord with a contemporary audience. This had the effect of elevating him from being a well-considered academic writer and relatively unsuccessful novelist to a commentator recognised and admired on both sides of the Atlantic.

The key to this success was *The Screwtape Letters*. Soon after the

letters started to appear in *The Guardian* magazine an influential
member of the BBC, the Director of Religious Broadcasting, Dr
James Welch, wrote to Lewis asking him if he would be interested
in trying his hand at radio broadcasting.

Jack turned out to be a natural and the first programme broadcast
live from the BBC in London, on Wednesday 6 August 1941, was
immensely well received. The subject of this talk was, as advertised
in the *Radio Times*, 'Right or Wrong: A Clue to the Meaning of Life',
and an audience of over one million listeners was drawn immediately
to Lewis's warm, slightly accented voice. The following week and
after each of his Wednesday broadcasts throughout that month, the
BBC received a huge response in the form of thousands of letters
from a wide cross-section of listeners. In fact, after the first broadcast Lewis received so much mail that he could not possibly reply to
every letter and so someone at the BBC suggested that in the second
talk he should devote some time to answering as many of the questions as possible raised by his fans. This, however, only made things
worse because after this broadcast the mailbag swelled still further.

The great appeal of Lewis's talks came from the fact that his
manner was down-to-earth and straightforward. He was never pre-
tentious but spoke about relatively complex matters in an easy-going
style. Christians and non-believers were receptive to this and whether
or not one subscribed to what he said, he made a convincing commentator who was also easy on the ear.

Not surprisingly, the BBC was much taken with Lewis's talks and
between August 1941 and April 1944 four series were made. The
second series, broadcast in January 1942, was entitled 'What
Christians Believe' and became even more popular than the first. For
the third set of talks, broadcast in July of that year, Lewis chose as
his subject 'Christian Behaviour', and still more listeners tuned in. By
the time he was ready to deliver a fourth series the BBC had come
up with the idea of pre-recording the programmes on to gramophone discs and broadcasting them later the same week, which
made scheduling more flexible. This had the added advantage that
copies could be sold afterwards.

Lewis was not so keen on this technique and believed it removed some of the spontaneity. But again the series was extremely popular and many believe that this final set, 'Beyond Personality: The Christian View of God', was the best of the four.

From the earliest series of broadcasts in 1941 Lewis and his publisher were astute enough to repackage the talks in book form. The first book, *Broadcast Talks*, was published by Geoffrey Bles in July 1942 and encompassed the first two series. A second, *Christian Behaviour*, appeared the following spring (on 19 April 1943, the day before *Perelandra* was published), and the third, *Beyond Personality*, during the autumn of 1944. Each became a best-seller very quickly.

Although Lewis was asked repeatedly to give more series of talks, he always refused. He was probably right to leave the project while he was on top, but there were two personal reasons for making this decision. The first was that he could not keep up with replying to even a fraction of the letters he received from around the world, which increased in number with each new series. The other was that he believed that he had said everything he could say to a lay audience and he did not want to repeat himself.

There is also the fact that Lewis thought that he was becoming 'too popular'. He was, we must remember, a man who succeeded in straddling the very different worlds of popular writing and academia, but he never found it easy to balance these two aspects of his life. By the time he had entered his forties he was becoming entrenched in his ways. He had always been a man older than his years, slightly out of tune with the normal run of everyday life, but this became more marked with age. Lewis was at heart an elitist, but most of the time he succeeded in quashing this trait. Ill at ease with many aspects of twentieth-century life, he hated the radio and detested television even more when it arrived. He had only accepted the offer from the BBC to talk on the radio because he rightly believed he could reach a large audience in this way and that it was his Christian duty to do so. He hated travelling to London and he hated the capital. He was repulsed by almost all aspects of popular culture, from Disney to jazz, and he deliberately ignored any form of modern art, music, theatre, film or literature. He locked himself in his very tall ivory tower, where he remained hermetically sealed until his last breath.

However, there is an ironic twist to this aspect of Lewis's life. In the eyes of many academics, Lewis was a rather vulgar popularist who tarnished the image of the Oxbridge don. They looked down on him for talking on the BBC to the general public; they despised *The Screwtape Letters* and the Ransom books and they hated Lewis's non-fiction even more. The general consensus among his colleagues was that matters of religion were too personal to be dissected in a book aimed at the mass market. In Oxford, and within some areas of the wider academic community, there was a sense that Lewis was cheapening the work of serious scholars and eroding the carefully constructed intellectual ramparts that kept the uneducated riffraff from the college gates.

A further irony, during a time when many thinkers and media figures were moving away from an orthodox stance on religion, is that Lewis's views went against the grain, making him unpopular with a large proportion of intellectuals and journalists. Renowned for being an old-fashioned intellectual Christian, diametrically opposed to many radical writers and critics, Lewis was reviled by a string of influential media figures of the time.

He was partly aware of the fact that he was falling between two stools, but his strong belief that he should do his utmost to communicate his views kept him writing and proselytising. He was never an evangelist and did not try to foist his beliefs on to others, but he was an excellent speaker and a gifted writer, and in spite of his natural elitism he had a talent for connecting with people. He could not deny what he felt was a calling.

It was almost entirely for this reason that in 1941, about the time he was spending much of his energies on the BBC broadcasts, Lewis agreed to undertake a series of talks to audiences at RAF stations up and down the country. These were not wholly successful, and were, in many respects, a waste of his time and energy. The idea to talk to RAF personnel had come from the Chaplain-in-Chief, the

Reverend Maurice Edwards, who believed that Lewis's blend of urbanity and warm delivery would be just right for servicemen, whether they were Christians or not. Lewis initially had his doubts about this theory but he finally accepted the invitation.

The first talk in Abingdon, near Oxford, was poorly attended and put Lewis off so much that he almost cancelled the rest of his tour itinerary, but gradually they improved. At some of the air bases he spoke before two or three hundred servicemen and servicewomen and was usually well received thanks to the fact that his profile had been heightened considerably by his BBC broadcasts each Wednesday.

However, the entire exercise, stretching from 1941 until close to the end of the war in the spring of 1945, placed quite a strain on Lewis. Although many Oxford students were away fighting, he still had some teaching commitments to fulfil as well as the obligatory administrative duties required of a tutor. He also had the BBC talks each Wednesday evening. Travelling to London and back took up half a day, while another day was lost in preparing for the talks.

One of the factors that had swayed Lewis when the Chaplain-in-Chief had first extended the invitation to give the talks back in early 1941 had been the financial aspect of the offer, for at this time Lewis was still rather hard up. He had earned almost nothing from his earliest books and his position at Magdalen just about covered the bills. He had given away his earnings from the serialisation of *The Screwtape Letters* in *The Guardian* between May and August 1941, and so, during the years before his books began to earn him a lot of money, he was pleased to be offered expenses and a generous fee for each talk.

However, this incentive soon became rather less important. With the publication and huge success of *The Screwtape Letters*, *Perelandra* and *The Problem of Pain* as well as the BBC-linked books, all published within the space of four years, by the end of the war Lewis had suddenly become rather wealthy. Each of the efforts he had made during the war years had assisted the others without his ever consciously planning anything. The BBC talks promoted his books and each book led readers to the other titles. Lewis's career had finally taken off.

At about the same time as Lewis was lecturing to servicemen and talking to the nation on air he found yet another forum for self-expression, this time in Oxford itself. A society calling itself the Oxford Socratic Club began in January 1942 and the founders invited Lewis to join them. It was established by a student at Somerville College, Stella Aldwinkle, and was in principle a standard debating society but it differed in that it specialised in religious rhetoric. The idea was to hold weekly meetings during which a member of the club would be pitted against a visiting speaker and the arguments of the rivals could then be thrown open to the floor for general discussion. Lewis went along a few times to see how it was going and was so drawn to the club that within a month he became its first president, after which he rarely missed a meeting until he gave up the post in 1954.

The highlight of the meetings was a verbal battle between Lewis and the guest speaker, who was often an agnostic or an atheist. Most weeks over a hundred students and faculty members attended and the meetings could sometimes become quite raucous affairs, with heated debate actively encouraged. For Lewis it was a perfect forum because he loved nothing better than a good argument with intelligent people whom he respected, and before its dissolution in 1972 the Socratic Club attracted some extremely distinguished guests, including the influential scientists J.B.S. Haldane and Konrad Lorenz, the writer Dorothy Sayers and the philosopher and author Joseph Bronowski.

This period, then, may be considered the halcyon days of Lewis's first wave of literary success. The second wave was to come with the publication of *The Lion, the Witch and the Wardrobe* in 1950, and with this he achieved far broader fame and a variety of celebrity that was not simply confined to his work as a writer on religious ideas. But between these two peaks there was a deep trough, a period of personal confusion, pain and loss that caused Lewis suffering but also awoke in him the creative energies that carried him from the world of Screwtape to Narnia.

The descent into this dark period began within hours of VE Day, 8 May 1945. Jack's close personal friend and fellow Inkling Charles Williams had begun to suffer intense abdominal pain. He was diagnosed with adhesions of the digestive system and an operation was arranged at the Acland Hospital, just north of the Bird and Baby, the Inklings' favourite pub. Jack, who had known Williams was due in surgery on the evening of 14 June, set off for the hospital late the following morning to see how his friend had fared under the knife. When he arrived there he was told by a nurse that Williams had died a few hours earlier.

Warren had already heard. The hospital had called Jack's rooms at Magdalen to pass on the news soon after Jack had left, and his brother, stunned by the news, had headed straight for a drink. Warnie chose the King's Arms and only realised as he sat down deeply depressed that this was the very pub he and Williams had retreated to on many occasions, just the two of them downing pints after Williams had finished his working day at the Oxford University Press. It did nothing for his mood. Writing in his diary, he reported prophetically: 'There will be no more pints with Charles: no more "Bird and Baby": the blackout has fallen, and the Inklings can never be the same again.'[2]

Jack was devastated by the news and thought that 'the very streets looked different'.[3] After leaving the hospital he walked back slowly to the Bird and Baby, where the other Inklings had gathered for their weekly meeting. None of his friends had realised that Williams was seriously ill, and Jack broke the news ashen-faced and barely able to hold back his tears.

Some argue that if there is a use at all for Christian faith it is to be found at times of crisis and personal grief, and it did indeed help Jack deal with his loss. He genuinely believed that Williams was closer to him and to his other friends in death than he had ever been during his lifetime. As a result, Jack felt a deep pain, but, he told himself, not a particle of depression or resentment over the fact that his friend had been snatched away. For him it somehow made the next world more real, and what he saw as one's inevitable destiny to go there had become something less frightening to contemplate. At the funeral service held at the cemetery of St Cross, he had the overwhelming feeling that Williams was still there, holding back from his final journey, watching over his friends.

At this time Jack found additional spiritual comfort in a correspondence with a nun named Sister Penelope who had made contact with him after she had read and enjoyed *Out of the Silent Planet*. Sister Penelope was herself an accomplished writer who authored some twenty books under the pseudonym 'A Religious of CSMV', which referred to her convent, the Community of St Mary the Virgin, in Wantage, Berkshire.

Jack used Sister Penelope almost as a confessor, telling her his problems in the numerous letters that passed between them, and in return she gave him what advice she could. As well as this, they exchanged books and criticised each other's work and she acted as a constant source of support for Jack, especially during the torturous times he faced late in life. Indeed, shortly before his death one of the last letters he ever wrote was to his 'elder sister in the Faith', as he called her.

The end of the war also brought changes at The Kilns. There were no more parties of evacuees from London and the house returned to being the quieter, duller place it had been before 1940. Janie was becoming increasingly infirm and her mental state was beginning to deteriorate. This meant that she was often irascible, unpredictable in her moods and more demanding than ever. Jack was tolerant and tried hard to keep her happy, but Warnie was never so calm nor so accommodating, and his relationship with her grew increasingly fraught.

The atmosphere at The Kilns was often unpleasant at this time. Jack sometimes found himself returning to find that Warnie and Janie were not talking because of some trifling disagreement that had escalated out of proportion, or to discover that his brother had stormed out to find solace in a whisky bottle. From 1945 Warren's alcoholism grew steadily worse, his drunken binges more frequent, his 'disappearances' from The Kilns more common and, for Jack, more worrying.

Warren's favourite form of escape was to take a trip to Ireland, where he could go on a bender away from the reproving gaze of his brother and Janie. He was driven to these binges through self-loathing and boredom and they became more frequent and more damaging as he grew older. While on one of these 'escapes' soon after the end of the war he found himself in Our Lady of Lourdes Hospital in Drogheda. Here he was looked after by a group of dedicated nuns who in later years treated him whenever he returned to the area for another bout of excessive drinking. Going far beyond the call of duty, they had even sent helpers to local pubs to find Warren when he was known to be in town and to get him to the hospital before he did himself too much harm.

As Janie grew weaker and more unstable the demands placed on Jack began to take their toll. Janie was obsessive about her dog, Bruce, and once she was housebound she insisted that Warnie take him for frequent walks. But when Warren had gone AWOL or was so drunk he could not get up, the job fell to Jack, who had to stop whatever it was he was doing to walk around the grounds of the house for half an hour. All of this was merely a supplement to the domestic duties he still had to perform. For a long time Janie refused to have any help in the form of a maid or housekeeper. A gardener and handyman named Fred Paxford had been employed soon after they had moved to The Kilns, but his domain did not extend to the inside of the house unless it was specifically to repair something.

Janie was eventually talked into allowing a young woman called June Flewett to help with the household chores. June worked at The Kilns from 1942 to 1945 and by the time she left (to begin training as an actor at RADA) Janie had come to consider her 'irreplaceable', as did Jack and Warren, for it meant that after she left they were once again in demand as factotums and dog walkers.

Janie's habit was to call Jack from her bed, or if she was up, from some far room of the house with a trumpeted: 'Barboys! Where are you?' Jack had to immediately put down his pen or his book and rush off to see what was required of him. Warnie (who had been in 'retirement' since his mid-thirties) constantly whined about Janie's demands, whereas Jack, who was working full-time and writing whenever he could, managed to retain his good humour. With typical stoicism he wrote to Arthur Greeves: 'The great thing, if one can, is to stop regarding all the unpleasant things as interruptions of one's "own" or "real" life. The truth is of course that what one calls the interruptions are precisely one's real life – the life God is sending one day by day.'[4]

This was a sentiment he shared with Tolkien, who also regretted that he could rarely find time to do the things he loved and often felt overwhelmed by domestic responsibilities. Tolkien wrote a story about this predicament called *Leaf By Niggle*, a perfect allegory of their situation and a tale much admired by Lewis. The central character, Niggle, is a painter obsessed with refining the most minute details of a painting he has been working on for many years. He knows that time is running out for him as he will soon die, but he is constantly being distracted and never completes the picture. The scene then shifts to Niggle's time in purgatory, where he discovers that the painting has been recreated so that he may finish it before travelling on to heaven.

The years 1947 to 1950 were a period during which the day-to-day reality of Lewis's life was set in stark relief against his growing commercial and critical success. On the one hand he was continuing to write at the same blinding pace he had established during the late 1930s and his fame was spreading apace: in September 1947 he appeared on the cover of *Time* magazine and had another best-seller with a non-fiction book, *Miracles*. On the other hand, these were the worst years at The Kilns.

During one of his solitary sojourns in Ireland, in June 1947, Warnie had gone on a drinking binge so extreme that he was forced to spend two weeks recovering at Our Lady of Lourdes Hospital.

This came at a particularly bad moment for Jack and merely compounded his woes. That summer the Professor of English Literature at Merton College, David Nicholl Smith, retired from his position and Jack thought that he would be the prime candidate for the Chair. For some years Tolkien had stated his wish that he could become the Merton Professor of English Language and Literature and that his friend Lewis could acquire the other English Chair at the college. Although Tolkien achieved one of these ambitions, his own professorship at Merton, Lewis was passed over and the position went eventually to his old college tutor, the elderly Shakespearian scholar F.P. Wilson.

Although Tolkien may have had naïve dreams of himself and Jack occupying the two English Chairs at Merton, Lewis never stood a chance. As far as his academic ambitions were concerned, his unpopular image among the powerful and influential at Oxford forever limited him. Weighing against his obvious merits – his scholarly works such as *The Allegory of Love* and *A Preface to Paradise Lost*, his skills as a lecturer, tutor and administrator – were his popular books such as *The Screwtape Letters* and what were perceived as crass science-fiction novels. These things tarnished Lewis's image irreparably.

There was also the little matter of the fiasco over the Poetry Chair ten years earlier, an incident that had certainly not been forgotten by those who counted at Oxford. To complete the grievances against him, Lewis had the reputation of being an argumentative, opinionated and sometimes rude individual who was never a good team player. The mighty of Oxford did not care a fig about covers of *Time* (indeed, most of them had probably never heard of it) and even among the most senile, memories of what they saw as wrongs committed against them were astonishingly long and vibrant. They were an unforgiving bunch and the last thing they wanted was a professor in their ranks who had the potential to rock the boat.

This rejection was a terrible humiliation for Lewis and disturbed him greatly. His commercial success satisfied only one aspect of his personality, it fulfilled the need for recognition on a large scale, a wish felt by almost all artists whether they admit it or not. But another powerful force within him was a desire for the respect of his academic peers; he wanted to be accepted as an intellectual equal and given due credit. He could not fully grasp the fact that it is rarely possible to have both. He had risen to become a Tutor of English Literature at Magdalen before he had found fame, and it was a position that could never be taken from him. But once he had entered the public domain with his writing and broadcasting any hopes of climbing to the top of the academic tree were doomed for ever.

Unfortunately for Lewis, this failure came at a particularly inauspicious moment because he was already facing a crisis of confidence that had been precipitated by a most unexpected source. Since his first appearance at the Socratic Club he had played a very active role there. Those invited to speak at the club were quite often respected figures in their field but also people whose work Lewis had criticised in newspaper articles and essays, or ones whose intellectual stance he personally opposed.

Lewis's favourite hate figures were atheists and scientists and he prided himself in the belief that on every occasion on which he had locked horns with either variety of intellectual he had trounced them. That, at least, was what his many supporters had led him to believe. The debates were often vehement, which the largely student audience loved, and if nothing else, the meetings were hugely entertaining.

At one gathering, in January 1944, over 250 students turned up, packing the lecture theatre to hear Lewis argue the subject of 'On Being Reviewed by Christians' when the guest speaker was the respected agnostic philosopher and writer C.E.M. Joad. On that occasion the two men grew so hot that Joad asked if he could remove his jacket. When the chair, club founder Stella Aldwinkle, asked Lewis if he would like to do the same, he told her that he could not because he had a large hole in his shirt.

On another famed evening at the club Lewis was pitted against a relativist who apparently ended his speech with the statement: 'The world does not exist, England does not exist, Oxford does not exist, and I am confident that *I* do not exist!' When Stella Aldwinkle asked if Lewis had any reply, he declared: 'How am I to talk to a man who's not there?'

But Lewis could not always win, and much to his lasting disgust and humiliation, it was a woman and a Christian who became the only speaker to embarrass him at the Socratic Club. The occasion was 2 February 1948, and a twenty-nine-year-old Cambridge philosopher named Elizabeth Anscombe had asked if she could debate with Lewis an issue that had been concerning her for almost a year.

The point in question had arisen from Lewis's book *Miracles*, which Elizabeth Anscombe had read soon after its publication in May 1947. In the book Lewis had claimed that God must exist because naturalism is self-refuting. What he meant by this arises from a series of reasoned arguments. First, he said, naturalism, a philosophy stating that all things are interrelated and interdepend-ent, must, by its nature, refute the existence of free will and free reasoning. He thought this because if there were such things as free will and free reasoning they would influence the universe and stop all things becoming simply mutually dependent. He went on to argue that if there is no such thing as free will or free reasoning, all belief in science and philosophy is invalid too. This would, of course, then mean that the concept of naturalism (a philosophical idea based on free reasoning) is also impossible. From this, Lewis went on to argue that if naturalism was a self-destroying concept and therefore invalid, supernaturalism, a belief in an omnipotent God, must be the only valid interpretation of the universe.

Elizabeth Anscombe took exception to this argument, and with very good reason. She was a 'modern philosopher', a disciple of Wittgenstein, and she was well acquainted with what were, by 1948, rather antiquated arguments of the type Lewis was employing. That fateful night, before two hundred adoring Lewis followers, she illus-trated just how fragile his thoughts were on the subject.

Using linguistic analysis pioneered by Wittgenstein, Elizabeth Anscombe showed that Lewis's premise was based entirely on the interpretation of the words used in his argument and that a belief in supernaturalism simply because naturalism *appeared* to be self-destroying was nonsense. Philosophical understanding, she showed, could no longer be based on the Hegelian system followed by Lewis, namely that religious ideas such as faith were unverifiable and only understood by calling on supernaturalism. Furthermore, Wittgenstein and others had made it clear that in order to speak and think rationally about philosophy there must be an agreed set of terms so that those engaged in discourse can understand one another.

This simple premise alone showed that the Hegelian argument was flawed. But, on top of this, Lewis's adversary pointed out that, if he thought supernaturalism could provide 'proof' that God existed, he was mistaken. Any supernaturalist, she said, must have received data from a naturalist perspective to place their argument on the table. In other words, if this was the case (and it had to be), then supernaturalism must also be a self-destructive concept.

Lewis was crushed by this defeat. Perhaps the fall was all the more painful because he had become so used to using the Socratic Club as a forum for his inflated ego. His friends and supporters tried to rally round, claiming that the debate was a draw, but Lewis knew better. The most painful aspect of this reverse was the fact that he had been forced to realise that his philosophical understanding was outmoded.

One might think that Elizabeth Anscombe's powerful arguments would have knocked Lewis's faith in God and Christianity, but they did nothing of the sort. By this time his religious convictions were so indelibly etched into his very being that he could never have lost faith as a result of a mere argument. It is significant that, as disturbing as this incident must have been, Lewis did not even begin to question the foundations of his faith. Instead he did something which was to have far more interesting consequences for his writing. He retreated into himself and internalised his pain and confusion.

After February 1948 Lewis never wrote another word of religious commentary. His last books on religious subjects were purely devotional and dealt with such matters as grief (*A Grief Observed*) and prayer (*Letters to Malcolm*). There was no more analysis, no more intellectualising, no more dissecting. Instead Lewis turned his energies to the most enduring of his creations, his religious allegory, or 'supposal', as he preferred to call it, *The Chronicles of Narnia*. In pain, and destined to lick his wounds for the rest of his life, he returned to the innocent and unquestioning dream world of his childhood.

Writing *The Lion, the Witch and the Wardrobe* and the other Narnia books brought Lewis great personal satisfaction and pleasure. The series provided an escape into a fantasy realm within which he could disappear for at least a part of his waking life. And yet, as magical as this sanctuary may have been for him, the chaos of his domestic existence could not be easily ignored for long. In June 1949 Lewis collapsed from exhaustion and his friend and physician Dr Robert Havard immediately had him admitted to hospital. There he was found to be suffering from a high temperature and swollen glands, which Havard considered dangerous in an unfit, overweight and stressed man of fifty.

Warren was furious at the news because for years he had been complaining about the way Jack could never say no to Janie. According to an account detailed lovingly in his diary, he stormed up to Janie's room and gave her a piece of his mind, demanding that she stop badgering his brother when he returned to health.

In reality Warren's tirade was almost certainly a waste of breath. By this time Janie had slipped into senility and probably forgot the incident within hours of his attack. And, for all his noble words, Warnie probably knew he had been wasting his time because the very next day he went off on one of his benders. That night he found himself in the same ward as his brother at the Acland Hospital. This time he had almost succeeded in killing himself with drink. Initially he was treated at the Acland, but he had drunk so much that he had descended into a temporary psychosis. His doctors decided to transfer him to the Warneford Hospital in Headington, a psychiatric hospital. There he sobered up with surprising speed.

The unavoidable image of The Kilns during the late 1940s is one of a rundown and battered old house filled with ageing eccentrics. Maureen had escaped the place in 1940 when she had married, and although she lived close by she visited rarely. Warren, who tried to absorb himself in helping Jack with his correspondence and writing books on French history, was prone to violent mood swings. He would veer from happy sobriety to such extreme states of alcohol abuse that he diced with death. Meanwhile Janie's form of dementia was particularly stressful for the Lewis brothers because it frequently sent her into malevolent moods and she would lash out at those around her. On many occasions she became impossible to talk to, yet she managed to dominate the house and upset everyone with her increasingly wild demands. It is not surprising that Lewis relished so much the writing of his Narnia books.

By the spring of 1950 even Jack had to admit that life at The Kilns was becoming intolerable. As patient and as caring as he had always been with Janie, the time had come for her to be admitted into care, and so she was moved to Restholme, a nursing home close to Oxford. She died there nine months later, in early 1951.

Jack received the news of Janie's death with painful resignation, but also an undeniable element of relief. He had certainly loved Janie, but his love expressed itself in a way no one will ever really understand. As discussed, the nature of their relationship is open to many interpretations and so all conclusions about it can be nothing more than pure speculation, but it is clear that no man could devote the best years of his life to a woman like Janie Moore without loving her deeply, and Jack was totally devoted.

Warnie was clearly relieved by Janie's death and wrote in his diary that his brother's relationship with her had been 'the rape of Jack's life . . . I wonder how much of his time she did waste? It was some years before her breakdown that I calculated that merely taking the dogs for unneeded "little walks" she had had five months of my life.'5

With Janie out of their lives, the two brothers were drawn together more than ever. By 1951 the Inklings was a dying institution, a sad, pale shadow of its glory days, and Lewis was deeply immersed in the world of Narnia. The week Janie died he was close to two-thirds through the fourth book in the collection, *The Silver Chair*, and her passing hardly broke his stride. By slipping into the warm cocoon of his self-created world, Lewis could blot out the real world. In Narnia there were no academic hierarchies beyond his control, no one could disapprove of him. In Narnia the only female demons were ones he could vanquish in the guise of Aslan; Narnia was a world in which young woman philosophers could not destroy his careful arguments and no drunkard brothers could threaten his perfect universe.

Tired and tarnished, weary of the real world and distracted by a fantasy realm entirely of his own creation, Lewis might easily have slipped into a state of isolation and self-contemplation. But, although he did not know it, the seeds of a new life had already been planted. In January 1950, two months before Janie was admitted to a rest home, he had received a letter from an American woman, a fan of his books who wished to begin a correspondence with her hero. Her name was Joy Davidman and she was about to transform his life.

9

Joy

Joy Davidman was Jack Lewis's greatest fan, a literary groupie who tracked down the object of her dreams, won him over and eventually married him.

Until she met Lewis, Joy's luck with men had been limited. She had been born Helen Joy Davidman in 1915 in New York City to Russian-Jewish émigré parents, Joseph and Jeanette. They had been an unhappy, ill-suited couple, not least because Joy's mother still practised Judaism and wished to embrace the American way of life, while her father was a confirmed atheist and active socialist. Joseph Davidman also suffered wild mood swings and an aggressiveness that sometimes spilled into mania. Joy responded by expending a great deal of effort in trying to please him, but her failure to do so precipitated her own neuroses.

One of the obvious outwards signs of the psychological damage Joy's father had caused her was that she found it extremely difficult to talk to people she had only just met. He had produced in her a sense of inadequacy that had become ingrained, and to compensate, she worked hard, performed well, but could not hold what many would consider a normal conversation. She was forever challenging the things others said, trying to win points in a conversation, and although she was an intelligent and eloquent woman she covered her own insecurities with what others perceived as an unattractive brashness bordering on the uncouth. These traits abated once she became comfortable with a person, but it did not make it easy for her to form friendships.

Joy studied English at Hunter College in New York and stayed in the city to take an MA in English Literature at Columbia University, all before her twenty-first birthday. Then, like many young people of her generation, she joined the Communist Party. She began writing for newspapers and journals and her skills were put to good use by the Party. In 1940, still only twenty-five, she had a novel published. *Anya* had developed out of the stories her mother had told her as a child about the times before Jeanette and Joseph had left Russia. On the strength of this book and her journalism she was recruited by MGM in Hollywood as a junior scriptwriter.

Things were going well for Joy, but then she met the man who would become her first husband, a divorcee named Bill Gresham. Bill had tried his hand at everything from journalism to nightclub singing, had volunteered to fight for the Communists in Spain in 1936 and had been in and out of psychiatric hospitals ever since. He was a womanising alcoholic who, between the bar, the gambling den and the brothel, was trying to write the 'Great American Novel'. But he was also charming, urbane and occasionally romantic, and Joy fell for him.

After a whirlwind romance Joy and Bill were married and for a short time at least she seems to have had a sobering influence on him. They lived in a tiny cramped apartment on East 22nd Street and had two children in quick succession. Their first, David, was born in 1944, followed a little over a year later by Douglas. Bill was working hard at writing and in 1944 he had a thriller called *Nightmare Alley* published which was snapped up by Hollywood for the then astronomical sum of $60,000 and made into a film starring Tyrone Power. This gave the family the means to move out of New York into the suburban idyll of Pleasant Plains.

But before long Bill Gresham had squandered the money and Joy discovered he had slid back into womanising and drinking. Soon she began to fear for the safety of her sons because sometimes when Bill got drunk he would become violent and unstable, firing pistols into the ceiling and throwing whisky bottles across the living room.

Then, in 1947, Bill suddenly walked out. Joy could not reach him anywhere and he left no word, not a letter, not a phone call. Although Joy had been in despair over the state of their marriage and hated her husband's behaviour, this latest turn of events threw her into a deep depression. It was then, she recalled years later, that God came into her life.

The similarities between Joy's conversion and Jack Lewis's are striking, and they tell a familiar story. God came to Joy in her moment of need, just as He had come into Jack's life soon after Albert died, when Jack was floundering around in intellectual and emotional confusion. As it had for Jack, Joy's 'awakening' was to become a pivotal moment in her life. Eventually it helped her to escape the dire situation she was in with Bill Gresham, led her to Jack and gave her life substance and meaning.

For a short time it even appeared that her discovery of God might help her patch up her marriage. A few months after her conversion Joy was reunited with Bill, who simply turned up one day at their home. Through her faith Joy even succeeded in bringing about a temporary change in her husband, so that by the end of 1948 Bill was apparently a Christian himself, praying with Joy for his salvation from the demon drink and the devil women he had pursued.

After a few years of piety and reform Bill reverted to his old habits. But, thanks to her devotion to Christ, Joy had by this time found other aspects to her life. She had met a preacher named Father Victor White while he was on a lecture tour of the United States. Joy was immediately drawn to his ideas and through his talks she was introduced to the work of C. S. Lewis, who had been an inspiration to the priest. After one of the lectures Joy plucked up the courage to approach White and to ask for his advice. How, she wanted to know, could she contact this writer Lewis?

Father White simply suggested she write to the great man in Oxford and reassured her that, as far as he knew, Lewis always answered sincere letters from readers. Thus began a correspondence which lasted for two and a half years before Jack and Joy actually met. The first letter Joy sent was received with delight by Jack and Warnie, who were amused by her alacrity and acute sense of irony – something the brothers had, until then, believed missing from the personality of all Americans.

For Joy the exchange of letters with Jack immediately became an inspiration, something that very soon developed into being the focus of her life. She could not wait for his letters to arrive from England and wrote back with great care and a growing sense that she had found in him a soulmate. To a friend she confided that she had already mentally 'married' Jack some time before she met him in the flesh, and it is clear that even in those heady days she had set her sights on somehow making him hers.

In her own mind at least, this was a magical time for Joy. Her correspondence with the world-famous Christian writer, a man whose views chimed with her own so perfectly and who wrote such witty, intellectually challenging letters to her, was, after her love for her sons, the most important thing in her life. But as this aspect of her existence grew more significant, her everyday, real-life problems were beginning to grow steadily worse. By the summer of 1952 she had resolved to do something about it. A cousin, Renée Pierce, who had recently separated from her own drunken, no-good husband, volunteered to move to New York to watch over the boys and to look after the home, allowing Joy to travel alone to England in search of Lewis.

Jack was naturally wary of Joy and, of course, Joy was intelligent enough to know that she had to feign detachment and not overwhelm her hero. She arrived in Oxford in September 1952, she and Jack having arranged in advance to meet for lunch at one of his favourite pubs, the Eastgate Hotel, across The High from his college. However, it is clear from this first meeting that Lewis was suspicious of Joy's intentions because he tried to persuade Warnie to act as a 'chaperone' for the afternoon. When his brother refused, Lewis was obliged to turn to a former student whom he trusted, George Sayer, who accompanied him to the engagement.

According to Sayer, the lunch went splendidly and Jack and Joy hit it off immediately. From their first minutes together Jack adored Joy's razor-sharp manner and her ability to slice through the small talk and get to the heart of a topic. It is easy to see why he would be drawn to such a woman. He liked nothing better than debate, which Joy also relished. Like her, he had a habit of assaulting people in conversation and had no time for pettiness or chit-chat. Joy took this further, to the point of bluntness, even rudeness at times. Her language was often coarse, especially to the delicate ears of dons' wives, and she only escaped being ostracised completely by the Oxford crowd because she was intelligent, knowledgeable, well read and, most importantly, a friend of C. S. Lewis.

Warnie summed it up well in his diary some time after the day he first met Joy Davidman. 'I was a little time in making up my mind about her,' he recalled. 'She proved to be a Jewess, or rather a Christian convert of Jewish race, medium height, good figure, horn rimmed specs, quite extraordinarily uninhibited. Our first meeting was at lunch in Magdalen, where she turned to me in the presence of three or four other men, and asked in the most natural tone in the world, "Is there anywhere in this monastic establishment where a lady can relieve herself?"'[1]

Joy was considerably younger than Jack, but she was not at all physically attractive, and this helped him. She made him laugh, which was a quality in others that always attracted him deeply, and she was the sort of American who genuinely did not much care for America. This appealed to the strong anti-American bias Lewis had nurtured since his youth. Joy hated big cities and loved country walking, she was scathing of Hollywood and American literature and loved everything English. Most crucially, she was a Christian and a genuinely devout one too. Furthermore, she was the type of Christian who shared many of Lewis's ideas and in many areas of doctrine and belief she had taken his position as a personal cue.

Ideologically, they were twins and after that first lunch Joy was totally convinced of her mission.

Lewis it seems was also rather interested in this woman, but he certainly did not take her as seriously as she took him. They continued to meet sporadically during Joy's visit to England and they talked about her personal problems, the situation with her husband at home and how she should deal with him and protect her sons. It all amounted to good Christian advice from Jack, offered by a master to an acolyte, and at this time at least, he felt no sense of emotional bonding, even if Joy's feelings were silently, secretly overbrimming.

Shortly before Christmas 1952 Joy returned to America, only to find that her husband was now having a physical relationship with her cousin Renée. This perhaps came as little surprise to Joy because for many years she had been aware of what sort of man Bill was. It is even possible that she had deliberately engineered the arrangement. By the time she left for England she had almost certainly decided that her marriage was over and she understood both her husband's weaknesses and her cousin's predicament. Once she was home, it became simply a question of how she could contain the mess.

By November the following year Joy had managed to arrange everything. She had secured legal custody of the boys and set up financial support from their father. Renée returned to Florida to file for divorce and Joy purchased three air tickets to London, one for her, one for David and one for Douglas. The Gresham marriage was effectively over and Joy was about to embark on her greatest adventure.

Back in England again, Joy was naturally keen to avoid raising any suspicions and she had made it as clear as possible to Jack that she was returning with her sons because her marriage had ended. She needed a change of scene, she disliked life in America, she adored England and she believed that the boys would be happier there. But Jack was not so innocent as to believe this was the entire picture. He may have lived the life of a pseudo-bachelor for many years, but he was also aware of his own attractiveness to a certain type of woman. He had even had a stalker. Over a period of a few months a slightly deranged woman had written him a stream of increasingly unhinged letters. Eventually he had given up replying and when the letters kept coming he stopped even opening them (he could always identify letters as hers because the envelopes were covered in tiny writing in red ink). This reaction seems to have made the poor woman worse. Soon after Lewis cut communication with her he was astonished to see an announcement she had put in the newspaper declaring that they had secretly married. The following day his stalker turned up at The Kilns. Lewis was out and the woman was taken away by the police. This had made Jack understandably suspicious of gold-diggers and deranged fans, and so for some time after Joy's return to England he did his best to avoid her as much as possible.

Nevertheless, they continued to correspond. Joy was living with her sons at a friend's house in London and the family visited Oxford occasionally. Joy and Lewis would sometimes meet for lunch or a drink and he even politely invited her to appropriate college functions. But it is clear that, at this time at least, Joy was driving the relationship and Jack was definitely taking a back seat. This is clear from anecdotes that may have been exaggerated by some of Lewis's friends who had taken an instant dislike to Joy. The best of these, and one that can be easily imagined, was the claim that on more than one occasion Joy had turned up unannounced at The Kilns, to be told by the housekeeper that Jack was out when really he was hiding in an upstairs room, peeking through a crack in the curtains and waiting for her to go.

But Joy was no mad stalker, and although he was slightly wary, Jack clearly began to develop a genuine interest in her. What held him back was the simple fear of allowing himself to slide into a relationship. He obviously found this blunt, intense, earnest and very bright American woman attractive, but what could possibly be gained from getting involved with her? She was still married, and, even ignoring the social stigma of beginning a relationship with a married woman, his religious convictions did not allow him to enjoy a romantic liaison out of wedlock, nor, looking a long way ahead, would they permit him to ever marry a divorcee. Following things through logically, he could see no point in allowing anything to develop. But then, when it came down to it, Lewis couldn't help himself.

In some ways their growing closer was inevitable. Joy was a determined and clever woman who had a genuine desire and love for Lewis. Jack was a lonely man who had no emotional outlet other than his writing and perhaps his intimacy with Warnie. Furthermore, he was the sort of character who liked to rebel a little. Knowing that many of his friends disliked Joy and aware that some were even concerned for him, he deliberately did the opposite of what they wanted.

But even when he had reached this conclusion, Jack played hard to get. He invited Joy and the boys to spend Christmas with him and Warnie at The Kilns in December 1953 and he grew to like the boys, but still he maintained his distance, rarely allowing Joy to spend time alone with him and only asking her to functions to which other female friends had also been invited.

At this time Lewis was also distracted by events in the academic world. In 1951 the Chair of Poetry at Oxford had again become vacant. This was the Chair fought for by the Inklings in 1938, to which they had succeeded in getting Adam Fox elected. Fox's tenure had been a great disappointment but he had been followed by an even poorer professor, Maurice Bowra, who, although renowned as something of a wit within his donnish coterie, was an appallingly bad lecturer. By 1951 the Oxford dons responsible for choosing their Professor of Poetry wanted to elect someone who would prove a little more colourful, a real poet, who could add a certain vitality to the position.

Lewis would have been the ideal man for the job. He was a respected writer, a very good academic and a lively, engaging lecturer. However, his enemies had not gone away and they ensured that his rival, a solid, conventional academic named Cecil Day-Lewis, was elected instead.

It appears that Jack was less bothered by this second failure to secure a professorship than were his followers and friends. It is likely that he did not really want the position but had gone along with the election effort because his closest associates thought he should. In typical style he quickly put the rejection behind him, and by 1954, when Joy and her sons were settled in England, he was considering an altogether more tantalising and exciting proposition.

In the summer of that year some of Jack's Cambridge friends succeeded in creating a new Chair and Fellowship at Magdalene College, Cambridge, for a specialist in the literature of the medieval and Renaissance periods. This post was, of course, deliberately designed with Lewis in mind. Not only had he concentrated on this area of literature throughout his thirty-odd years at Oxford, but a few months earlier he had delivered to Oxford University Press his most important (and longest) academic book, a 700-page opus entitled *English Literature in the Sixteenth Century Excluding Drama*. Published in September 1954, this was part of a series called *The Oxford History of English Literature*. In moments of exasperation Lewis referred to the latter as 'OHEL'.

Jack was greatly honoured by the invitation, but he was also quite thrown by it. He had lived in Oxford all his adult life and was not the sort of person who could uproot himself very easily. During the war he had found travelling to London to give his BBC broadcasts hard going, and he had never dreamed he would ever leave the college he had worked in for almost three decades. There was also Warnie to worry about. Jack was only too aware of the mess his brother was in. He knew the man was a baby who could no more look after himself than he could have done when he was ten years old. In trying to find a solution to this problem, Jack briefly considered the idea of selling The Kilns and buying a house with Warnie in Cambridge, but, apart from the financial considerations of this drastic move, he could not face the idea of cutting all his ties with the city he had lived in and loved for so long.

But, equally, the offer was too good to let pass, so the problems it brought simply had to be resolved satisfactorily. Jack and Warnie eventually worked out that Jack should spend his weekdays in Cambridge, arriving there late on Monday and leaving for Oxford early on Friday afternoon. In that way he could spend all weekend and most of Monday with his brother. There were also changes in the way the house was looked after. A new housekeeper, Mrs Miller, was employed, while the faithful Fred Paxford took on a greater role in running things, helping out with shopping and cleaning and soon proving himself to be an accomplished cook.

Jack gave his inaugural lecture at Cambridge to a packed theatre on 29 November 1954. It was entitled 'De Descriptione Temporum' and dealt with the idea that there was a massive culture schism dividing the time of Jane Austen and the mid-twentieth century. The lecture was a brilliant piece of oratory and a carefully formulated argument, but it was also a perfect example of Lewis's habit of kicking against all the things he disliked, especially science and the advancement of technology. For him the old world was infinitely superior to the new, and science was a vehicle for cultural regression rather than advance.

The audience gave Jack a rare standing ovation, but reading the transcript of the lecture today there is no denying that, for all his cleverness, wit and inventiveness, he had by this time slid inexorably into the cronyism he had only just avoided by great effort throughout his life.

Lewis's arguments were those of a man who knew nothing of technology, a man who had no suspicion of the poetry and beauty of science. He had no realisation at all that physics and its offspring, technology, grew from minds every bit as creative as those of the poet or the painter. Furthermore, he had no inkling that science engenders creativity, that it nurtures inventiveness. These were concepts Lewis never wished to grasp, and because of this failing he became fixed in the mould of a highly educated, marvellously talented and expressive individual who could nonetheless only ever understand and appreciate one aspect of human genius.

When it came close to the time for Lewis to take up his new

position as Professor of English Literature at Cambridge, he rather dreaded the thought. He suddenly began to fret about leaving Oxford and felt uncomfortable with the thought that he would have to get used to new routines and a quite different lifestyle. In addition, he was unsure what exactly was expected of him, and although he was pleased that he would never again have to sit in tutorials listening to mediocre essays, part of him believed that at fifty-six he was too old for such a change.

He had been given a set of rooms in Cambridge that were very well appointed but rather stark compared with those in which he had worked for so long in Oxford. Friends in Cambridge helped out with offers of a few creature comforts, but they hardly needed to worry, for Jack was never one to care much about his surroundings. If it had not been for the charity of his friends, he would have settled into his rooms quite happily with only the desk, rug, two chairs and bed that were there already.

This monastic approach had long been a characteristic of the man. As a student he had paid some attention to the place in which he worked, but this had in part come from a wish to settle into college life and be accepted by his contemporaries. Under Janie Moore's influence he had tried to take some pride in his home, but after her death The Kilns had fallen into disarray and was considered dirty and rundown by most visitors who spent any time there. One guest of the Lewises, a young academic named Helen Gardner, who visited the house in the early 1950s, was shocked to find that there was not a single ornament or picture to admire and that the furniture was falling apart. In the same way, although Lewis's rooms in Oxford were always kept clean thanks to long-suffering college servants, his papers were often deposited in piles around the floor, his furniture had not been replaced since 1925 and his desk was a battlefield of paper.

It would be nice to imagine that in January 1955 Lewis was particularly uninterested in his environment because he was deep in thought, lost in plots for future books or mulling over his next academic venture. But this was not the case at all. For the first time in

anecdote —
Bereft —

his life he was at a loss for ideas for any new books or projects, and as a result he was sliding into depression. This mood was exacerbated by the fact that he was alone most of the week and did not even have his brother for company. It was perhaps inevitable that Joy would move in to fill the void.

Joy visited Jack in Cambridge and again at weekends, when he was back at The Kilns. Learning very quickly the source of his sadness, she offered something he had never before sought and had little idea how to respond to. She realised that there were many more ideas for Jack to follow up and that he merely needed coaxing. It was from this gentle guidance that he formulated the central premise of his next book, *Till We Have Faces*.

The novel was a development of the ancient story of Cupid and Psyche, first recorded in *The Golden Ass*, written by the poet Apuleius in the second century AD. It is a tale of love, loss and ego, a quest to find a perfect intellectual love. Jack always considered *Till We Have Faces* to be the most important piece of fiction he had ever written and he cherished it above all his other published works. However, when the book appeared in 1955 it confused his regular readers and confounded the critics so thoroughly that it was to be his least successful fictional work, now largely forgotten by all but devotees.

Till We Have Faces may have been a commercial and critical failure but Joy played a major role in its gestation and it was this collaboration that truly cemented their relationship. This is clear from the fact that by the summer of 1955, as the novel was reaching completion, she felt confident enough to make the move from London to Oxford, and with her sons in tow, she rented a house at 10 Old High Street, Headington, less than a mile from The Kilns.

It was soon after this that Jack completed his autobiography. *Surprised by Joy* is a book rich in anecdote and opinion but almost totally bereft of real personal detail. The subtitle is 'The Shape of My Early Life' and that is what it is, a mere outline. We learn of the schools Lewis attended and his feelings about his teachers and the rites of learning. We discover the influences on his intellect and the literature and art that moved and moulded him. But any reader who wishes to find more than clues to Lewis's feelings towards others will come away disappointed. Although the description of his mother's death and the days that followed are rendered with painful brilliance, his recollections of his father are both cruel and one-sided. Furthermore, Lewis tells us precious little about his feelings towards anyone else. We glean almost nothing about his relationship with Warnie, and, staggeringly, there is almost no mention of Janie; nor are there more than a few vague pages about Jack's role in the First World War.

For many people these glaring omissions make *Surprised by Joy* an almost meaningless book, but there are precise reasons why Lewis made it so. Although a man who found it difficult to express emotion, he could write with enormous honesty about his deepest drives just so long as they were disguised by fiction. Using this device he could express both his pain and his sense of joy. In attempting to tell the story of his early life in a straightforward autobiographical style, all he could manage was a desiccated tale from which the great Lewis voice was absent, the narrative bloodless.

But in writing the book Jack had also to contend with Joy's feelings. By the time he was reworking the final draft she was already looking over his shoulder and sharing every word with him. As a consequence, he could not have written the plain truth about his relationship with Janie, his earliest sexual feelings or his most personal drives and motivations even if he had been able to overcome his own deep-rooted inhibitions.

To compound this emotional constipation and Joy's censorial presence there was another self-imposed pressure that led him to write such an antiseptic account. By 1955 C. S. Lewis was a name synonymous with religiosity and strict Christian morals, which meant he could not write a book in which he revealed anything about his intimate life with Janie. We must also bear in mind that 1950s British society was not ready for emotional or sexual honesty. Any truthful revelation in such a book would have ruined Lewis's profile as a Christian apologist and greatly embarrassed his friends. It might even have damaged his image as a serious scholar.

One area in which *Surprised by Joy* is strong and intimate is the sections in which Lewis deals with his conversion to Christianity. These give the book greater appeal as they go some way towards explaining the source and inspiration for Lewis's creativity and the driving force behind almost all of his writing from the early 1930s onwards. Because of this, the book was generally well received and reviewed extensively.

Ironically, if it had been published a year or two earlier, it would have been yet another nail in the coffin of Lewis's reputation at Oxford because, for the stony-faced academics who despised Lewis, it was far too honest and eloquent about his religious awakening. This may go some way to explaining his delay in getting round to writing the book, for by 1955 Lewis was far beyond the reach of prejudiced Oxford dons.

Soon Joy and Jack were pretty much inseparable. Jack paid the rent on Joy's house and took over her sons' school fees as these had become a serious drain on their mother's meagre resources. From the summer of 1955 Jack and Joy saw each other almost every day and Jack now rarely appeared at social functions and gatherings without his American 'friend' beside him.

Lewis's Oxford friends were split into two camps by this new situation. Some, like his ex-pupil George Sayer, embraced the relationship, and his wife, Moira, liked Joy. Warnie had also grown used to her. Indeed he had discovered to his delight that she knew a surprising amount about French history, his own specialist subject, and this did much to foster their relationship.

Others were far from impressed with the new woman in Jack's life. Tolkien, whose friendship with Jack was, by the 1950s, a pale shadow of its former self, did not like Joy at all. He was strongly anti-American, and like Jack, was inclined towards misogyny. He disliked Joy's bluntness and considered her rude and uncouth, but beyond this he was deeply suspicious of her. He was also jealous, although he disguised this with his (admittedly genuine) belief that Jack was wrong to get involved with a divorcee.

Ironically, Tolkien's wife, Edith, was rather taken with Joy and the two women became good friends. By contrast, Jack had barely exchanged two words with Edith during the three decades he had known her. Whenever he had visited Tolkien at home in Northmoor Road, north Oxford, he and Edith both felt uncomfortable and their conversation never went beyond mumbled greetings. Tolkien was aware of this, of course, and in the early days of the Inklings Edith's often barbed opinions about his friend did little to encourage domestic bliss. For her part, Edith had been quite miserable for most of her married life. She did not get along well with most of the other dons' wives and felt intellectually inferior to them. With Joy Gresham she could relax and she did not have to battle against the snobbery and scarcely concealed elitism of the wives living close by.

The four-way relationship between Edith and Ronald Tolkien, Joy Davidman and Lewis must have made for an interesting social dynamic during the early 1950s. Tolkien disliked Joy and at best displayed a rather patronising gentlemanly reserve in her presence. Edith relished Joy's company but clammed up with Lewis. Jack and Tolkien were no longer intimates and there was a growing undercurrent of resentment between them. Meanwhile Jack and Joy were growing closer by the day.

Within two years of Joy's return to England, Jack no longer cared what some of his friends thought, for he knew he was falling in love with her. Far more of a problem was the conflict this love created for him, a conflict between his emotions and his religious convictions. He knew that he could neither marry Joy nor have her live at The Kilns without their being married, and this presented him with what he was beginning to suspect was an insoluble dilemma. If it had not been for fortuitous timing, this dilemma could have developed into a genuine emotional crisis for Jack.

Early in 1956 Joy had applied for a renewal of her visa so that she and her sons could remain in Britain, but the Home Office turned her down. It soon became clear that the only way she could stay in the country was to marry an Englishman. Loath to tell Lewis or to put any pressure on him, she kept this news to herself for some time. It was only as her deadline for leaving the country grew close that she concluded that she had to break the news.

Lewis had also been struggling in silence, trying to resolve the conundrum created by his feelings for Joy. In letters to Arthur Greeves he had been weighing up the matter and had tried to resolve the problem, but he kept hitting a brick wall. Canon law was very clear on the matter. In the view of the Christian Church, divorce was a false concept of man's making and it did not really dissolve a marriage, so Joy could never be free of Bill Gresham while he was alive. Consequently, no clergyman in England would sanctify a marriage involving a divorcee, and the only form of service possible in such cases was a civil marriage, which Lewis could not recognise as genuine before God.

However, Lewis had to act. On 23 April 1956 he and Joy were married in a civil service at Oxford Registry Office in St Giles, close to the Eagle and Child. It was an extremely quiet affair with only two friends in attendance as witnesses, Jack's doctor and old drinking partner Robert Havard and Father Austin Farrer, a brilliant Oxford theologian whom Lewis had known for many years. At the time no announcement of the wedding was made in the press and almost no one in Lewis's circle of friends even knew that it had taken place. It was not until the couple finally put a notice in *The Times* on Christmas Eve 1956, eight months after the event, that many of Jack's closest friends knew he had married.

For Tolkien, Lewis's decision was a crucial act that hastened the degeneration of their friendship. He had been upset that he had not even been told of the wedding and only learned about it from the newspaper, but at the heart of the matter he was far more disturbed by the religious consequences of Lewis's actions. To an orthodox Catholic like Tolkien, Jack had committed a grave sin. Therefore he felt it his religious duty, as well as his responsibility as a friend, to pretend that the marriage had not taken place at all and to shun both Jack and Joy. For men with the sort of convictions Tolkien held, when it came to God's law there could be no bending the rules.

For the first six months of this new relationship both Jack and Joy were happy. Jack still did not consider them to be married in the strictest sense because they had only shared a civil ceremony; and because of this he insisted that Joy should continue to live in the rented house in Headington with David and Douglas. But then, as the summer of 1956 dissolved into autumn, a new personal crisis was poised to shatter the couple's temporary idyll.

During September 1956 Joy had begun to suffer from sharp pains in her legs and was feeling unusually tired. She had told Jack of her symptoms and they had both concluded it was probably a touch of rheumatism and simply hoped the problem would go away. When Jack started back for the new university term at the beginning of October he could have had no idea that something was about to transform his and Joy's life.

After suffering for weeks and with the pain in her legs growing much worse, Joy consulted a doctor. By the following day she was an outpatient at the Wingfield Morris Orthopaedic Hospital in Oxford, undergoing a series of investigatory X-rays and tests. Before the week was out she had learned the dread news. She had cancer in her left thigh and her femur had broken. She also had a malignant tumour in her left breast and other lumps in her right leg and shoulder.

Jack was poleaxed. It seemed that, just at the moment he had achieved some sort of personal happiness, his world was unravelling. Throughout the winter of 1956 and into the spring of 1957 Joy underwent a succession of operations to remove the tumours and was started on the primitive treatments then available to halt the progress of the disease. She escaped a full mastectomy, the surgeons managing to remove the lump in her breast with as little invasion as possible, but she had a section of her left femur removed and both ovaries taken out.

The fact that the cancer had spread from its source in her thigh was a bad sign and the doctors were not optimistic. The only thing they could do was wait and see how the operations and therapy had helped. But by February 1957 tests showed that Joy's condition was steadily growing worse.

This shattering blow only intensified Jack's feelings for Joy. 'Never have I loved her more than since she was struck down,' he told Arthur Greeves.[2] And, crucially, it made him wonder again about the complex issue of his marriage to Joy. With her condition degenerating by the day, Jack was forced to wrestle with the conflicting forces of his faith, the rules of the Church and his love for the woman he had taken as his wife in civil law. He was struggling to find a let-out clause, an argument by which he could have the marriage solemnised without breaking the canon law that meant so much to him and on which he had structured his life and his career as a writer. After talking to his closest confidants, Arthur Greeves and Robert Havard, and finally finding himself with too much conflicting advice and too many imponderables, Jack simply took some personal choices, assumed an intellectual position on matters he believed nebulous and acted on them.

The argument that led Jack to organise a blessing for his marriage to Joy ran as follows. The Church claimed that a marriage is not ended by divorce and that a divorcee who remarries before their spouse dies is committing adultery and bigamy and putting their immortal soul at risk. Jack argued, however, that Bill Gresham, who had married Joy in a civil ceremony, had already been married and divorced once before. Therefore his marriage to Joy was not a proper marriage at all. This meant that he and Joy were not committing adultery because, according to Church law, Joy had not been married in the first place. The Church, Jack declared, could not have it both ways.

In March 1957 Joy's doctors gave her a terrifying prognosis. In their opinion she had, at best, a matter of weeks to live. Hearing this, Jack approached a trusted friend, a priest named Peter Bide, who agreed with his analysis of the situation and offered to perform a service to sanctify the marriage.

Jack, Bide and Warren gathered around Joy's hospital bed at 11 a.m. on 21 March. Father Bide conducted a mass and gave Holy Communion before solemnising the marriage. Warren wrote afterwards: 'To feel pity for anyone so magnificently brave as Joy is almost an insult.'[3] The service was a dramatic scene filled with pathos, but Jack and Joy also saw it as a celebration.

Joy's son Douglas sounded rather hyperbolic when he wrote many years later: 'There were never two people alive in the history of the world more in love than Jack and Joy.'[4] Even so, it is obvious that the couple were deeply committed and adored each other, and that their love was deep, true and clear to all who knew them.

But it seems the doctors had misjudged the situation. Joy was not to die so soon as predicted. Indeed, almost immediately after the marriage service her condition began to improve noticeably. The doctors were amazed by this sudden change and Jack was naturally guarded about how genuine it might be, but could not help feeling excited and hopeful.

By April, Joy was able to leave hospital and to move into The Kilns. A few weeks later she was making her way slowly around the house using a walking frame, and by the end of the year she could walk several hundred yards without collapsing.

Jack naturally perceived this to be a miracle in action, but there was a strange twist to the story of Joy's recovery. Lewis was a believer in the theory of substitution. He was convinced that if he prayed intensely enough he could take on Joy's pain and that she would be relieved of it by an equivalent amount. And Jack prayed very hard. By the summer of 1957, as Joy was regaining her health, Jack was falling ill. This apparent transference of symptoms eventually eased off towards the end of the year as Joy's condition plateaued.

Much has been written about the so-called miracle of substitution experienced by Jack and Joy, but it has almost always come from Jack's devout Christian followers. It is therefore not surprising that many of these people have written unquestioning accounts of the process. In his biography of Lewis, George Sayer wrote: 'Joy lived to enjoy three years and four months of married life with Jack. Although they were often both in great physical pain, it was the happiest period of their lives. Prayer made this possible. Prayer and sacrifice.'[5] And years after the experience Jack unquestioningly declared: 'The intriguing thing was that while I (for no discernible reason) was losing the calcium from my bones, Joy, who needed it much more, was gaining it in hers.'[6] But, from an objective standpoint, it is easy to see that divine intervention might not qualify as the best explanation.

Jack, we must remember, was under immense stress. Only a short time earlier he had taken up a new position at Cambridge which had forced him into a change of lifestyle that had left him unsettled. Naturally, he had been terribly shaken by Joy's sudden illness, and by the late 1950s his writing career was all but over, his latest novel an abject failure. He no longer had great, original ideas demanding to be put on to paper, nor did he have the energy to write anything that might compare with the Narnia books, *The Screwtape Letters* or *That Hideous Strength*. Most importantly, he was facing up to the fact that the woman he loved was still gravely ill and might die at any time. He must surely have been feeling sick and exhausted at this time.

Beyond this there is another factor to consider. In marrying Joy and having their relationship sanctified by Father Bide, Jack had succeeded in battering his way through the situation using purely intellectual weapons. Deep down, the guilt of the pious raged on, for although he had convinced himself and his friend the priest that the Church could not have things both ways, a part of him was still not convinced that he had done the right thing. A nagging doubt remained that, as Tolkien would have it, he had committed a terrible sin.

In such circumstances guilt can be a powerful force and can make the mind play tricks on itself. By praying to take on Joy's pain, Lewis was in fact trying to ease his own guilt by allowing himself to be punished. Indeed he was *asking* God to punish him, for in so doing he believed he could relieve Joy of her own agonies.

Whatever the cause, Joy really did feel better. For more than two and a half years she remained in remission and she and Jack entered the happiest period of their lives. This was a time during which they could live as husband and wife. Lewis no longer needed to hide his feelings and he did not care what anyone thought of their relationship.

Once Joy was more or less well again, they decided, they would live life to the full, enjoy the time they had left and spend as much of it together as they could.

Joy relished the role of wife again and the atmosphere at The Kilns could not have been more different to when Janie was growing senile. Joy and Warnie got on well and such domestic bliss even encouraged Jack to return to writing. The house itself seemed to take on a new lease of life after Joy called in decorators, replaced the old decaying curtains with new brightly patterned ones, swept away the cobwebs and spruced up the garden with flowers alongside the vegetables.

They enjoyed a sex life too. In typical style, Jack consulted his friend Robert Havard, asking him if it would be safe for a man of his age and a woman in Joy's condition to make love. Havard told him it would be fine so long as neither of them overexerted themselves. Not surprisingly, this invigorated both of them and led Joy to declare, in her own inimitable style, to a journalist that Jack was 'a wonderful lover' and that she was so glad she had not had a mastectomy because he was so fond of caressing her breasts.[7]

The couple also enjoyed a full social life together. They had many friends, although by marrying they had alienated the doubters and the objectors. They even took a trip abroad, a ten-day holiday in Greece, where, by all accounts, they had a wonderful but exhausting time exploring ruins and museums with friends Roger Lancelyn Green and his wife June.

For Lewis, married life brought enormous changes. Although he still worked as an academic, he was now a married academic. Once he had relished bachelor life, enjoying the intimacy of male friendship, drinking until closing time and staying up until the small hours discussing weighty matters; now he had become domesticated, his life dominated by his wife and other couples. Given the choice he certainly would not have changed a thing, but, initially at least, it was a difficult adjustment to make.

Joy's remission may have seemed the stuff of fantasies, but there could be no fairy-tale ending. In October 1959 Jack accompanied her to the Churchill Hospital in Oxford for what was scheduled to be her final check-up before getting what they both expected to be the all-clear from her doctors. The couple were in high spirits and filled with hope and optimism. All of which made the news that day even more devastating. The cancer, they learned, had returned more aggressively than before and the disease had again metastasised.

As before, operation followed operation and Joy was treated with the latest drug therapies, but she soon entered what would this time be a slow and irreversible decline that sapped the life from her. The end came on 13 July 1960. Warren was woken at 6.15 a.m. by the sound of screaming coming from Joy's room. In his room at the other end of the house, Jack was roused and a doctor called. Joy was taken to the Radcliffe Infirmary, where, with Jack beside her, she died at around 10.15 that night.

Close to the end, Jack said to her: 'If you can − if it is allowed − come to me when I too am on my death bed.' 'Allowed!' she exclaimed. 'Heaven would have a job to hold me; and as for hell, I'd break it into bits.'[8]

10

Life Without Joy

Nothing since the death of his mother had affected Lewis so intensely as the loss of his wife. The end of Joy's life had been a slow, painful degeneration, expected and even partially prepared for, but this did nothing to ease the agony. Douglas Gresham expressed this well when he wrote in his autobiography published many years later: 'Jack was never again the man he had been before Mother's death. Joy had left him and also, it seemed, had joy.'[1] And Jack now entered a period of decline which left him a sad and often lonely man in whom the light of creativity and intellectual fervour was fading fast.

Douglas, fourteen at the time of Joy's death, had been aware the end was close during the closing weeks of his mother's life, but he had been sent back to his boarding school, Lapley Grange in Wales, a few days before she died. Learning of Joy's death from the kindly headmaster's wife, Mrs Cross, he was immediately driven back to The Kilns to attend the funeral on 18 July.

He found Jack in a truly pitiful state. Quite out of character, his stepfather burst into tears as Douglas entered his study and the two of them hugged, sobbing into each other's shoulder. It was the first time Lewis had shown either of his stepchildren any sign of physical affection and it had the effect of drawing Douglas closer to the man he had respected and loved from a distance. Joy's older son, David, had always been a more distant figure, and by all accounts he remained detached even after his mother's death. In 1960 he was a pupil at Magdalen College School in Oxford and had begun a life-long fascination with Judaism. Two years later, in April 1962, he left The Kilns to study in London.

Joy's death brought about a massive change in Lewis's outward persona. Throughout his life he had been unable to let his emotions show and had bottled everything up. This completely altered after his wife's death. Suddenly he could not help displaying his emotional side. He was distraught and he did not care any more if his friends saw it. On many occasions he broke down in tears while in the company of the other Inklings or after having a few glasses of wine at a friend's home.

Even more profound was the possibility that his loss might totally destroy his belief in God. From Lewis's writing during the period immediately after Joy's death, it is clear that his faith did indeed waver. 'Go to him when your need is most desperate, when all help is vain,' he wrote. 'And what do you find? A door slammed in your face and a sound of bolting and double bolting on the inside. After that, silence.'[2] But now he needed God more than ever, and his Christianity was so deeply ground into his very being that he could not part from it. Furthermore, Lewis was no ordinary Christian. He had founded his entire career on the faith he had acquired during the 1930s, a faith he had carefully nurtured for some three decades. This need to believe must have helped him through the most desperate times.

But if Jack did not give up on God entirely, he at least altered his perception of the divine. He continued to see God as a force that had created the world and guided it still; but whereas he had once seen God as actively 'good', after Joy's death this vision changed dramatically. From 1960, Jack could only conceive of a deity who deliberately set up problems and traumas for humans to overcome, almost as a parlour game. Man's lot, he now believed, was to endure, and God could not be relied on to help you out of a scrape. 'My idea of God is not a divine idea,' he declared a year after Joy died. 'It has to be shattered time after time. He shatters it Himself. He is the great iconoclast. Could we not say that this shattering is one of the marks of His presence?'[3]

And as Jack struggled with his emotions and tried to find a way through his grief, his brother dealt with the trauma in the only fashion he knew how: he drank. Warren was almost no help to Jack in his time of need, and just as he had always done and always would do until his own death in 1973, he simply drowned his pain in whisky. Jack would have had ample justification to feel resentful of this if he had been able to find the emotional energy, but he had other things on his mind. Even so, Warren's escapism did pour salt into the gaping wound in his brother's heart. Given the job of announcing Joy's death, he placed a notice in the newspaper he habitually bought, the *Daily Telegraph*, but forgot to also put it in *The Times*, the paper read by most of their friends. As a result, very few of those who had known Joy were even aware that she had died until it was too late, and so only a handful of mourners appeared at the funeral at the Oxford Crematorium. This hurt Jack deeply and it was not until hours after the service and the few mourners had gone that he learned the truth of what had happened.

The Kilns very quickly reverted to the rather dingy place it had been between Janie's demise and Joy's arrival. The two increasingly eccentric brothers lived there in hermit-like isolation, the one trying desperately to overcome his grief, the other in an alcoholic haze. Douglas spent the school holidays at The Kilns and grew closer to Lewis than he had ever done before his mother's death. To a degree both of them managed to overcome their public-school reserve and an inability to express emotion drilled into them through years of indoctrination.

The Lewis brothers continued to be looked after by the same servants who had worked for them for many years. Fred Paxford tended the gardens and did his best to maintain the property, and the cook-cum-housekeeper, Mrs Miller, was provided with an assistant, Mrs Wilkins, who was not much liked by any of the men in the house and quickly acquired the nickname 'the Wilk'.

The pain Lewis felt during the first months after Joy's death had, at some point, to be faced or else he was in danger of sinking into self-absorption and despair. A large part of him knew he was sinking, but he had no clear idea how to deal with the agony of loss. Lewis was learning, very late in life, that the intellect could not always be relied on to solve a dilemma. This realisation itself initially added another layer to his pain, for he was a man who had built his universe around his mind. Even his Christian faith had been intellectualised, a thing dissected and explained to his audience using the tools that had always sustained him, ink and paper. And although he came to realise that mere intellect could not save him now, it was to his most cherished cerebral activity, writing, that he turned in order to search for a road that might lead him to some form of emotional stability.

He began to write as a form of catharsis, but was soon finding his way into a project that drew from him a level of genuine commitment he had not felt for a long time, and with this came a new, raw energy that ultimately produced one of his most honest and beautiful books.

A Grief Observed was written during the depths of Lewis's personal tragedy, but because he possessed a special talent for always being able to communicate with the reader, what went on to the page was not a mawkish, prurient piece of literature but a work that was appreciated by anyone who was suffering the agony of grief. It was also a very personal book, with Joy as the central 'character' around whom Lewis could explain his feelings. In *A Grief Observed*, Jack managed to strip Joy's personality back to its primal essence. He could call her 'rather a battle-axe' and elsewhere declare that his wife and himself were 'a sinful woman married to a sinful man; two of God's patients not yet cured'.[4] He could reveal Joy to be an often stubborn, difficult woman but he also illuminated her inner being, her core personality. 'We are taken out of ourselves by the loved one while she is here . . . ,' he wrote, 'we must learn still to be taken out of ourselves though the bodily presence is withdrawn, to love the very Her . . .'[5]

It was a book that not only helped Lewis and others but also illustrated to all what a profound love he had felt for Joy. Most importantly, although it is a book written by a Christian and imbued with his orthodoxy, it transcends this viewpoint to become a 'spiritual' work, a book that speaks of things that go beyond simplistic Christian theology.

Lewis wrote *A Grief Observed* under the pseudonym N.W. Clerk. He did this because he considered the work too personal to be published under his own name. This anxiety had little to do with what his academic peers might have thought and more to do with the fact that it revealed so much of his own inner life without the protection of fiction. Indeed, the only reason he wished to have the book published at all was because he realised quite rightly that it might help a great many people. But he thought this not because he considered himself to be a magus or a seer. He simply believed that by sharing his emotional reaction to Joy's death and the thought processes that had led him to a place of acceptance beyond the pain, he might offer some small insights to his fellow sufferers.

Lewis chose to send the book not to his regular publisher but to the London firm of Faber & Faber, whose Managing Director at the time was T.S. Eliot. He sent off the manuscript just as any first-time author without an agent might, and the book was duly put on the slush pile, eventually to be picked up by one of the company's readers. The resulting report was extremely negative. While admitting that the book was well written and soul-searching, the reader thought that the subject matter was far too morbid and would simply alienate anyone who read it.

Eliot, who had also read the short manuscript, was not totally convinced by this assessment. He observed in the text what many thousands have found since, an intellectualised spirituality that could help rather than repel, and so he sought a third opinion. He approached a young director of the publishing house, Charles Monteith, who was also then a Fellow of All Souls College, Oxford. Unknown to Eliot, Monteith had been a student of Lewis's a decade earlier and when he received the manuscript with his former tutor's handwritten corrections, he immediately became suspicious. He then recalled that, years earlier, Lewis had published some poems in *Punch* under the pseudonym Nat Whilk (Old English for 'I know not who') and he was aware that Lewis's wife had died recently. Putting all these facts together, he realised that N.W. Clerk was C. S. Lewis.

Once Lewis's harmless charade had been exposed, Faber & Faber were naturally falling over themselves to publish *A Grief Observed*. However, although the book received some very complimentary reviews, it is perhaps not surprising that it made little impact when it was first published in 1961. It sold no more than fifteen hundred copies in Lewis's lifetime and only after his literary executor, Owen Barfield, gave Faber & Faber permission to republish the book under Lewis's name a year after the author's death did it became a best-seller and go on to sell a hundred times as many as the first, pseudonymous edition.

In June 1961, as *A Grief Observed* was being made ready for publication, Jack's health began to go into decline. It began without pain but he found that he had problems urinating. At first he told no one about it and instead went on holiday to Ireland to visit Arthur Greeves. His old friend thought he looked ill and remarked on it, prompting Jack to visit his doctor in Oxford soon after his return.

Dr Havard gave Jack a thorough physical examination and quickly discovered that he was suffering from a severely enlarged prostate and infected kidneys. He was immediately booked into the Acland Hospital and Havard arranged for him to be seen by a surgeon friend, who conducted a series of blood tests and other investigations. The surgeon found Lewis had a serious prostate problem but also realised that he was suffering from toxaemia, which causes dangerous heart irregularities. The fact that Lewis was also significantly overweight and in generally poor shape for his age meant that an operation on his prostate would be risky. Instead he was given strong antibiotics, put on a low-protein diet, fitted with a catheter and told that he had to sleep sitting upright in a chair. He was also advised not to return to Cambridge for the entire autumn term.

All of this caused Jack great discomfort, but he was stoical. However, he ignored much of the medical advice he was given and utterly refused to give up the things he most enjoyed in life, such as beer, tea and cigarettes, claiming that he would rather live a shorter, happier life than prolong an existence in which he was deeply unhappy and denied the things he enjoyed.

Although the symptoms began to subside by the end of 1961, allowing him to return to Cambridge in January the following year, Lewis soon discovered that the treatment he was receiving was actually woefully inadequate. During the summer of 1962 he began to suffer acute pain and was forced to consult a local doctor. The young medic who saw him, Dr Tony Haines, was horrified by the contraption that his patient had been fitted with to collect urine. It was a primitive affair thrown together using bits of cork, rubber tubing and tape. A year after it was first fitted it was falling apart, leaking and smelling badly, but most crucially it was poisoning Jack's system: his urinary tract was infected.

Dr Haines was amazed that such an important man as Lewis was not receiving the very best medical treatment on offer and insisted he take over his case. A modern catheter was fitted and a course of more modern and effective drugs prescribed, specifically aimed at treating the new infection as well as the original symptoms of Lewis's disease.

Robert Havard, who was by this time in his sixties, was obviously behind the times when it came to treatment methods and he shouldered much of the blame for the rapid decline in Lewis's health witnessed between 1961 and 1963. Douglas Gresham was particularly scathing of the man's efforts, and probably with some justification.[6] However, it cannot be denied that Lewis's inability to change his lifestyle exacerbated his symptoms. He had also been slow to go to Havard in the first place and had subsequently refused to listen to much of the advice he was given. Most importantly, by the time his condition had been identified he was too ill for surgery.

Dr Haines certainly made Jack more comfortable, but his body was rebelling. Two summers after he had first noticed signs of illness, Jack was just putting the finishing touches to his plans to travel to Belfast to visit Arthur when he suffered a heart attack at The Kilns and was rushed to the Acland Hospital.

A few days after the attack, while in intensive care, Lewis took another turn for the worse and was thought to be so close to death that a local priest was called in to administer extreme unction. But then, to the amazement of the doctors attending Lewis, as the priest recited his words, the patient opened his eyes and smiled before asking for a cup of tea.

Jack stayed in the Acland Hospital for over six weeks. During much of this time Warnie was nowhere to be seen. In June he had set off for Ireland, having arranged to meet up with his brother later that month, but when he learned of Jack's heart attack he did what came most naturally to him when faced with the harsh realities of life and headed for the nearest pub. Determined perhaps to make himself as least as ill as his brother, this time Warren really hit the booze hard and found himself once more in Our Lady of Lourdes Hospital in Drogheda. Learning that their patient's famous brother was seriously ill in Oxford, the nuns eventually sent word to Havard to tell him that Warren was with them and that he was in such a serious condition he might not be well enough to return to England until as late as October.

Meanwhile, at the Acland Hospital, Jack's condition had stabilised, but, through a combination of illness and treatments, he became delusional. At times he would wake up suddenly and demand his clothes because he had important matters to attend to in college or at home. On another occasion he told a bemused friend that he had in his possession an unpublished novel by Charles Williams but that he was being prevented from publishing it because Williams's widow, Michal, was demanding £10,000 from him before it could be released.

During this time Jack had his final meeting with Tolkien. The two men had met for tea at The Kilns the previous winter and it had not been a happy encounter. Tolkien's youngest son, Christopher, had arranged things, hoping that they might bury the hatchet and find some closure to their differences; but this had not happened. Although both Lewis and Tolkien had been courteous, on that day there seemed to be no spark of friendship remaining and they had parted at the door to The Kilns no better friends than before.

Tolkien visited Lewis at the Acland Hospital in July 1963 but there was no one else with them in the room that day to record the encounter, so we will never know if they managed to begin healing their relationship. It must have been obvious to both men that Lewis would not live for long, but even this may not have been enough to heal the rift that had opened up so many years before.

By late July, Jack was back at The Kilns being looked after by a group of friends and helpers. Warren, having recovered faster than the nuns in Ireland had predicted, turned up rather shame-faced in late August. In his own inimitable way he did his best to make amends for his desertion. Jack was extremely frail and easily tired, but he doggedly refused to let things get him down and was pleased to see his brother. He was constantly short of breath but could not resist smoking whenever he could get away with it and insisted on being allowed to continue drinking his beloved tea.

He had two nurses tending him around the clock and college associates visited while his close friends rallied round. Jack was able to maintain a cheerful demeanour, but when the friends had gone and only his close family were there to witness it, his suffering became impossible to disguise completely. According to both Douglas Gresham and Warren in accounts written long after this time, it was apparent that by September 1963 Jack had begun to look forward to his own death, and this was a factor that almost certainly hastened his end.

Letters written to his oldest friend, Arthur Greeves, offered a little comfort, but they were soon developing into desolate missives that simply illustrated just how depressed and despondent Jack had become. 'But oh Arthur, never to see you again,' he wrote during the late summer of that year.[7]

Then the clouds seemed to part and during the final few months of his life Jack enjoyed a semblance of earthly peace. He was suffering physically but he began to find both an emotional and an intellectual calm at The Kilns. The surety of approaching death brought Jack and Warnie closer than they had ever been before. It was now a time when nostalgia was welcomed and no harm could come from revisiting the past. The two brothers dipped into the deep well of memory and pulled out treasures to savour. They could be children again.

Jack also found that being completely detached from the rushing turmoil of life was really rather pleasant. In August he wrote to the authorities at Cambridge resigning his professorship and his fellowship at Magdalene and he stepped away from his last contacts with the academic world, a world in which he had been totally immersed since he had gained a scholarship to Oxford almost half a century earlier. Now he allowed himself to simply enjoy books, enjoy the substance of his life, all those beautiful words on a page. Long days passed in reading and rereading the books he had loved for most of his life and he could experience again the pleasure he had derived from being ill in bed as a small child. Perhaps during long sleepless nights, sitting up in bed, he felt the gentle caress of his mother's hand and saw her face leaning over him slowly morphing into that of Joy.

On Monday 18 November Jack decided he felt well enough to make a final gesture towards his old life, the life now racing away from him. He was driven into Oxford to a pub called the Lamb and Flag, where the remnants of the Inklings met sporadically. The group, still occasionally joined by Lewis whenever he was well enough during his final years, had, several months earlier, given up on the Bird and Baby because it had become 'intolerably cold, dark, noisy and child-pestered'. Sadly, on the occasion of Lewis's last-ever

Inklings meeting, only one of his old friends appeared, Colin Hardie, whom he had known since the early 1930s. Nevertheless, the pair talked merrily and Jack enjoyed his beer just as he had always done. 'It was perhaps the best of all such Mondays,' he later told Warren.[8]

But the clock was ticking and for Lewis life was ebbing away. On 22 November 1963, a day writ large in any history of modern times, as President John F. Kennedy was making final amendments to his itinerary several thousand miles away in Dallas, Jack Lewis was approaching his final hours. Warren was the last person to see him alive when he brought him a tray of tea in bed at four in the afternoon, and he later recalled that Jack seemed drowsy but cheerful. After helping his brother to sit up, he returned downstairs to the kitchen to read the newspaper. Then, at around 5.30, Warnie heard a loud crash from the bedroom overhead. Rushing upstairs, he found Jack unconscious on the floor beside the bed. A few minutes later C. S. Lewis was dead.

11

Legacy

Only a small group of friends and relatives attended Lewis's funeral at Holy Trinity Church in the village of Headington Quarry, a short walk from The Kilns, and even then one member of the inner circle was missing. Warren Lewis could not face seeing his brother lowered into the ground and instead spent the day in bed drinking whisky. Tolkien attended the service with his son Christopher, and other mourners included Jack's stepsons, Douglas and David, Maureen Blake (née Moore) and the ever-faithful Fred Paxford. A few members of the Inklings were in attendance, along with one of Jack's oldest friends, Owen Barfield. Arthur Greeves was unable to make the crossing from Belfast.

After the funeral, Owen Barfield, who was one of the two executors of the Lewis estate (along with Alfred Cecil Harwood, who, like Barfield, had met Lewis during their earliest days at Oxford), led a small party into the living room (which Jack always referred to as the 'common room') in order to read the will.

Dispensing quickly with the legalities, Barfield told the gathering of Lewis's simple wishes. His estate was to be used to finish the education of his stepsons and then the money would pass to Warren for life. On Warren's death the legacy would revert to David and Douglas. However, the biggest surprise for many there that day was the relatively small size of the estate. After taxes, at the time of his death Lewis was worth £37,772 (equivalent to about £700,000 today).

Throughout his life Lewis had never really understood financial matters. It was one of the things that never figured much in his thinking; it was all too nuts and bolts and boring for his type of mind. While he was alive the majority of his earnings from writing had gone to charity, and although his fiction was popular during his lifetime, it became much more so from the early 1960s onwards, so that his estate grew enormously during the first decade after his death.

There was also The Kilns. When Jack, Warren and Janie had bought the house together in 1930, it had been agreed that each of the partners would only be a life tenant of the property. This had been reinforced in Janie's will before she died in 1951, and it was a condition designed precisely to protect her daughter, Maureen. At the time it seemed beyond doubt that on the death of Jack and Warren (neither of whom ever looked likely to marry and have children of their own) the house should be passed to Maureen and her children. But then Joy entered the picture.

Joy was extremely protective of the interests of herself and her children. All was well concerning Jack's earnings and the shared property of the Lewis family until she discovered she had cancer and would probably not live long. Suddenly her sons' future became a matter of utmost concern. Bill Gresham was keen to have the boys in America after his former wife's death and Joy needed to find a way to ensure this would never happen. It was therefore extremely important to her that her boys inherit The Kilns after the Lewis brothers had died.

In 1957 there had been an embarrassing showdown over the matter at Maureen and Leonard Blake's home. Over tea one Sunday afternoon Joy, as blunt as ever, simply told Maureen that the boys would one day inherit The Kilns. Shocked, Maureen replied that this was certainly not how things had been arranged legally and that she, her husband and their children were the only rightful heirs to the estate. Joy grew angry and an intense, deeply unpleasant argument ensued. To his later shame Jack sided with Joy on the matter, which caused enormous ill feeling for some time.

Fortunately for the Blakes, short of a nasty court battle, there was nothing Joy or Jack or anyone else could do about Janie's will and the legally enshrined agreement made years before. No one wanted the matter to go to an expensive and damaging court case, and eventually Jack managed to convince Joy that he would provide for the boys whoever was one day to take over The Kilns.

The figures in Jack's will are no indication of what the Lewis estate is worth today. A survey of more than 50,000 people, carried out in 1997 by the Waterstones book chain and Channel 4 in the UK, placed *The Lion, the Witch and the Wardrobe* at number twenty-one in the Top 100 most-loved books of all time. (*The Lord of the Rings* was voted number one.) The book was the fourth most popular children's book after *The Wind in the Willows* (sixteenth), *Winnie the Pooh* (seventeenth) and *The Hobbit* (nineteenth).

Although polls tell us very little about the quality of a book, they should be respected for the fact that they indicate what people like, and popularity does not preclude a book from being good, of course. However, after the poll was published, a huge debate raged in the British media over the fact that *The Lord of the Rings* had been ranked first. Sniffy elitists wrote ill-considered disclaimers and journalists who had always hated Tolkien complained bitterly. Many of these people also despised Lewis, but they had at least been able to dismiss much of his output as 'mere children's literature'. During the years after this chart others appeared, and each time they vindicated those who had voted in the original poll. Tolkien and Lewis were repeatedly voted two of the best-loved authors of the twentieth century.

Lewis's fame, and consequently the sales of his most popular books, have grown steadily over the years. Estimates of the number of copies of the Narnia books sold since their publication range from fifty to one hundred million and they have been translated into every major language. But, even if they dwarf the sales figures for Lewis's other titles, the Narnia books were not his only successes. The Ransom trilogy – *Out of the Silent Planet*, *Perelandra* and *That Hideous Strength* – have sold in the tens of millions, the statistics relating to *The Screwtape Letters* fall into the same category, and even Lewis's most serious works of religious apologetics, books such as *Letters to Malcolm*, *The Four Loves*, *Miracles* and *The Great Divorce* have sold hundreds of thousands of copies.

Four different small-screen adaptations of the Narnia books have been made in recent years. The best and most true to the original spirit of Lewis's creation is the BBC version, seven series collectively called *The Chronicles of Narnia*, which were first broadcast in 1989. There are also tapes available of a Radio 4 series and a set of audio books (published by HarperCollins) which were read by the acclaimed actors Ian Richardson, Claire Bloom, Sir Anthony Quayle and Michael York.

The Lion, the Witch and the Wardrobe has also been successfully adapted as a stage play. The best-known production was that by Adrian Mitchell with the Royal Shakespeare Company's artistic director Adrian Noble, a show that enjoyed a box-office record-breaking run at Sadler's Wells Theatre in London at the end of 2001. Since the book was first published in 1950 there have been literally thousands of stage performances of Lewis's most famous work, from little amateur dramatics groups presenting the story in village halls to multimillion-pound world-touring productions that reach cultures far beyond the cosy confines of Oxford. (At the time of writing there is a production of *The Lion, the Witch and the Wardrobe* in Perth, Western Australia. This production, for which Douglas Gresham was an adviser, has been touring the country for the past few months.)

For many years the Lewis estate resisted all proposals to sell the film rights for the Narnia books. It is said this is because Lewis had a very low opinion of Disney and would have hated his stories to have been adapted into American-style cartoons or a sugary-sweet version with sparkling-toothed American children taking the roles of his four main characters.

In 1969 J.R.R. Tolkien had been forced to sell the film rights to *The Lord of the Rings* for £104,602, allegedly to pay a tax bill. This need had arisen because he had failed to manage his finances properly when the earnings from the sudden success of his books began to roll in. Lewis was as inexperienced with money as Tolkien and if he had been alive at this time he may well have found himself in the same sort of predicament. This did not happen because after his death his earnings were carefully managed by the estate, which meant that Hollywood had no claim over the Narnia books. But during the late 1990s both Paramount and Disney began to work up proposals for big-screen adaptations of *The Lion, the Witch and the Wardrobe*, which they hoped eventually to produce with the support of Lewis's literary heirs.

These Hollywood plans were totally misguided. According to some sources, the British director John Boorman was briefly involved with one of the proposals and had begun working on a version of the story that bore almost no relationship to the original book. Hollywood rumours tell of a script plan in which the setting of the story had been changed to present-day LA, the children were no longer escaping the Blitz but were evacuated from Los Angeles because of the threat of earthquakes and Edmund was tempted by the Witch with hamburgers instead of Turkish Delight.

If these stories are true, then the Lewis estate was wise to avoid having anything to do with Hollywood until a sensible proposal came its way. Because Tolkien had sold the rights to his great work, neither he nor the Tolkien estate ever again had a say in what was to happen to *The Lord of the Rings* in Hollywood, and over the years there were some dreadful suggestions for adaptations (and indeed one very bad film was made, Ralph Bakshi's 1978 production). Legend has it that during the mid-1960s the Beatles were seriously considering a cartoon adaptation of *The Lord of the Rings* featuring the voices of the four band members. Fortunately for everyone with the slightest regard for Tolkien's creation, the group decided instead to make *Yellow Submarine* and the project eventually fell into Peter Jackson's very capable hands.

In 2000 the Lewis estate began to consider seriously again the idea of a movie adaptation of the Narnia books. This was partly inspired by the fact that both *The Lord of the Rings* and J.K. Rowling's Harry Potter books were then in production with responsible film-makers and producers. The estate was still very resistant to Disney and in the end they sold the rights for £50 million to a new company, Walden Media, created by the American billionaire mogul Philip Anschutz.

Walden Media is now run by Cary Granat under the umbrella of the Hollywood giant Miramax Films. Asked recently how he intends to steer the production of the film, Granat said: 'The truer we are to the written word the better the film will be. There are so many rich characters and emotional scenes.'[1] It is clear from this and from the style and quality of recent film adaptations that the decision makers in Hollywood have come to realise that the public who love and cherish books like Lewis's classic, *The Lord of the Rings* and *Harry Potter* do not want to see them gutted and reworked by committee in Los Angeles.

As well as promising to stick faithfully to the original book, Walden Media have also made the wise decision to make a series of films, one for each of the Narnia books, rather than trying to shorten and merge the stories as some would have been tempted to do. Douglas Gresham, who sold his stake in the Lewis estate in the 1970s, still acts as a consultant and adviser for those who have taken on the role of Lewis's literary executors, and he will be intimately involved in the making of the films, the first of which is to have a budget rumoured to be in excess of $200m and is set for global release in mid-2005.

In 2002 the highly successful director Andrew Adamson was appointed by Walden Media to mastermind the Narnia films. His previous credits include the superb animated movie *Shrek*, starring Eddie Murphy, and he is a long-time Lewis fan. 'Narnia was such a vivid and real world to me as a child, as it is to millions of other fans,' he has said. 'I share Walden's excitement in giving those fans an epic theatrical experience worthy of their imaginations and driving new generations toward the work of C. S. Lewis. Making a film that crosses generations is a far easier task when the source material resonates with such themes as truth, loyalty and belief in something greater than yourself.[2]

There is little doubt that this movie has huge commercial potential and if Walden Media get it right they cannot possibly fail to make a great deal of money from Lewis's creation. *The Lord of the Rings* trilogy and the first three films in the Harry Potter series netted $6 billion between them during their first year of theatre and video release. *The Lion, the Witch and the Wardrobe* should appeal to an audience just as large and have just as many opportunities for lucrative merchandising spin-offs.

However, one interesting element in the Lewis books that has not been an issue at all with *The Lord of the Rings* or Harry Potter is their religious content. How will the movie-makers handle the Christian aspect of the stories?

One clue to help answer this question comes from a literary precedent. In 2001 rumours began to circulate on the internet about a deliberate plan engineered by the Lewis estate and HarperCollins (the publisher of almost all of Lewis's works) to produce new versions of the books with all Christian allegory removed and to arrange for more Narnia books to be written that left out any connections with Christianity.

These rumours were precipitated by a leaked memo from HarperCollins that was quickly posted on the net. Since then, these rumours have not been satisfactorily denied nor have they been confirmed, but many Lewis devotees are suspicious and anxiously await the publication of the planned books. A spokesperson for HarperCollins, Lisa Herling, has gone on record as saying: 'The goal of HarperCollins is to publish the works of C. S. Lewis to the broadest possible audience and leave any interpretation of the works to the reader.' Douglas Gresham, who is himself a non-denominational Christian preacher (and has nothing to gain financially from the decision made by HarperCollins) concurs. 'What is wrong with trying to

get people outside of Christianity to read the Narnian Chronicles?'
he asks. 'The Christian audience is less in need of Narnia than
the secular audience and in today's world the surest way to
prevent secularists and their children from reading the Narnia
books is to keep it in the Christian or Religious section of the
bookstores or to firmly link Narnia with modern evangelical
Christianity.'[3]

It will be interesting to see if a similar path will be followed by
the makers of the film adaptations of the Narnia books. Shortly
after the appointment of Andrew Adamson, the Emmy Award-
winning screenwriter Ann Peacock was given the job of adapting the
books. She has said of the task: 'The Lion, the Witch and the Wardrobe is
one of my five children's favourites and I'm thrilled to be writing the
screenplay for the story, which encapsulates universal principles all
young people need an introduction to, such as truth, honour, compassion, loyalty and courage.'

Herein lies the modern interpretation of the Narnia books that
will, by force of artistic and financial power, become the overwhelmingly significant one in the future. Some of the parents who
will in future years read The Lion, the Witch and the Wardrobe to their children (just as past generations have) may remember how the book
was once seen as a paradigm for the Christian story. They may
recall how Aslan represented a Christ-type figure and that his torture at the hands of the Witch was a 'supposal', an alternative
crucifixion. But future generations will receive a slightly different
message from Lewis's stories. Instead of re-enacting the story of
Christ's incarnation the books will offer a less focused spiritual
message, teaching, as Ann Peacock implies, the spiritual and ethical
values that play a key role in building a moral infrastructure in society.

The jury is still out as to whether this slow metamorphosis of
Lewis's most famous creations will work, but it is undeniably true
that one of the most attractive things about the Narnia books is
their universality, and a reader does not have to be a Christian to
enjoy them. Anthony Hopkins, who played Lewis in the film

Shadowlands, apparently claimed that reading Lewis's work had no more made him want to become a Christian than playing Hannibal Lecter in *The Silence of the Lambs* had made him want to be a cannibal. The Narnia books are fairy stories possessed of a timeless quality. They appeal to Christians and non-Christians alike and adults and children enjoy them in different ways and for different reasons. It would seem safe to assume the stories are strong enough to sustain remoulding as 'pure entertainment with a spiritual message' rather than in their original form, 'pure entertainment with an orthodox Christian message'.

We inhabit a world very different from the one in which Lewis lived when he wrote the books. Today fewer people are orthodox Christians and more of us are able to differentiate between strong personal moral values and morals based solely on Christian doctrine. Therefore many would agree that a version of the Narnia books in which, as Ann Peacock puts it, universal principles of truth, honour and compassion are encouraged, will have a greater impact and be more in tune with our time than the originals. The only dubious aspect about following this path is that Lewis would have absolutely hated the decision.

Lewis's great fame and the nature of some of his ideas have attracted, at one end of the scale, overzealous praise, even discipleship, while at the other end they have drawn opprobrium. Much of this has, rightly or wrongly, helped sustain his importance as a writer and commentator, keeping some of his themes and beliefs in the literary and religious spotlight.

In this book I've tried to portray Lewis the writer, but many perceive the man as a religious commentator first and as an author second. Most of Lewis's original manuscripts are now kept in a permanent exhibition dedicated to him and other religious apologists in the Marion E. Wade Center, at Wheaton College, Illinois. The college, which includes as an alumnus the preacher Billy Graham, is also in possession of such weird memorabilia as a wardrobe from Lewis's house purported to be *the* wardrobe that inspired his most famous book, and a table from the kitchen of The Kilns. Wheaton College is run by and for conservative Christians, a place where the name C. S. Lewis is revered. Sadly, though, such adulation is based on confusion and misinterpretation.

It is clear to see why Lewis would appeal most to bigoted, hard-line, old-fashioned Christians. He was an old-fashioned Christian when he was alive and today those who consider the Church to be too interested in modernising and who wish to keep the institution in thrall to retrograde thinking see Lewis as a hero of religious orthodoxy and conservative values.

This would be harmless except for the fact that they have managed to morph the real Jack Lewis into a version of himself even he would have had trouble recognising. Lewis loved a drink, he loved to smoke and he even continued to enjoy his 'soaks', as he called cigarettes, when his doctors told him that smoking would hasten his end. For more than forty years he smoked sixty cigarettes a day between pipes and he actively disliked non-smokers and merrily mocked teetotallers. Lewis also had sex with at least one woman. When he was young he masturbated, detailing his experiences to his intimate friend Arthur Greeves; and as a youth he revelled in vivid cruel fantasies. He also loved bawdy songs and ancient poetry bordering on the pornographic. However, the evangelists who collect his furniture and place it in glass cases in American colleges, and Lewis societies that work hard to project a fabricated image of the writer in England and elsewhere, claim that Lewis was not at all the man history has recorded him to be.

Most forthright in expressing these views is a man named Walter Hooper, who has done a great deal to keep Lewis's work alive through encyclopedic volumes, including companions and worthy Lewis guides, along with a rather oblique biography (written with Roger Lancelyn Green and published in 1976). But Hooper has also, for his own reasons, been most vociferous in his claims that Lewis was not the man everyone else thought he was; nor indeed the man some people closer to Jack knew him to be.

By hero-worshipping Lewis and making himself so indispensable to the man's legacy, Hooper has created the impression that he knew Lewis extremely well. But, compared with some of Jack's life-long friends and colleagues, he really only encountered him in passing. He spent a few months acting as Jack's secretary and amanuensis in the final year of the writer's life. He did not know the young Lewis, he did not know Lewis while he was married to Joy and he was probably given few genuine insights into those times by Lewis himself. However, Hooper has tried to remould C. S. Lewis as a 'Perpetual Virgin', believing that he died without ever having engaged in sexual intercourse and that therefore his marriage to Joy was never consummated. It is difficult to understand why this means so much to Hooper, a fundamentalist Roman Catholic (who was once a strict Anglo-Catholic deacon). But, for him, an objective, log-ical portrayal of Lewis based on the facts of his life, an image of Lewis as a man like any other, is simply not good enough.

What is most odd about this is that Lewis himself wrote of his sexual relationship with Joy. In the pages of his most honest book, *A Grief Observed*, he details the fact that he and Joy fell in love, that they quelled their long-unsatisfied hunger, that they were one flesh. As well as this, Lewis implied (even if he did not make it entirely clear) that he had at one time enjoyed a sexual relationship with Janie Moore. 'All I can or need to say is that my earlier hostility to the emotions was very fully and variously avenged,' he wrote of his relationship with Janie in *Surprised by Joy*, and that with Joy Gresham leaning over his shoulder.[4] Furthermore, at least two of those who knew Jack well, Maureen Moore and Joy's brother, Dr Howard Davidman, have lent weight to the notion that he certainly did not die a virgin.

But to Hooper and the other disciples who wish to offer us 'St Jack of Oxford', Lewis's own descriptions in such accounts as *A Grief Observed* or the implied statements he offered in letters to his closest friend, Arthur Greeves, were actually works of fiction. As for per-sonal testimony from close associates and family, well, as far as Hooper is concerned, rather than being genuine recollections, these could only have been imagined.

Walter Hooper is not the only one to attempt to rewrite history. Far from the weekly meetings of the C. S. Lewis Society in Oxford (an organisation Hooper founded), the puritans of America (ironically, a breed Lewis always loathed) have tried desperately hard to furnish the world with another sanitised version of the real Lewis. Their influence has infiltrated some of the smaller publishers who have certain rights over Lewis's works in America and for their own misguided reasons these parties have made it their business to ensure that all references to alcohol and tobacco in his writing are eradicated.

Thankfully, most fans of C. S. Lewis are sensible enough to recognise as self-serving the transparent nature of efforts to remodel their hero or to neuter his more interesting characteristics and there has been no shortage of well-written and carefully produced books, plays and films about his life.

In 1985 Brian Sibley's *Shadowlands* was published, a book that focused on the intense and life-altering relationship between Jack Lewis and Joy Gresham. ('Shadowlands' is a term Aslan refers to when talking about the 'real' world outside Narnia.)This was later made into a successful play which toured with the late Nigel Hawthorne as Lewis and later a TV adaptation starring Joss Ackland and Claire Bloom. Then, in 1994, a Hollywood movie of the same name starring Debra Winger and Anthony Hopkins was released to critical acclaim and commercial success.

These have done much to revitalise public interest in C. S. Lewis, particularly in America. If you need some proof of this, travel to Oxford and join the weekly 'Inklings Tour', which begins at 11 a.m. every Wednesday morning during the summer. Along with stops at the Eagle and Child and Holywell Street, where Tolkien lived during the early 1950s, one of the highlights is a brief pause at the Eastgate Hotel, where Joy and Jack first met. It is at this point in the tour that one of the middle-aged American ladies who invariably skew the demographic of the group will suddenly develop renewed interest and enquire whether this was the very room in which the scene in *Shadowlands* was filmed. It was not: the scene where Lewis and Joy met was filmed in a room at the Randolph Hotel a few hundred yards from the Eastgate Hotel in the centre of Oxford. This was done because the room at the Eastgate in which they met in reality was too small to be filmed.

Naturally, Lewis is not universally loved and those who dislike the man they perceive him to have been and who remain unimpressed by his work are as scathing of Lewis, and in some cases as unfair, as the eccentric disciples who have worked so hard to canonise the man.

For many years Lewis has been the target of those who believe he was a misogynist bully, a man who tried to foist his retarded vision of religion on to people insidiously through his fiction, a man who worked to promote his Luddite opinions and one who spoke out against technological and social progress, in short, a man keen to hold back the natural evolution of the intellect.

Most vocal in their dislike of Lewis and his work are some members of the British literati who see Lewis as old-fashioned and politically incorrect. The writer Philip Hensher, who has been a Booker Prize judge, has called Lewis's Narnia books 'poisonous, ghastly, priggish and half-witted' and he detests what he describes as 'Lewis's creed of clean-living, muscular Christianity'.[5] More passionate still is the acclaimed author Philip Pullman, writer of the highly successful and ingenious *His Dark Materials* trilogy, for which he won the Whitbread Prize in 2002. Pullman has described Lewis's books as 'detestable' and believes he was 'cruel' to his characters, that he used fiction to glorify backward thinking, morals and beliefs, and that he was a misogynist racist with a 'sneering attitude to anything remotely progressive in social terms or to people with brown faces'.[6]

Pullman's particular loathing centres on one of the final passages in *The Chronicles of Narnia*, towards the end of *The Last Battle*, in which Susan Pevensie, one of the four children who first enter Narnia through the wardrobe in *The Lion, the Witch and the Wardrobe*, is excluded from the barn (which represents heaven or paradise). The reason Lewis gives for her exclusion from paradise is that 'she likes lipstick and nylons and invitations'. To Pullman this has suggested that Lewis considered a girl reaching sexual maturity to be such a terrible thing she should be banished to hell.

There can be no denying that there are many aspects of the Narnia books that are, even on a casual reading, appalling. Lewis indeed refers to 'darkies', and the bad guys (the Calormene) who threaten the very British kings and queens (the four children, Susan, Lucy, Edmund and Peter) are very clearly stereotypes based on Muslims. The social structure of Narnia is overtly modelled on the British imperial system, and the portals into this fantasy world (of which the wardrobe is one) are all located in Britain, which some believe offers as a subtext the concept that Britannia rules. Women are often attacked in the books, as is any suggestion of modernity. In one passage Lewis achieves a double whammy by having one of his characters, Jill Pole, come from a 'progressive' school, which he dubs 'Experiment House' and which is such a ridiculous institution it actually has a headmistress.

But, as often happens when commentators offer up for public digestion their strongly held opinions, Pullman and other critics of Lewis choose to ignore facts that counter their argument. First, they make no mention of the Calormene Emeth, who dies in battle while saving others and comes before Aslan, who then offers him entry into the Kingdom of Heaven. Second, they conveniently ignore the fact that although one of the two female lead characters, Susan, is indeed banished from heaven at the end of *The Last Battle*, during the earliest parts of the series of books it is her younger sister, Lucy, who is the most active, adventurous, brave and honest character.

There is also the simple matter of taking into account the era in which Lewis lived and wrote. It is so very easy for people living in the twenty-first century to brand as bigots, misogynists and racists those who lived in past, possibly less enlightened ages. We rightly object to terms such as 'darkie' but we must not forget that this was simply the generic term for black people used almost universally until as late as the 1970s. It might well be that in five decades from now some contemporary children's fiction will be considered politically incorrect and dated.

So, in conclusion, what may be decided about this man Lewis? Like all great achievers, his character was one replete with contradictions. He was certainly old-fashioned, backward-looking, scared of change and progress. He had a problem with women. He despised uneducated females, who to him appeared to be wasting their lives as drones and therefore deserved no sign of respect. However, he was equally uncomfortable with many of the educated women he met, and he disliked the thought that they could be intellectually precocious or play crucial roles in society and education. And yet he loved Joy, an intellectual woman, and was utterly devastated when she left his life.

Lewis hated the idea of being a popular writer, but revelled in the fame his success brought him. He considered the very notion of fandom simple-minded and childish, but he faithfully replied to every sincere letter written to him by his fans. This illustrates his dedication to his role and the faith he kept in what he saw as the deal made between author and reader. Indeed, he ended up marrying his most devoted fan.

Lewis disliked children and knew very few of them, but he wrote one of the best-loved and most successful children's stories ever published. He found absolutely no pleasure in teaching, he hated college ritual and many university traditions and he was mocking of some of his fellow dons, whom he considered dull and narrow-minded. But he could never have endured leaving academia.

In sum, Lewis was clearly a man who held contradictory views when it came to 'principles' and 'examples'. He did not care for most women, but loved three women deeply: his mother, Janie and Joy. He did not understand or approve of homosexuals, but his oldest and most cherished friend, Arthur Greeves, was gay. He did not like children, but he came to love his younger stepson Douglas and he adored his fictional children Lucy, Susan, Edmund and Peter.

Lewis was a man deeply scarred by childhood pain. He was

drawn backwards all his life, tempted by a desire to return to that most simple and comfortable time – the few years through which he had lived when things were whole – those few years before his mother died. For most of his life he could, with great effort, resist this tug of the past through denial and transference of his desires. And perhaps this is part of the reason he needed to find a substitute in religion; a substitute that also proved incredibly useful to his career.

Whether he is now in heaven, as he himself hoped, reincarnated in a new form, as some religions describe, or, as atheists would have it, only his words have survived, in the end the greatest of his achievements came from his ability to offer enormous pleasure to many millions of people around the world and across generations. Whatever the guiding forces that drove him to create both his works of fiction and his many non-fiction books, it cannot be denied that the world is a richer place because of them.

Notes

1: 'Call Me Jack'

1 C. S. Lewis, *Surprised by Joy*, Harcourt Brace and Co., New York, 1955, p.8.
2 Ibid., p.3.
3 Also published as *Boxen: The Imaginary World of C. S. Lewis*, Harcourt Brace Jovanovich, San Diego, California, 1985.

2: The Call of Learning

1 C. S. Lewis, *Surprised by Joy*, Harcourt Brace and Co., New York, 1955, p.17.
2 Ibid.
3 For a more detailed description of this aspect of Tolkien's character, see my life of Tolkien, *Tolkien: A Biography*, Little, Brown, London, 2001.
4 *Surprised by Joy*, p.17.
5 Ibid., p.56.
6 Ibid., p.100.
7 Ibid., p.103.

3: Scholarship and War

1 C. S. Lewis, *Surprised by Joy*, Harcourt Brace and Co., New York, 1955, p.180.
2 Walter Hooper (ed.), *They Stand Together: The Letters of C. S. Lewis to Arthur Greeves 1914–1963*, Collins, London, 1979, p.185. Postmarked: 3 May 1917. Note that Lewis mentions the OTC at Malvern. Until recently almost all public schools in Britain had their own OTC in which young boys received basic military training as part of the curriculum.

3   Albert Lewis to Warren Lewis, 30 April 1917, The Lewis Papers: Memoirs of the Lewis Family, 1850–1930, transcript in the Wade Collection, Marion E. Wade Center, Wheaton College, Wheaton, Illinois, USA, vol. 5, p.208.
4   Ibid., p.159.
5   Ibid., p.189.
6   Letter to Albert Lewis, The Lewis Papers, vol. 5, pp.212–13.
7   Ibid., p.213.
8   These poems appeared in Lewis's first published work, *Spirits in Bondage*, Heinemann, London, 1919.
9   The Lewis Papers, vol. 5, p.243.
10 *Surprised by Joy*, p.183.

4: 'Mother'

1   30 May 1918, The Lewis Papers: Memoirs of the Lewis Family, 1850–1930, in the Wade Collection, Marion G. Wade Center, Wheaton College, Wheaton, Illinois, USA, vol. 5, pp.320–1.
2   20 June 1918, The Lewis Papers, vol. 5, pp.330–1.
3   The Lewis Papers, vol. 6, p.134.
4   Ibid., p.79.
5   C. S. Lewis, *Surprised by Joy*, Harcourt Brace and Co., New York, 1955, p.160.
6   George Sayer, *Jack: A Life of C. S. Lewis*, Harper and Row, New York, 1988, p.154.
7   The Lewis Papers, vol. 6, pp.118–23.
8   Bodleian Library, Oxford, Ms. Facs.d.264, f.140.
9   W.H. Lewis (ed.), *The Letters of C. S. Lewis*, Geoffrey Bles, London, 1955, p.12.
10 The Lewis Papers, vol. 6, p.226.

5: Fellowship

1   W.H. Lewis (ed.), *The Letters of C. S. Lewis*, Geoffrey Bles, London, 1955, p.104, C. S. Lewis to Albert Lewis, 21 October 1925.
2   George Sayer, *Jack: A Life of C. S. Lewis*, Harper and Row, New York, 1988, p.203.
3   John Lawlor, 'The Tutor and the Scholar', in *Light on C. S. Lewis*, edited by Jocelyn Gibb, Geoffrey Bles, London, 1965.
4   Ibid.

5 John Lawlor, *C. S. Lewis: Memoirs and Reflections*, Spence, Dallas, Texas, 1999.

6 The Lewis Papers: Memoirs of the Lewis Family, 1850–1930, in the Wade Collection, Marion E. Wade Center, Wheaton College, Wheaton, Illinois, USA, vol. 9, p.148.

7 Roger Lancelyn Green and Walter Hooper, *C. S. Lewis*, Harvest Books, London, 1994, p.91.

8 *Jack: A Life of C. S. Lewis*, p.204.

9 The Lewis Papers, vol. 10, p.94.

10 C. S. Lewis, Diary entry for 11 May 1926, The Lewis Papers.

11 *The Letters of C. S. Lewis*, p.12.

6: Fantasy

1 A.N. Wilson, *C. S. Lewis: A Biography*, W.W. Norton, New York, 1990, p.161.

2 From Warren Lewis to Albert Lewis, 28 January 1919, The Lewis Papers: Memoirs of the Lewis Family, 1850–1930, in the Wade Collection, Marion E. Wade Center, Wheaton College, Wheaton, Illinois, USA, vol. 6, p.84.

3 Walter Hooper (ed.), *They Stand Together: The Letters of C. S. Lewis to Arthur Greeves 1914–1963*, Collins, London 1979, pp.474–5.

4 Horace Williams, *New York Times Book Review*, April 1939, p.304.

5 *The Times Literary Supplement*, 1 October 1938, p.625.

6 Graham Greene, *Evening Standard*, 24 August 1945, p.6.

7 Orville Prescott, *New York Times*, 21 May 1946. *Time*, vol. XLVII, no. 23, 10 June 1946, p.36.

8 C. S. Lewis to Warren Lewis, 20 July 1940, quoted in Walter Hooper, *C. S. Lewis: Companion and Guide*, HarperCollins, 1996, p.267.

9 Leonard Bacon, *Saturday Review of Literature*, 26, 17 April 1943, p.20.

10 *Times Literary Supplement*, 28 February 1942, p.100.

11 Charles Williams, *Time and Tide*, 21 March 1942. Williams also reviewed the book in *Dublin Review*, no. 423, October 1942.

12 C. S. Lewis, 'It All Began with a Picture', *Radio Times*, vol. CXLVIII, 15 July 1960.

7: Friendship

1 C. S. Lewis, *Surprised by Joy*, Harcourt Brace and Co., New York, 1955, p.209.

2   Humphrey Carpenter, *J.R.R. Tolkien: A Biography*, George Allen and Unwin, London, 1977, p.3.

3   C. S. Lewis and Charles Williams, *Arthurian Torso*, Oxford University Press, 1948, p.1.

4   Unpublished letter to Arthur Greeves, 11 January 1944, quoted in Clyde Kilby, *Tolkien and the Silmarillion*, Harold Shaw Publishers, USA, 1976, p.73.

5   *Tolkien and the Silmarillion*, p.67.

6   Nigel Reynolds, *Daily Telegraph*, 20 January 1996.

7   W.H. Lewis (ed.), *The Letters of C. S. Lewis*, Geoffrey Bles, London, 1966, p.287.

8   Quoted in George Sayer, *Jack: A Life of C. S. Lewis*, Harper and Row, New York, 1988, p.222.

9   Letter to Sheldon Vanauken, 17 April 1951, The Lewis Papers: Memoirs of the Lewis Family, 1850–1930, in the Wade Collection, Marion E. Wade Center, Wheaton College, Wheaton, Illinois, USA.

10 *Surprised by Joy*, p.189.

11 Roger Lancelyn Green and Walter Hooper, *C. S. Lewis: A Biography*, Collins, London, 1974, p.197.

12 Humphrey Carpenter, *The Inklings: C. S. Lewis, J.R.R. Tolkien, Charles Williams and their Friends*, George Allen and Unwin, London, 1978, p.52.

13 *C. S. Lewis: A Biography*, p.241.

14 From an unpublished memoir of Lewis by Peter Bayley, quoted in Humphrey Carpenter, *The Inklings*, p.120.

15 *The Letters of C. S. Lewis*, pp.196–7.

16 Ibid.

17 Charles Williams, *Divorce*, Oxford University Press, 1920.

18 C. S. Lewis et al., *Essays Presented to Charles Williams*, Oxford University Press, 1947, p.x.

19 A.N. Wilson, *C. S. Lewis: A Biography*, W.W. Norton, New York, 1990, p.174.

20 Henry S. Resnick, *Niekas*, vol. 18, no. 43.

21 Humphrey Carpenter, *W.H. Auden*, Unwin, London, 1981, p.224.

22 C. S. Lewis, Bodleian Library, Oxford, MS.Eng lett. C.220/5, fol.77.

23 Edwin Muir, *Observer*, 22 August 1954.

8: From War to Joy.

1 Walter Hooper (ed.), *They Stand Together: The Letters of C. S. Lewis to Arthur Greeves 1914–1963*, Collins, London, 1979, p.485; 15 September 1939.

2 The Diary of Warnie Lewis, 15 May 1945, in the Wade Collection, Marion E. Wade Center, Wheaton College, Wheaton, Illinois, USA.

3 Humphrey Carpenter, *The Inklings: C. S. Lewis, J.R.R. Tolkien, Charles Williams and their Friends*, George Allen and Unwin, London, 1978, p.204.

4 *They Stand Together*, p.499.

5 The Diary of Warnie Lewis, 13 January 1951.

9: Joy

1 The Diary of Warren Lewis, p.276.

2 Walter Hooper (ed.), *They Stand Together: The Letters of C. S. Lewis to Arthur Greeves 1914–1963*, Collins, London, 1979, pp.542–3.

3 The Diary of Warren H. Lewis, p.246.

4 Douglas H. Gresham, *Lenten Lands: My Childhood with Joy Davidman and C. S. Lewis*, Harper San Francisco, San Francisco, California, 1988, p.127.

5 George Sayer, *Jack: A Life of C. S. Lewis*, Harper and Row, New York, 1988, p.369.

6 C. S. Lewis to Sheldon Vanauken, quoted in Sheldon Vanauken, *A Severe Mercy*, Harper and Row, New York, 1977, pp.227–8.

7 Quoted in *Jack: A Life of C. S. Lewis*, p.373.

8 C. S. Lewis (under pseudonym N.W. Clerk), *A Grief Observed*, Faber & Faber, London, 1961, p.263.

10: Life Without Joy

1 Douglas Gresham, *Lenten Lands: My Childhood with Joy Gresham and C. S. Lewis*, Harper San Francisco, San Francisco, California, 1988, p.130.

2 C. S. Lewis, *A Grief Observed*, Faber & Faber, London 1961, p.7.

3 Ibid., p.16.

4 Ibid., p.44, p.37.

5 Ibid., p.41.

6 *Lenten Lands*, p.134.

7 Walter Hooper (ed.), *They Stand Together: The Letters of C. S. Lewis to

Arthur Greeves 1914–1963, Collins, London, 1979, p.564.

8   Quoted in Roger Lancelyn Green and Walter Hooper, *C. S. Lewis: A Biography*, Harcourt, Inc., New York, 1976, p.307.

11: Legacy

1   'Magic of Narnia is Hollywood's Next Trick', Adam Sherwin, *The Times*, Saturday 8 December 2001, p.3.

2   'The Lion, the Witch and the Wardrobe', Entertainment News website, 31 July 2002.

3   Doreen Carvajal, 'Marketing Narnia Without a Christian Lion'; interview with Carvajal at TheOneRing.net website, 3 June 2001.

4   C. S. Lewis, *Surprised by Joy*, Harcourt Brace and Co., New York, 1955, p.61.

5   'In Defense of Lewis', Greg Easterbrook, *The Atlantic Online* (*The Atlantic Monthly*), October 2001.

6   Ibid.

A Guide to the Publications of C. S. Lewis

Fiction and poetry

Spirits in Bondage (Heinemann, 1919)
A collection of poems which deal mostly with Lewis's response to his experiences during the First World War. Originally published under the pseudonym Clive Hamilton.

Dymer (Dent, 1926)
An extended narrative poem.

The Pilgrim's Regress: An Allegorical Apology for Christianity, Reason and Romanticism (Dent, 1933)
Lewis's first attempt at religious allegory. Loosely modelled on Bunyan's famous tale, it tells of the journey to salvation of an everyday man whom Lewis named John in honour of Bunyan.

Out of the Silent Planet (John Lane the Bodley Head, 1938)
The first in the Ransom trilogy, the book is set on Mars and centres on Dr Elwin Ransom, a Cambridge philologist who becomes embroiled in an interplanetary battle between good and evil.

The Dark Tower (fragment written around 1938, published by Collins, 1977)
This was an abortive attempt at a sequel to *Out of the Silent Planet* in which

Lewis tries his hand at writing a novel about time travel. It is far darker and more sinister than anything else he wrote, but because the surviving text is only some 30,000 words in length it is difficult to know how Lewis would have developed the story if he had completed it.

The Screwtape Letters (Geoffrey Bles, 1942)

Originally written as a series of magazine articles, *The Screwtape Letters* consists of a correspondence between a trainee devil named Wormwood and his powerful senior devil, his Uncle Screwtape. It is an amusing and thought-provoking fantasy that uses satire to delve deep into theological concerns.

Perelandra (John Lane the Bodley Head, 1943)

Later retitled *Voyage to Venus*, this is the second book in the Ransom trilogy and describes Elwin Ransom's mental battle with the devil in the form of his old enemy from *Out of the Silent Planet*, Dr Weston. This battle takes place on a virginal planet Venus (Perelandra) and the book may be considered a recasting of the story of the Garden of Eden.

That Hideous Strength (John Lane the Bodley Head, 1945)

Subtitled 'a modern fairy-tale for grown-ups', this is the third and last book in the Ransom trilogy. Set on earth, it tells of the final battle between the forces of good and evil. Ransom, now revealed to be the Pendragon of Arthurian legend, enlists the help of a resurrected Merlin to fight the N.I.C.E., a demonic organisation bent on corrupting humanity.

The Great Divorce: A Dream (Geoffrey Bles, 1946)

A work of religious allegory in which Lewis describes a dream involving a journey to both heaven and hell.

The Lion, the Witch and the Wardrobe (Geoffrey Bles, 1950)

The first book in the seven-volume series *The Chronicles of Narnia*. Four English children, Lucy, Susan, Edmund and Peter, accidentally discover a magic land which lies beyond the real world and which they may reach through an ordinary wardrobe in the bedroom of an old house. In this land, Narnia, Edmund betrays his brother and sisters to the White Witch, who has suspended all of Narnia in a state of perpetual winter. Only when the lion Aslan agrees to die at the Witch's hand can Edmund's betrayal be forgiven and spring be allowed to return to Narnia.

Prince Caspian: The Return to Narnia (Geoffrey Bles, 1951)
In the second book in the Narnia series the four children return to a Narnia in which many centuries have passed. Here they encounter the mouse Reepicheep and are enlisted to help Prince Caspian to defeat the Telmarines and to bring back the Old Things.

The Voyage of the Dawn Treader (Geoffrey Bles, 1952)
The third book in the Narnia series is another adventure involving Caspian, who is now a king. Edmund and Lucy join their cousin Eustace and the three become involved in a voyage to the World's End aboard a ship captained by Caspian. At the World's End the children encounter Aslan, who tells them that they are now too old for Narnia and must endeavour to see him in their own world.

The Silver Chair (Geoffrey Bles, 1953)
The fourth Narnia book sees the children's cousin, Eustace, and a friend, Jill Pole, embark on their own adventure when Aslan sends them to find the imprisoned Rilian, who is the true heir to the Narnian throne. Guided by a new character, Puddleglum, the children help Rilian to escape from Underland.

The Horse and His Boy (Geoffrey Bles, 1954)
The fifth book in the series is a tale which, except for its setting and historical backdrop, has little to do with many of the other Narnia books. It centres on a character named Shasta, who, aided by the Tarkheena Aravis and two talking horses (Hwin and Bree), helps save Archenland from invasion.

The Magician's Nephew (The Bodley Head, 1955)
The sixth Narnia book begins in late-Victorian London, where two children, Polly and Digory (whose Uncle Andrew is a rather ineffectual magician), meet an evil queen during their travels. The queen unintentionally leads the children and Uncle Andrew to witness the creation of Narnia, the moment when Aslan gives the gift of speech to the animals.

The Last Battle (The Bodley Head, 1956)
The final book in the series is set in the final days of Narnia, when a clever ape has created a false Aslan, which disturbs the citizens of Narnia as well as the original travellers Lucy, Susan, Peter and Edmund (now kings and queens of Narnia). Close to the end of the book, all four children die in a railway accident in England at the same time that Narnia ceases to exist. Three of the children, Lucy, Peter and Edmund, find a new Narnia or 'heaven'.

Till We Have Faces: A Myth Retold (Geoffrey Bles, 1956)
Written with a substantial degree of input from Joy Gresham just as she and Lewis were drawing close, this was the least commercially successful of all the writer's novels. It is a modern recasting and retelling of the ancient story of Cupid and Psyche, in which Psyche, a beautiful mortal princess, is loved by Cupid (or Eros), the god of love. Psyche then loses Cupid through lack of trust. The title comes from the notion understood eventually by one of the lead characters, Orual, that we cannot look the gods in the face until we have acquired faces, a metaphor for our souls.

Poems (Geoffrey Bles, 1964)
A collection published posthumously and edited by Walter Hooper. These poems were written by Lewis between the 1920s and the 1950s. The collection does not include the poems published in *Spirits in Bondage* in 1919.

Screwtape Proposes a Toast and other Pieces (Fontana, 1965)
This is Lewis's one-off return to the Screwtape story and recounts a speech delivered by Screwtape at the 'annual dinner of the Tempter's Training College for young Devils'. It was originally written for the *Saturday Evening Post* in London and first published in December 1959.

Non-fiction

The Allegory of Love (Clarendon Press, 1936)
Lewis's first scholarly work, subtitled 'A Study in Medieval Tradition', this is a survey and a critique of allegorical love poetry from Ovid to Spenser.

Rehabilitations and Other Essays (Oxford University Press, 1939)
A collection that includes the essays 'High and Low Brows', 'William Morris' and 'Christianity and Literature'.

The Personal Heresy: A Controversy (Oxford University Press, 1939)
Co-authored by E.M.W. Tillyard, this is a collection of six essays (three by each author) debating the question of whether poetry is a true expression of a poet's personality.

The Problem of Pain (Geoffrey Bles, 1940)
Controversial in its day, this remains a thought-provoking work. Lewis attempts to address the question, If God is good and God is omnipotent, why is there pain and evil in the world?

A Preface to Paradise Lost (Oxford University Press, 1942)
This book derives from a series of lectures Lewis gave on the subject of epic poetry (concentrating on Milton's *Paradise Lost*). He believed that a reader could not understand or appreciate Milton's masterpiece without first comprehending the beliefs that it presupposes.

Broadcast Talks (Geoffrey Bles, 1942)
A set of essays based on Lewis's radio talks at the BBC.

Christian Behaviour: A Further Series of Broadcast Talks (Geoffrey Bles, 1943)

The Abolition of Man (Clarendon Press, 1943)
A set of three lectures defending the concept of Natural Law.

Beyond Personality: the Christian Idea of God (Geoffrey Bles, 1944)
A final set of essays linked with Lewis's BBC broadcasts.

Miracles: A Preliminary Study (Geoffrey Bles, 1947)
Lewis questions whether we have grounds for believing in the supernatural, how this would then relate to the 'natural' and how each may be linked with the Christian assertion of the Miracle of the Incarnation.

Transpositions and Other Addresses (Geoffrey Bles, 1949)
A set of religious essays which includes 'Learning in War-Time' (1939),

'The Weight of Glory' (1941) and 'The Inner Ring' (1944).

Mere Christianity (Macmillan, New York, 1943)
Another collection based on Lewis's broadcast talks at the BBC. These
were written specifically for a lay audience and the author undertakes
throughout to confine himself to the common Christian core of belief
and steer clear of disagreements between denominations.

English Literature in the Sixteenth Century Excluding Drama (Clarendon Press, 1954)
This is one of Lewis's most successful academic works and is still considered a classic by specialists and lay readers alike.

Surprised by Joy: The Shape of My Early Life (Geoffrey Bles, 1955)
Lewis's not-very-revealing autobiography.

Reflections on the Psalms (Geoffrey Bles, 1958)
Lewis addresses questions that occurred to him while praying or studying
the Psalms.

The Four Loves (Geoffrey Bles, 1958)
In this book, which was greatly influenced by his wife, Joy, Lewis analyses
four different kinds of love, taking as his starting point the ancient Greek
words for them.

Studies in Words (Cambridge University Press, 1960)
An academic work in which Lewis discusses the changes from century to
century in the meaning of a selection of words.

The World's Last Night and Other Essays (Harcourt Brace and Co., 1960)

A Grief Observed (Faber & Faber, 1961)
Originally written under the pseudonym N.W. Clerk, this is Lewis's most
honest and profoundly moving book. He explains how he reacted to his
wife's death and began to deal with his loss.

An Experiment in Criticism (Cambridge University Press, 1961)
Lewis on the subject of how to approach a book or any piece of art and
how to distinguish between the different sorts of pleasures that may be
derived from 'good art' and 'bad art'.

They Asked for a Paper: Papers and Addresses (Geoffrey Bles, 1962)
A collection which includes the papers 'Psycho-analysis and Literary Criticism' (1941) and 'De Descriptione Temporum' (1954).

Letters to Malcolm: Chiefly on Prayer (Geoffrey Bles, 1964)
Lewis on how to pray.

The Discarded Image: An Introduction to Medieval and Renaissance Literature (Cambridge University Press, 1964)
Lewis explains how the image of the universe in medieval and renaissance times is reflected in the literature of the era.

Letters and other material

After Lewis's death several books were published that were based on manuscripts he had left complete, and many others were compiled from collections of essays, letters, notes and fragments.

Of Other Worlds: Essays and Stories (edited by Walter Hooper; Geoffrey Bles, 1966)

On Stories: and Other Essays on Literature (edited by Walter Hooper; Harcourt Brace Jovanovich, London, 1966)

Christian Reflections (Eerdmans, 1967)

Selected Literary Essays (edited by Walter Hooper; Cambridge University Press, 1969)

God in the Dock: Essays on Theology and Ethics (edited by Walter Hooper; Eerdmans, 1970)

Fern Seed and Elephants (Collins Fount, 1975)

The Weight of Glory (Macmillan, 1980)

Boxen: The Imaginary World of C. S. Lewis (Harcourt Brace Jovanovich, San Diego, California, 1985)
A collection of some of Lewis's childhood fantasy writing.

Present Concerns (edited by Walter Hooper; Harcourt Brace Jovanovich, London, 1986)

Lewis's diaries and letters have been published in many editions, including:
Letters to an American Lady (Eerdmans, 1967)
Letters to an American fan whom he never met, written between 1950 and 1963.

They Stand Together: The Letters of C. S. Lewis to Arthur Greeves 1914–1963 (edited by Walter Hooper; Macmillan, New York, 1979)
The intense and honest correspondence between Lewis and his closest and oldest friend.

Letters (Servant Books, Michigan, 1988)
A set of letters exchanged between Lewis and two Italian priests between 1947 and 1961.

Letters to Children (Collier Books, Macmillan, 1988)
A collection drawn from Lewis's vast correspondence with his younger fans.

All My Road Before Me: The Diary of C. S. Lewis, 1922–1927 (Harcourt Brace Jovanovich, San Diego, California, 1991)

The Letters of C. S. Lewis (edited by W.H. Lewis; Geoffrey Bles, 1994)

Appendix 2

A Chronology of the Life and Times of C. S. Lewis

18 May 1862: 'Flora' Augusta Hamilton, Lewis's mother, is born.

23 August 1863: Albert James Lewis, Lewis's father, is born.

28 March 1872: Janie Moore (née King) is born.

3 January 1892: J.R.R. Tolkien is born.

29 August 1894: Albert and Flora marry in St Mark's Church, Belfast.

27 August 1895: Warren Hamilton Lewis, Lewis's brother, is born.

29 November 1898: Birth of C. S. (Clive Staples) Lewis.

1899–1902: Boer War.

22 January 1901: Queen Victoria dies.

21 April 1905: The Lewis family move to their new home, Little Lea, on the outskirts of Belfast.

12 July 1908: Lewis enrols at Wynyard School, Watford, Hertfordshire.

23 August 1908: Flora Hamilton Lewis dies of cancer.

6 May 1910: King Edward VII dies.

September 1910: Lewis attends Campbell College boarding school in Belfast, but leaves in November the same year.

January 1911: Lewis is sent to school at Cherbourg House, Malvern, England, and remains there until June 1913.

3 January 1914: Warren Lewis enrols at Sandhurst.

June 1914: Lewis and Arthur Greeves begin corresponding after their first meeting in April that year.

4 August 1914: Britain declares war on Germany.

19 September 1914: Lewis begins his studies with William Kirkpatrick at Great Bookham, Surrey.

14 November 1914: Warren Lewis goes to fight in France.

18 April 1915: Joy Davidman born in New York City.

5–9 December 1916: Lewis sits scholarship exams at Oxford University. On 23 December he receives news that he has been awarded a scholarship to attend University College, Oxford.

26 April 1917: Lewis arrives at Oxford.

May 1917: Lewis meets Paddy Moore.

8 June 1917: Lewis meets Janie Moore.

November 1917: Lewis goes to fight in France.

15 April 1918: Lewis is wounded during the battle of Arras.

May 1918: Lewis re-establishes his relationship with Janie Moore while convalescing in England.

September 1918: Paddy Moore (Janie Moore's son) is officially declared dead.

11 November 1918: First World War ends.

13 January 1919: Lewis returns to his studies at Oxford. The same month Janie Moore and her daughter, Maureen, move to the city.

20 March 1919: Lewis's first book, *Spirits in Bondage*, published.

31 March 1920: Lewis takes a First in Classical Honour Moderations.

22 March 1921: Lewis's tutor, William Kirkpatrick, dies.

4 August 1922: Lewis takes a First in Greats.

16 June 1923: Lewis takes a First in English.

20 May 1925: Lewis is elected Fellow of Magdalen College, Oxford.

11 May 1926: Lewis meets J.R.R. Tolkien. The same month Britain is thrown into chaos by the General Strike.

11 April 1927: Warren Lewis is posted to China.

25 September 1929: Albert Lewis dies.

10–11 October 1930: Lewis and Janie and Maureen Moore move into The Kilns.

Late 1930: The Inklings first meet in Oxford.

September 1931: Lewis returns to a belief in Christianity.

December 1932: Warren Lewis retires from the Army and moves into The Kilns.

21 May 1936: Lewis's *Allegory of Love* is published.

12 December 1936: King Edward VIII abdicates.

21 September 1937: Tolkien's *The Hobbit* is published in Britain.

23 September 1938: *Out of the Silent Planet* is published.

3 September 1939: Britain declares war on Germany.

May 1940: Warren Lewis evacuated from Dunkirk.

27 August 1940: Maureen Moore marries Leonard Blake.

April 1941: Lewis gives his first RAF talk.

2 May 1941: The first of the thirty-one *Screwtape Letters* is published in *The Guardian* magazine.

6 August 1941: Lewis gives the first of his BBC radio broadcasts.

26 January 1942: The Socratic Club meets in Oxford for the first time.

9 February 1942: *The Screwtape Letters* is published.

20 April 1943: *Perelandra* is published.

27 March 1944: Joy Gresham's first son, David, is born in New York.

9 May 1945: Second World War ends.

15 May 1945: Charles Williams, one of Lewis's closest friends, dies.

6 August 1945: An atomic bomb is dropped on Hiroshima, Japan.

16 August 1945: *That Hideous Strength* is published.

10 November 1945: Douglas Gresham is born in New York City.

8 September 1947: Lewis appears on the cover of *Time* magazine.

20 October 1949: The last recorded Thursday-night meeting of the Inklings takes place; Tuesday-morning meetings at the Eagle and Child on St Giles continue.

1950–3: The Korean War.

10 January 1950: Lewis receives his first letter from Joy Gresham.

16 October 1950: *The Lion, the Witch and the Wardrobe* is published.

12 January 1951: Janie Moore dies.

15 October 1951: *Prince Caspian* is published.

15 September 1952: *The Voyage of the Dawn Treader* is published.

24 September 1952: Lewis meets Joy Gresham (née Davidman) for the first time over lunch at the Eastgate Hotel in Oxford.

7 September 1953: *The Silver Chair* is published.

1953: Collins buys Geoffrey Bles and so becomes Lewis's publisher.

4 June 1954: Lewis accepts the Chair of Medieval and Renaissance Literature at Cambridge.

6 September 1954: *The Horse and His Boy* is published.

18 April 1955: Albert Einstein dies.

2 May 1955: *The Magician's Nephew* is published.

August 1955: Joy Gresham and her sons David and Douglas move to Oxford.

19 September 1955: *Surprised by Joy* is published.

19 March 1956: *The Last Battle* is published.

23 April 1956: Lewis and Joy Gresham are married in a civil ceremony in Oxford.

10 September 1956: *Till We Have Faces* is published.

19 October 1956: Joy is diagnosed with cancer.

21 March 1957: Lewis and Joy have their marriage sanctified by the Reverend Peter Bide in a ceremony in Joy's hospital room.

June 1958–October 1959: Joy's cancer is in remission.

3–14 April 1960. The Lewises visit Greece on a ten-day holiday.

13 July 1960: Joy dies.

18 August 1960: The Beatles first play in Hamburg.

29 September 1961: *A Grief Observed* is published under the pseudonym N.W. Clerk.

22 November 1963: C. S. Lewis dies the same day as John F. Kennedy and Aldous Huxley.

9 April 1973: Warren Lewis dies at The Kilns.

2 September 1973: J.R.R. Tolkien dies.

1994: The film *Shadowlands*, starring Anthony Hopkins and Debra Winger, is released

17 February 1997: Lady Dunbar of Hempriggs (née Maureen Moore) dies.

2000: Film rights to the Narnia books are sold for £50 million to Walden Media, who begin production of the first film in a projected series.

Appendix 3

Those Who Survived C. S. Lewis

A guide to the main characters in Lewis's life and what happened to them after his death in 1963.

Owen Barfield

A brilliant academic and talented writer, Barfield was a close contemporary of Lewis. The two men met within weeks of their arrival in Oxford in 1916 and stayed firm friends for the rest of Lewis's life. After graduating from Wadham College, Oxford, Barfield worked as a freelance writer but found that he could not support his growing family in this way and became a lawyer in his father's legal firm, where he worked until 1959. After he retired he was, in 1964–5, Visiting Professor at Drew University, New Jersey, before returning to writing. Barfield published many highly regarded works, including *Saving the Appearances: A Study in Idolatry* (1957) and *Worlds Apart* (1963).

Barfield was a contributor to meetings of the Inklings whenever he was in Oxford. As one of Lewis's most trusted friends, he became the executor of Lewis's estate after his death in 1963. Barfield died in 1997 aged ninety-nine.

Peter Bide

The Reverend Bide was the clergyman who conducted Lewis's marriage to Joy Gresham in Wingfield Morris Hospital, Oxford, on 21 March 1957. Born in 1912, he studied English at Oxford and got to know Lewis first as a student attending his lectures and later as a friend. He served in the Royal Marines and rose to the rank of captain before being ordained as an

Anglican deacon in 1949. He became a good friend of Lewis soon after this and stayed close to the writer's family for the rest of his life. He retired from the Church in 1980.

Maureen Blake (Lady Dunbar of Hempriggs)

Maureen Moore was the daughter of Janie Moore, with whom Jack lived for over thirty years. She grew up in a variety of homes she shared with her mother and Lewis in and around Oxford, including The Kilns from 1930. Some writers have described Maureen as a 'lifelong friend' of Lewis but a more accurate description would be to call her his common-law step-daughter. Maureen attended the Royal Academy of Music and began to work as a music teacher in 1930. In 1940 she married Leonard Blake, who was Director of Music at Worksop College, Derbyshire. In early 1963 Maureen discovered that she was titled: a distant relative, Sir George Cospatrick Duff-Sutherland-Dunbar, had died the previous year and she was next in line for a baronetcy, becoming Lady Dunbar of Hempriggs. After the death of Lewis's brother Warren in 1973, she and her husband inherited The Kilns.

Maureen's title brought her and her husband no financial reward and they continued to teach all their working lives. Leonard Blake became Director of Music at Malvern College in 1945 and remained in the post until he retired. The couple had two children. Leonard died in 1989 and Maureen died in 1997.

Hugo Dyson

Born in 1896, Dyson was an academic and a soldier. He was educated at Brighton College before graduating to Sandhurst. He was seriously wounded at Passchendaele in 1917. In 1919 he went up to Exeter College, Oxford, to read English. He became a lecturer at Reading University in 1924 but moved back to Oxford in 1945, becoming a Fellow of Merton College. Dyson died in 1975.

Arthur Greeves

Three years older than Lewis, Arthur Greeves was a close friend from 1914. Elements of their relationship have been preserved in the many letters they exchanged over some fifty years, which were published in 1979 as *They Stand Together*. Greeves was a sickly child and suffered poor health throughout his life. He left his native Belfast only for relatively short periods, but was educated at the Slade School of Fine Art in London and then lived for a short while in Paris before becoming a professional artist who exhibited in Ireland. Greeves was a homosexual and a deeply religious man, although he abandoned orthodox Christianity late in life to become a Quaker. He died in 1966.

David Gresham

The elder son of Joy Gresham (née Davidman), David Gresham never felt comfortable with his mother's decision to move to England in 1953 and this, along with many unhappy childhood experiences, scarred him. He and his younger brother, Douglas, became Lewis's stepsons upon his marriage to Joy, but whereas Douglas became deeply involved with the Lewis family and the writer's legacy, David, from his early teenage years, chose to follow his own, quite different road. In 1961 he became interested in the study of Judaism and took a degree in Oriental Studies at Magdalene College, Cambridge, in 1972. Since then he has travelled widely, continuing his study of languages and cultures. He moved to Dublin in 1985, married in 1992 and he and his wife have one son, born in 1994. He and Douglas are no longer in communication.

Douglas Gresham

Lewis's younger stepson, Douglas Gresham was born to Joy and Bill Gresham in New York in 1945. He moved to England with his mother and brother David in 1953 and was educated at a succession of public schools. After studying agriculture he married in 1967. He and his wife, Merry, have had four children and adopted a fifth in 1990. In 1993 Douglas and his family settled in Ireland, where he has worked ever since as a non-denominational minister. His account of his childhood with Joy Gresham and Lewis, *Lenten Lands*, was published in 1988. He is now a creative consultant for all matters linked with Lewis's books and is working closely with Walden Media, who are making the film of *The Lion, the Witch and the Wardrobe*.

Colin Hardie

Born in 1906, Hardie was an Oxford graduate and later a Fellow of Balliol who was a member of the Inklings when he lived and worked in Oxford. He was Director of the British School in Rome between 1933 and 1936 before returning to Oxford, where he became a Fellow of

Lewis's college, Magdalen. Between 1967 and 1973 Hardie was Public Orator for Oxford University and was made Honorary Professor of Ancient Literature at the Royal Academy of Arts in 1971. He died in 1998.

Robert ('Humphrey') Havard

For many years Havard was Lewis's personal physician. He began his academic life studying chemistry at Keble College, Oxford, before taking a medical degree and qualifying as a doctor. He lived for a while in Leeds before returning to Oxford in 1934, when he met Lewis and his friends. Although not a literary man, Havard was for many years a regular and much-loved member of the Inklings. He ran medical practices in Headington, just outside Oxford, and St Giles in the city centre, and died in 1985.

Walter Hooper

Born in 1931, Hooper met Lewis in Oxford a few months before the author's death in November 1963. For a short time in the summer of that year he acted as part-time assistant to Lewis and has been responsible for a large number of books about Lewis and his work. These include *C. S. Lewis: Companion and Guide* (1996), which won the Gold Medallion Book Award in 1997. Many Lewis scholars claim that Hooper has described his relationship with the writer as being closer and more significant to the older man than the facts show, and that he has created a myth around himself to heighten his own profile.

For twenty-four years between 1964 and 1988 Hooper was a deacon of the Anglican Church before converting to Catholicism. He continues to work as an editor and self-appointed 'literary heir' to Lewis.

Warren ('Warnie') Lewis

Born in 1895, Warren Lewis lived with his younger brother Jack and their parents at Little Lea until 1905, when he left home to attend Wynyard School in England. Later he went to Malvern College and was educated for a short time by William Kirkpatrick in Great Bookham, Surrey. He graduated to Sandhurst in 1914 and was a professional soldier until 1932.

Throughout his adult life Warren was a victim of alcoholism. He was devoted to his brother and lived with him at The Kilns from 1932 until 1963. He was a leading light in the Inklings and read his own literary

efforts to the group. His keen interest in French history led him to publish several books on the subject, including *The Splendid Century* (1953), *The
Sunset of the Splendid Century* (1955) and *Louis XIV: An Informal Portrait* (1959).

After Jack died, Warren became a rather pathetic figure who could not
break out of his mourning. He let The Kilns, but returned to live there
sporadically. He completed the collection known as the Lewis Papers,
which contains letters, diaries and assorted documentation concerning
his family, and in 1966 he published a collection of Jack's letters. Warren
died in 1973 aged seventy-seven.

Fred Paxford

Employed as a gardener and general repair man at The Kilns, Fred Paxford
was also a genuine friend to Jack and Warren Lewis and was much loved
by Janie Moore. He began working for the Lewises soon after the move to
The Kilns in 1930 and served there for three decades until Lewis's death
in 1963, when he retired to his house and allotment in the Oxfordshire village of Churchill. He died there in 1979.

Sister Penelope (Ruth Penelope Lawson)

Sister Penelope became a spiritual guide and friend to Lewis soon after she
wrote to him with her thoughts on his novel *Out of the Silent Planet*. Lewis
referred to her as his 'elder sister in the Faith' and he shared many of his
most intimate thoughts with her from 1939 until 1963. Lewis dedicated
Perelandra to 'some Ladies at Wantage', a reference to Sister Penelope and
her convent, the Community of St Mary the Virgin at Wantage, Berkshire.
Sister Penelope was herself an accomplished writer who published some
twenty books on theology under the pseudonym 'A Religious of CSMV'.
She died in 1977 aged eighty-seven.

George Sayer

A student of Lewis's at Magdalen College, Oxford, between 1933 and
1936, George Sayer was greatly inspired by Lewis's brand of Christianity
and stayed close to him after their academic relationship ended. He
became an Inkling in the late 1930s and in the late 1940s he left Oxford
to become an English master at Malvern College, which both Jack and
Warren Lewis had attended as children. He kept in touch with his Oxford
friends and the Lewis brothers often stayed with him in Malvern. Sayer
wrote a biography of Lewis called *Jack: A Life of C. S. Lewis* (1988).

Christopher Tolkien

Christopher Tolkien is the youngest of J.R.R. Tolkien's three sons (his sister Priscilla was born in 1929). Born in 1924, Christopher was a successful academic at Oxford University and an important member of the Inklings. After his father's death he became the literary executor of the Tolkien estate. He edited and completed *The Silmarillion*, his father's account of the history of Middle-earth, which had been left incomplete and unpublished at the time of his death in 1973. Christopher, who now lives in France, has since written a vast canon of books that fill in the historical detail of Middle-earth.

J.R.R. Tolkien

For close to two decades, between the late 1920s and the late 1940s, Tolkien and Lewis were inseparable friends. Together they founded the Inklings and each scrutinised the other's writing, helping each other to become published and successful authors. Tolkien was born in South Africa in 1892 and became a scholar at Exeter College, Oxford, before taking the Chair of Anglo-Saxon at Oxford in 1925.

Although a highly successful academic, Tolkien is most famous as the author of *The Lord of the Rings*, which has been voted the most influential and best-loved book of the twentieth century. This book has sold over one hundred million copies and has been made into a much-praised trilogy of films by the New Zealand director Peter Jackson. Lewis's encouragement pushed Tolkien into completing this epic work and Tolkien always appreciated the fact that he might never have delivered the book to his publisher if it had not been for the influence of his friend and fellow academic. In return, Lewis acknowledged Tolkien as being in major part responsible for converting him to Christianity. However, from about the late 1940s the friendship between the two men cooled and towards the end of Lewis's life they saw little of each other. Tolkien died in 1973.

Bibliography

Books

L. Adley, *C. S. Lewis: Writer, Dreamer and Mentor*, Eerdmans, Grand Rapids, Michigan, 1998

H. Carpenter, *The Inklings: C. S. Lewis, J.R.R. Tolkien, Charles Williams and their Friends*, George Allen and Unwin, London, 1978

Joe R. Christopher, *C. S. Lewis*, Twayne, Boston, Massachusetts, 1987

J.T. Como, *C. S. Lewis at the Breakfast Table and other Reminiscences*, Macmillan, New York, 1979

R.B. Cunningham, *C. S. Lewis: Defender of the Faith*, Westminster Press, Philadelphia, 1967

C. Duriez, *The C. S. Lewis Encyclopedia: A Complete Guide to His Life, Thought and Writings*, Crossway Books, Wheaton, Illinois, 2000

K. Filmer, *The Fiction of C. S. Lewis: 'Mask and Mirror'*, St Martin's Press, New York, 1993

E. Fuller, *Books with Men Behind Them*, Random House, New York, 1959

J. Gibb (ed.), *Light on C. S. Lewis*, Geoffrey Bles, London, 1965

Evan K. Gibson, *C. S. Lewis, Spinner of Tales: A Guide to His Fiction*, Eerdmans, Grand Rapids, Michigan, 1980

D.E. Glover, *C. S. Lewis: The Art of Enchantment*, Ohio University Press, Athens, Ohio, 1981

Beatrice Gormley, *C. S. Lewis: Christian and Storyteller*, Eerdmans, Grand Rapids, Michigan, 1998

David Graham (ed.), *We Remember C. S. Lewis: Essays and Memoirs*, Broadman and Holman, 2002

Roger Lancelyn Green and Walter Hooper, *C. S. Lewis: A Biography*, Collins, London, 1974

Douglas H. Gresham, *Lenten Lands: My Childhood with Joy Davidman and C. S. Lewis*, Harper San Francisco, San Francisco, California, 1988

William Griffin, *Clive Staples Lewis: A Dramatic Life*, Harper & Row, San Francisco, California, 1986

M.P. Hannay, *C. S. Lewis*, Ungar, New York, 1981

D.A. Hart, *Through the Open Door: A New Look at C. S. Lewis*, University of Alabama Press, Montgomery, Alabama, 1984

D. Holbrook, *The Skeleton in the Wardrobe: C. S. Lewis's Fantasies, a Phenomenological Study*, Bucknell University Press, Lewisburg, Pennsylvania, 1991

L. Paul Holmer, *C. S. Lewis: The Shape of His Faith and Thought*, Sheldon Press, London, 1977

Walter Hooper, *C. S. Lewis. A Companion and Guide*, HarperCollins, London, 1996

Clyde S. Kilby, *The Christian World of C. S. Lewis*, Eerdmans, Grand Rapids, Michigan, 1964

G. Knight, *The Magical World of the Inklings*, Element, Longmead, UK, 1990

Wesley A. Kort, *C. S. Lewis: Then and Now*, Oxford University Press, 2001

P. Kreeft, *C. S. Lewis: A Critical Essay*, Christendom College Press, Front Royal, Virginia, 1988

Kathryn Lindskoog, *C. S. Lewis, Mere Christian*, Inter-Varsity Press, Downers Grove, Illinois, 1981

C. Manlove, *C. S. Lewis: His Literary Achievement*, Macmillan, London, 1987

G. Meilaender, *The Taste For the Other: The Social and Ethical Thought of C. S. Lewis*, Eerdmans, Grand Rapids, Michigan, 1978

Doris T. Myers, *C. S. Lewis in Context*, Kent State University Press, Kent, Ohio, 1994

R.L. Purtill, *The Lord of the Elves and Eldils: Fantasy and Philosophy in C. S. Lewis and J.R.R. Tolkien*, Eerdmans, Grand Rapids, Michigan, 1974

R.J. Reilly, *Romantic Religion: A Study of Barfield, Lewis, Williams and Tolkien*, University of Georgia Press, Athens, Georgia, 1971

L.D. Rossi, *The Politics of Fantasy: C. S. Lewis and J.R.R. Tolkien*, University of Michigan Press, Ann Arbor, Michigan, 1984

George Sayer, *Jack: C. S. Lewis and His Times*, Harper & Row, San Francisco, California, 1988

P.J. Schakel and C.A. Huttar (eds.), *Word and Story in C. S. Lewis*, University of Missouri Press, Columbia, Missouri, 1991

Jeffrey D. Schultz and John. G. West Jnr, *The C. S. Lewis Readers' Encyclopaedia*, Zondervan Publishing House, HarperCollins, USA, 1998

B. Sibley, *C. S. Lewis through the Shadowlands*, Revell, Grand Rapids, Michigan, 1994

R.H. Smith, *Patches of Godlight: The Pattern of Thought of C. S. Lewis*, University of Georgia Press, Athens, Georgia, 1981

Gunnar Urang, *Shadows of Heaven: Religion and Fantasy in the Writing of C. S. Lewis, Charles Williams, and J.R.R. Tolkien*, Pilgrim Press, Philadelphia, 1971

Chad Walsh, *The Literary Legacy of C. S. Lewis*, Harcourt Brace Jovanovich, New York, 1979

Michael White, *Tolkien: A Biography*, Little, Brown, London, 2001

A.N. Wilson, *C. S. Lewis: A Biography*, Collins, London, 1990

Websites

There are many thousands of websites devoted to C. S. Lewis and his work, of which this is a small selection.

The C. S. Lewis Foundation: http//:www.cslewis.org

Cair Paravel: website dedicated to the world of Narnia
http//:www.netten.net/-dpickett/narnia.html

C. S. Lewis and the Inklings:
http://personal.bgsu.edu/~edwards/lewis.html

Into the Wardrobe: http//:www.cache.net/-john/cslewis

C. S. Lewis's legacy: http//:www.sidcovery.org/lewis/cslewis.html

C. S. Lewis Institute: http://www.cslewisinstitute.org

Index